Misjudged Murderesses

Misjudged Murderesses

Female Injustice in Victorian Britain

An investigation into eight cases in Victorian England resulting in sentence of death

Stephen Jakobi

The tribulations of Mary Ball, Sarah Chesham, Ann Merritt, Sarah Barber, Priscilla Biggadike, Mary Lefley, Lizzie Pearson and Florence Maybrick in a misogynistic legal system.

PEN & SWORD
HISTORY
AN IMPRINT OF PEN & SWORD BOOKS LTD.
YORKSHIRE – PHILADELPHIA

First published in Great Britain in 2019 by
Pen and Sword History
An imprint of
Pen & Sword Books Ltd
Yorkshire - Philadelphia

ISBN 9781526741622

A CIP catalogue record for this book is available from the British Library.

Typeset in INDIA By IMPEC e Solutions

Printed and bound in the UK by TJ International Ltd.

Pen & Sword Books Ltd incorporates the Imprints of Pen & Sword Books
Archaeology, Atlas, Aviation, Battleground, Discovery, Family History, History,
Maritime, Military, Naval, Politics, Railways, Select, Transport, True Crime,
Fiction, Frontline Books, Leo Cooper, Praetorian Press, Seaforth Publishing,
Wharncliffe and White Owl.

For a complete list of Pen & Sword titles please contact

PEN & SWORD BOOKS LIMITED

47 Church Street, Barnsley, South Yorkshire, S70 2AS, England
E-mail: enquiries@pen-and-sword.co.uk
Website: www.pen-and-sword.co.uk

Contents

Chronology of events in this book

The major cases are printed in **bold**

1836 *Poison Testing*. In this year James Marsh, who was a chemist at the Royal Arsenal in Woolwich, published a paper giving a detailed methodology for testing for traces of arsenic and for measuring the actual quantity found. In the same year the government decreased the tax on newspapers from fourpence to a penny, creating the popular press.

1839 *Police*. The County Police Bill introduced to Parliament was a voluntary one; each group of county justices of the peace could take the decision whether or not to adopt it.

1840 *Police*. Essex police formed. Superintendents were expected to detect.

1841 *Poison Testing*. A German chemist named Hugo Reinsch published a description of a second method whereby metallic arsenic was deposited on copper foil from hydrochloric acid solution. The test was easier to perform than Marsh's, since it could be applied to a liquid containing organic matter.

1844 *Trial*. Eliza Joyce, Boston town.

1846 *The Times* Monday 1 June, Happisburgh.
Summer and autumn – a major cholera epidemic rages throughout Britain, with symptoms identical to arsenic poisoning.

The Times 21 September, conflation of Happisburgh with Sarah Chesham.

1847 March *trials*. **Sarah Chesham** acquitted.

1849 28 July *trial*. **Mary Ball.**

1851 *Trial*. **Ann Merritt (London)**, faulty medical evidence. **Reprieved.**

14/15 March *trial*. **Sarah Chesham (Essex)** for attempted murder.

24 March *public event*. Bill on sale of arsenic debated and passed by House of Lords.
25 March. **Sarah Chesham** executed.

1852 *Trial*. **Sarah Barber (Nottingham)**, lover was guilty party. **Reprieved.**

1861 *Police*. Promotional exams instituted and the system introduced in Lincolnshire.

1862 *Trial*. Catherine Wilson, native of Boston.

1868 *Trial*. **Priscilla Biggadike, Boston.**

1871 French Civil War Pétroleuses were accused of burning down much of Paris.

1873 *Trial*. Mary Ann Cotton, notorious serial killer. Durham.

1875 *Trial*. **Lizzie Pearson, Durham.**

1884 *Trial*. Catherine Flanagan and Margaret Higgins, sisters. Serial killers, Liverpool.

1884 *Trial*. **Mary Lefley, Boston.**

1889 *Trial*. **Florence Maybrick, Liverpool,** 'mad judge'. **Reprieved.**

Prologue

The subterranean cell was dark and noisome. There was no direct light under the local courtroom, lighting being supplied on occasion by a candle that flickered and cast shadows of the figures on the walls of the small room. It was noisome, The smell of urine and faeces from the bucket in the corner combined with the Tanner's yard reek of the smoke when tallow candles were employed for a visitor. These smells mingled with the body odour of the 'great unwashed' as the middle classes were prone to call working men and women. Much of this probably went unnoticed by the prisoner. She was used to this background as part of her daily living before her arrest.

As the *Coventry Herald Observer* reported (17 August 1849):

> The prison chaplain, the Rev Richard Chapman in the absence of the prison governor visited Mary Ball in her cell for a second time, intent on extracting from her the admission of guilt and repentance she had until then failed to deliver. Already frustrated and inwardly prepared for a repetition of this resistance, Chapman entered Mary's cell and immediately called for a lighted candle, which was brought to him. He took the candle in one hand and on the other hand had hold of the hand of the prisoner Mary Bell which he held over the candle and asked if she felt it. After a time she snatched her hand away having previously endeavoured to withdraw it saying at the same time she did feel it. Chaplain: think that would be compared to the torments of hell, where her whole frame would be burning for a hundred years? The witness, the assistant matron Susanna Winter, stated that the painful ordeal last two minutes and that Mary's hand was blistered. The chaplain afterwards read some prayers then went away apparently unaware of any notion of wrongdoing, and only 'wanted to give her some idea of what the torments of hell were'. It is a sign of Mary's yet unbroken defiance that when she complained to the governor, Mr Stanley, 'she declared she would relate on the gallows what had happened'.
>
> Bellairs, the visiting magistrate to the prison (and a fellow cleric) was informed and called for a hearing to be held on 7 August, having already suspended Chapman from his duties until further notice. At the same time Bellairs notified to the governor's intention to perform the morning duty and preached (sic) the condemned sermon in the gaol Chapel on the fifth instant, which he subsequently did.

It must be said that the terrible assault on Mary was as shocking then as it is today. *Punch*, the famous London-based magazine, carried a short satirical report on the incident on 22 August 1849 comparing Chapman's cruelty with the worst excesses of the Spanish Inquisition (itself having been abolished in 1830.)

Five days later the thirty-one-year-old Nuneaton mother was publicly strangled by a noose in Coventry, with a blistered hand in bandages.

Introduction

In 1994, right at the beginning of Fair Trials, I received a letter from Alan Davies, then a prisoner in the Bangkok Hilton. He had been arrested in December 1989 on a trumped up drug charge, lost all his appeals and was then serving 25 years. I replied saying that I had a poor reputation in Thai official circles and the wisest course for him now would be to plead guilty and agree to a prison transfer which would result in a release on parole at the latest in another 4 years. He insisted that he would never accept guilt and instructed me to represent him. In May 2001 we managed to get Robin Cook to send a full letter of support for a royal pardon to his counterpart in the Thai government. There was then a cock-up and Davies was still not released. He eventually returned home in 2007, 13 years after instructing me, and was my longest running case. He told me that it was only his burning sense of anger at the injustice of his case that kept him going. Almost all my clients refused to plead guilty even though in some cases it would have been a 'get out of jail free' card. Innocent people do not confess.

In my last book, *The Mind of a Female Serial Killer*, I described how my lifelong battle against capital punishment and the Ruth Ellis case had led me to commence an investigation into possible miscarriages of justice resulting in the execution of innocent women during the twentieth century. By the law of unintended consequences, this finished up as a study of violent female psychopaths in the late nineteenth and early twentieth centuries. It was during the research for that book that I came across a website devoted to Priscilla Biggadike, executed for poisoning her husband in 1868, and how she refused to confess although pursued to the scaffold by a clergyman who said he couldn't offer her the consolation of salvation unless she did so. The end of the website stated that 15 years afterwards one of the possible alternative murderers confessed on his deathbed and that as a result, in 1882, she received a posthumous pardon.

It seemed a clear example of a miscarriage of justice. An innocent woman being executed coupled with the hallmark of innocence, a refusal to confess.

The Victorian era was perhaps the high point where, in the name of salvation, pressure was applied to the brink of the scaffold by clergy, in at least one case even involving physical torture (see prologue), in an effort to compel confession.

As Patrick Wilson[1] observed:

> The crimes of such unattractive creatures as Mary Cage (a mid-Victorian poisoner) caused local clergyman to fulminate against the godlessness of the unlettered poor. From condemned cells were issued progress reports of the chaplains' struggles to bring prostrate women to a proper sense of repentance. Certainly very few of the women executed showed signs of coming from homes where religion was important. The apparent piety of the last century scarcely affected the poorest of agricultural labourers and slum dwellers.

Another striking feature of the early cases was the way the clergy were not only ministers to the condemned, but also sat in judgement as part of the judicial process. At least a quarter of the active magistracy were Church of England clergy[2], and it is notable in the Mary Ball case that the final minister involved was both visiting magistrate to the prison and the prison chaplain.

There were various elements to the panic over female poisoners which reached a peak in the 1840s and persisted for a generation. The role of the press and the misogynistic and class-based legal system, whose main elements persisted until the late twentieth century, interacted. The love hate relationship of the Victorians with arsenic and the apparent existence of local poison rings in relatively remote rural areas (East Anglia and Lincolnshire) fanned the flames. The exploits of sensational female serial killers over the period were locally remembered and created knock-on injustices contributing to many of the cases discussed here. (Priscilla Biggadike, Mary Lefley, Elizabeth Pearson and Florence Maybrick).

Here, the malign influence of *The Times* is examined through its interaction with the Sarah Chesham debacle. Then there was also the misogynistic bias of the legal process. As the case work demonstrates, the entire legal system during the Victorian period was male, middle-class and therefore had prejudices against the working class women before them. The defendants were often unrepresented at trial, or poorly represented by barristers who were appointed at the last minute. It is interesting to speculate what would have happened if Sarah Chesham had been represented at her final trial by the excellent legal team who obtained her acquittal in the early series. As it was she was unrepresented. Over this period defendants were not allowed to give evidence in their own defence. There was no appeal from the trial verdict until the Court of Appeal was established in the twentieth century. If the Jury were misdirected or got it wrong that was it. The Home Office were never concerned with the merits of the case (that was for Juries), and poisoners were almost always hanged.

The possible miscarriages of Justice[3]

During the period 1843–1900, 53 women were hanged for murder, 30 of them for poisoning, while 15 of the poisoners refused to confess.

Of course not all the clearly guilty confessed – they included notorious serial killers with ample proof against them.

Clearly guilty

1844 Sarah Westwood. Ten-year-old daughter heard her father ask her mother what was the white stuff mixed with his gruel and mother feigned ignorance.

1845 Mary Sheming bought arsenic and registered her hated baby grandson's death on the same day, though he did not die until a fortnight later!

1845 Sarah Freeman, serial killer with ample evidence she had poisoned her brother, mother, husband and son. She had obtained £20 from her husband's insurance and wished to use it as a dowry for marriage to a local butcher.

1850 Margaret Hamilton poisoned sister-in-law for £20 in the victim's bank account, and committed forgery and fraud to withdraw the money.

1851 Mary Emily Cage purchased arsenic, was indifferent to husband's suffering and there was evidence of her being involved in a series of unexplained deaths.

1862 Catherine Wilson, notorious serial killer, was native of Boston 'a town notorious for its female poisoners', was always a beneficiary of victims' wills. By the time of her death it was discovered she was responsible for at least two murders in Bolton, though she had been tried and executed for murder in London some years later.

1863 Alice Holt, murder of her mother. In January 1863 Alice insured the life of her mother for £25. Poison found.

1873 Mary Ann Cotton, another notorious serial killer.

1883 Louisa Jane Taylor. Victim killed for her pension.

1884 Catherine Flanagan and Margaret Higgins, sisters. Serial killers for insurance money. Discovered an innocent new source of arsenic – soaked flypaper.

Not proven?

The following convicted murderesses did not confess and suffered trial problems

Executed
1849 Mary Ball, Nuneaton near Coventry. Connections with George Eliot and Hetty Sorrel.

1851 Sarah Chesham, convicted of attempted murder of her husband.

1868 Priscilla Biggadike, was her lover the guilty party?

1875 Lizzie Pearson, Durham. Mary Ann Cotton's last victim?

1884 Mary Lefley, Boston. Convicted of murder of husband. Guilty by association with her friend Priscilla Biggadike?

Condemned to death but reprieved
1851 Ann Merritt (London), faulty medical evidence.

1852 Sarah Barber (Nottingham), lover was guilty party.

1889 Florence Maybrick served 18 years in prison because Queen Victoria was apparently, not amused.

These are the cases that are examined in this book.

In my previous book, I was greatly assisted in my search for primary sources by the existence of the Home Office 'death files' files that were automatically created in all cases where the death penalty had been invoked. These not only contain the judge's notes and Home Office thinking, they in fact were a collection of all known information about both convict and crime and surrounding circumstances known to the authorities at the time.

Unfortunately there are no Home Office records relating to Mary Ball, Sarah Chesham, Ann Merritt, Sarah Barber or Priscilla Biggadike since these cases were all decided before the death file system was introduced. There are death files for Lizzie Pearson, Mary Lefley and Florence Maybrick. For the other cases, the primary sources relied upon are the local papers of the time.

I am most grateful for the assistance of the following works published by local devotees and descendants of the accused.

The Life, Trial and Hanging of Mary Ball (Broadlands books) written by Robert Muscutt, the great great grandson of Mary Ball.

A Shadow of Doubt: The Story of Lizzie Pearson Written by Mike Stow of the Gainsford local history group.

Arsenic Sally: Or the Curious Case of the Eastwood Poisoner by Mike Sheridan (the Sarah Barber case) to whom I'm particularly indebted for the Tasmanian end to her story.

They have not only made available to me copies of their books but generously given permission to draw freely on them and save me a lot of time and trouble in research.

It would be wrong not to mention in this context the best source book on Florence Maybrick. Victoria Blake's *Crime Archive: Mrs Maybrick* is not only the best modern study of the case I came across. Her use of the National Archives saved me an enormous amount of time and trouble in providing an explorer's guide through the massive jungle of papers on that case at Kew.

As I intend to demonstrate, the concept of fair trials for working class women accused of poisoning was meaningless, since the classic trilogy for charge and conviction, proof of means, motive and opportunity was virtually presumed. It is my intention to play fair with the reader in putting all essential evidence in each of the eight cases under discussion so that the reader can draw different conclusions from my comments. The Victorian habit of, in effect, having four trials of capital cases (coroner's courts, magistrate's courts grand jury and Assize) meant one could concentrate on the trial. Within the trial, keeping in mind Scott's motto for *The Guardian* 'comment is free, but facts are sacred', opening and closing speeches and to some extent even the presiding judge's remarks can be abbreviated since they are all comments on the facts/evidence.

I had two advantages over most authors in this field.

My training as a lawyer before the 1960s radical reform in our criminal law system meant I was familiar with the workings of the mid-Victorian legal system which until then had survived almost intact.

My experience over the last 15 years of my legal career in dealing with Mickey Mouse justice systems all over the world where unfair trial could be presumed. One had to dig into the merits of the case for the defence as best one might from third-party sources. Indeed, many of my cases had 'smoking gun' evidence such as the crime being committed before the victim of injustice had arrived in the country. While smoking guns are scarce in these cases, Sarah Chesham's father's evidence and Mrs Maybrick's prescription come close.

PART 1

Background

Chapter 1

Arsenic and the Victorian Psyche[1]

On Wednesday, 13 December 1848 the following article appeared in *The Times*:

The following article was published in the form of a letter in last Saturdays *Lancet* by Mr Henry William Fuller, assistant physician to, and lecturer on medical jurisprudence at, St George's Hospital: –

'In these days of alarm respecting cholera, any effect suggesting an occasional and hitherto unsuspected source of gastric irritation cannot fail to prove interesting to the medical practitioner: – the circumstances I am about to communicate have an important bearing, not only upon the sanitary condition of our population, but upon the whole question of poisoning by arsenic, I need make no apology for laying them at once before the profession.

'For some months past, in certain parts of Hampshire, partridges have been found dead in the fields, presenting a very remarkable appearance. Instead of lying prostrate on their site, as is usually the case with dead birds, they have been found sitting, with their heads erect and their eyes open, presenting all the semblance of life. ...I was requested to undertake the investigation, and the result of my experiments I will now briefly detail.

'I first examined the seeds taken from the crops of the birds heads, detected, as I anticipated, a large quantity of arsenic. I will not take up your valuable space by detailing the various steps of my analysis. ... sulphate of copper, each of which gave its characteristic result.

'Having thus ascertained the presence of arsenic in the food of the partridges, I proceeded to examine the birds themselves. They were plump and in good condition, but the oesophagus was in both cases highly inflamed throughout.... I proceeded to ascertain whether the flesh of birds so poisoned might not of itself prove poisonous when eaten, and, with this view, I carefully cut the flesh off the breast and legs of one of the birds, and gave it, together with the liver, to a fine healthy cat. She ate it with ability, but in about half an hour she began to vomit, and vomited almost incessantly for nearly 12 hours, during the whole of which time she evidently suffered excessive pain. After this, nothing would induce her to eat any more Partridge.... I now felt satisfied from my observation of the symptoms induced in the cat, borne out as they were by many facts we are acquainted with respecting the action of poisons, that the arsenic which the partridges had swallowed been absorbed in sufficient quantity into the system to render the flesh of the bird poisonous, and to induce poisonous effects in anyone partaking of it.

'However, I was anxious to leave nothing to hypothesis, and as the cat so soon rejected by vomiting the greater part of the bird she had eaten, and pertinaciously refused to repeat the experiment by again partaking of the poisoned food, I was obliged to have recourse to chemical analysis, with the view of ascertaining, with certainty, the existence or nonexistence of arsenic in the flesh itself. I therefore, cut the flesh off one side of the breast of the other Partridge ...I obtained, by Reinsch's process a thin encrustation of metallic arsenic, thus demonstrating, beyond question what the previous experiments that left little room for doubt. I was now anxious to ascertain the source of the poison, and very little enquiry served to satisfy me on this point. ...I will simply mention the leading facts – viz., that in Hampshire, Lincolnshire, and many other parts of the country, the farmers are now in the habit of steeping new wheat in a strong solution of arsenic previous to sewing it, with the view of preventing the ravages of the wire-worm on the seed, this process is found to be eminently successful, and is therefore daily becoming more and more generally adopted; that, even now many hundreds weight of arsenic are yearly sold to agriculturalists with this express purpose; that although the seed is poisonous when sown, its fruit is in no degree affected by the poison; that wherever this plan has been extensively carried out, pheasants and partridges have been poisoned by eating the seed, and the partridges have been almost universally found sitting in the position I've already described; and, lastly, that the men employed in sowing the poisonous seed, not infrequently present the earlier symptoms which occur in the milder cases of poisoning by arsenic. Now the fact just enumerated suggests several most important points for consideration.

'Firstly It is notorious that many of the dealers in game are supplied through the agency of poachers ...It is certain, moreover, that if men of this sort were to find a covey of partridges in the field, dead, but fresh and good condition, they would not hesitate to send them, with the remainder of their booty, to the poulterer, who would certainly, without suspicion sell them to his customers. ...It is obvious, therefore, that in all cases of supposed cholera, or of suspicious bellyache, occurring at this season of the year, we shall do well to make particular enquiry as to whether our patient has recently partaken of pheasants or partridges purchased at a poulterer; and it is further manifest, that in all cases of poisoning; or suspected poisoning, by arsenic, the fact of persons having lately eaten the partridges and pheasants must form an important element <u>in the enquiry and must at least cast suspicion on the evidence adduced to prove a criminal intent in the administration of the poison</u>. *[My underlining]*

Secondly if it should prove, on further enquiry, that the practice of steeping seed wheat in arsenic is, even indirectly, producing an injurious effect on our population, it may become, in these days of sanitary reform, a matter for the anxious consideration of the legislature....

'Thirdly, as in the event of a practice, so destructive of game, becoming universal, pheasants and partridges, in their wild state at least, must, at no distant day, become extinct in this country, it is a question whether landlords may not henceforth be induced to insert a clause in their leases prohibiting the use of arsenic on their farms.

This wide-ranging article commencing from a specific incident and moving through experiment and deduction to general conclusions and recommendations encapsulates most of the concerns of the Victorian panic on arsenic. It covers the widespread use of arsenic as a general pesticide, the difficulty of diagnosis in cases of death until the mid-century, its extreme toxicity, its effects as an occupational hazard and even a tinge of paranoia in his recommendations.

White arsenic or arsenic trioxide (As_2O_3) is a metallic oxide that was widely used in the nineteenth century as a pesticide to kill vermin (it was commonly known as 'Ratsbane') and insects, a herbicide, a tonic and a component in medicines and wallpaper. The article concentrates on a specific agricultural use, the preservation of wheat seed against insects and blights and through it we learn that several hundred weight of white arsenic was used for this purpose alone: though possibly its main agricultural use was as a dip for sheep. It was very cheap, freely available up to 1851, odourless, soluble in water and largely tasteless.

As the article observes at the beginning, cholera epidemics were not uncommon at this time with major outbreaks in 1831/2, 1848/9, 1853/4 and 1866 which killed in total some 140,000 people. The symptoms produced by cholera almost mirrored the symptoms of arsenic poisoning when taken in food. These included vomiting, diarrhoea and severe stomach cramps. Apparently, according to the article, the same symptoms afflicted the experimenter's wretched cat (though luckily not fatally) and even the game birds.

Arsenic is one of the most dangerous of the irritant poisons: enough powder to cover the surface of a penny invariably killed. The effect on humans was not instantaneous. It caused a painful death several hours, sometimes days, after a lethal dose had been consumed. Even when taken in small quantities its effects are cumulative, i.e. it builds up in the body. Where death occurred and there were no obvious suspicious circumstances, doctors often certified the cause as cholera and did not order an autopsy.

Even then, there was no reliable test for the presence of small quantities of arsenic in the body until 1836.

In this year James Marsh, who was a chemist at the Royal Arsenal in Woolwich, published a paper giving a detailed methodology for testing for traces of arsenic and for measuring the actual quantity found. He had been involved with the case of James Boodle in 1832 and Boodle was acquitted due to lack of good forensic evidence, although he later admitted poisoning his grandfather's coffee. The process was very sensitive and could detect as little as a fiftieth of a milligram of the substance. The basis of the test was the readiness of arsenic in any form to combine with hydrogen to form the gas arsine (AsH_3). The addition of one of the strong acids, sulphuric or hydrochloric, to a sample of arsenic compounds is followed by adding zinc. Zinc forms the bond by generating hydrogen which immediately forms the bond with the gas. The Marsh system set light to the gas participating the arsenic in a mirrorlike metallic form.

However, arsine is extraordinarily poisonous when inhaled and the experimenter must ensure that there are no leaks in the cumbersome apparatus involved. As Wharton[2] observed, 'by 1900, nine fatalities would have been recorded amongst analysts inhaling arsine during the Marsh test.'

Moreover, the arsenic could be picked up from impurities in the zinc, copper tubing or any other material in the experimenter's apparatus. This particular problem damaged the reputation of Alfred Swain Taylor[3], perhaps the foremost expert witness of the late 1840s onwards during a major arsenic poisoning case, the Smethurst case, at the end of the 1850s. Having given evidence in the case he discovered the accidental contamination of his materials and being a scrupulous man declared it to the court. The test on the samples in question had to be performed anew by another experimenter but the damage had been done to the prosecution case against Dr Smethurst, a physician, and he was acquitted of murder.

Despite all the drawbacks, the Marsh Test soon became the standard forensic procedure, and samples of food, drink, stomach contents and tissue were examined using it.

In 1841 a German chemist named Hugo Reinsch published a description of a second method whereby metallic arsenic was deposited on copper foil from hydrochloric acid solution. The test was easier to perform than Marsh's, since it could be applied to a liquid containing organic matter.

Expertise at carrying out these tests built up in the newly opened teaching hospitals and there were soon a number of expert witnesses available to prosecutors. This proved to be some deterrent; the instances of arsenic poisoning began to diminish from the 1850s onwards.

* * *

The final observation in collaboration with Dr Heale, of occupational arsenic poisoning amongst agricultural workers handling the seed, introduces the topic of occupational arsenic poisoning in general.

Again, it was an article in *The Lancet* of July 1890 that demonstrated an instance of occupational arsenic poisoning as weird, in its way, as the partridge case. Under the prosaic medical title 'Two cases of arsenical peripheral neuritis', submitted by Dr Samuel Barton, the honorary physician to the local Norfolk hospitals, it related the medical history of a Norwich couple, both aged 28. In the autumn of the previous year the pregnant wife was carried to the hospital on a stretcher unable to walk or even stand. She told the doctors there that she was frightened by a thunderstorm which had given her a severe headache and for several weeks she'd been getting worse. Green vomiting, watery diarrhoea and the loss of her baby in premature labour all occurred during the first week in hospital. The second week saw progressive numbness through her limbs and by the end of the third week she could neither stand nor hold anything in her hands. Over the next few months she slowly improved, but even after three months she could only stand with the support of a chair. By this time the husband joined her with the same symptoms. The doctors were baffled as to how a couple who were not serious drinkers were exhibiting symptoms usually observed in alcoholics. However, the husband on admission giving his history explained he was a taxidermist and spent much time rubbing a mixture of arsenic and plaster of Paris into birds. When his urine was analysed a lot of arsenic was found. The wife's only contact was cleaning the husband's workroom twice a week, but it was enough to give her arsenic poisoning. It took them several months before they were able to walk unassisted the mile between their home and the hospital. This well-recognised occupational hazard even extended to people who bought the preserved animals and kept them in their bedrooms. Occupational arsenic poisoning was a cause of premature death and ill-health everywhere one turned. From mining through to wallpaper manufacture, even when the hazards had become recognised, little was done during this period to limit its effects.

William Morris (1834–1896) was the iconic advocate of a return to traditional craft styles and materials – and a defendant of poisonous wallpaper, according to a new study.

Andy Meharg[4] of the University of Aberdeen in Scotland has found arsenic in the green pigment in an early sample of Morris's patterned wallpaper, produced some time between 1864 and 1875. Production continued, even though the pigments were suspected in the mid-nineteenth century of releasing toxic fumes if they become damp.

The alarm about arsenic greens in wallpaper had been raised several years earlier. Morris was not ignorant of the health hazard. He was a shareholder and sometime director of his father's mining company, Devon Great Consols (DGC), the largest arsenic producer of the age. DGC workers were plagued by arsenic-related illnesses, and many died from lung disease. The company's activities caused immense environmental damage.

Nonetheless he dismissed public concerns about arsenic-based pigments in wallpapers, Meharg quotes him writing in a letter in as late as 1885: 'a greater folly is hardly possible to imagine: the doctors were bitten by witch fever.' 'If there was really a problem,' Morris asserted, 'we should be sure to hear of it.'

The alarm about arsenic greens in wallpaper had been raised several years earlier. And the producers of his wallpaper, Jeffreys and Co, were sufficiently worried to switch to an arsenic-free green in 1875.

Chapter 2

The Press

As a modern article in the *New Yorker* stated:

> In 1836, right before the poisoning craze peaked, the government decreased the tax on newspapers from four pence to a penny. This development coincided with another important change: a rapid rise in literacy among the working class. Working-class people liked murder stories. (So, no doubt, did readers of higher rank.) Consequently, the number of newspapers shot up, as did the sales of any paper willing to report vividly and at length on poisoning cases.... In 1856, when the *Illustrated Times* published a special edition on the trial of the 'Rugeley poisoner,' Dr. William Palmer – circulation was said to have doubled to 400,000.

The articles probably inspired a few poisonings. Indeed, they more or less provided instructions... People accustomed to believing that poisoning was something done by foreigners now saw it at their own front door.

This depiction of the popular and local press as occupying the current role of the dark web in disseminating antisocial material as a manual for poisoning may have been overdone. Not only was the illiteracy rate 50 per cent throughout the period until the passing of the Foster education act in 1871, it was much higher for working class females. With the exception of Florence Maybrick, in all of the dubious cases examined in this book the defendants were at best semi-literate. The function of the general British press during this period would appear to frighten precisely those who formed juries: the shopkeepers and other ratepayers who could now afford the penny press. These juries may well have been prejudiced by previous cases with local connections having been reported in local newspapers. Essentially, local gossip about women who got away with it and what probably motivated those females who were convicted.

The four-stage progress of the Victorian murder case, with the prosecution witnesses and evidence fully rehearsed and reported through coroners court, magistrates court and grand jury meant that everyone concerned, from witnesses to jurors, knew all about the case from the prosecution view through the local press before the opening of the trial.

In one of the best source books on the Victorian justice system of the nineteenth century David Bentley[1] opens the chapter on pre-trial publicity with a quote from an Old Bailey judge:

'It was much to be lamented that… No cases now occur… Which was not forestalled by accounts in the newspapers which created a prejudice against accused persons from which it was very difficult, if not impossible, to divest themselves.'

As the law stood and still stands, stirring up prejudice against an accused awaiting trial was prohibited on pain of committal for contempt. Not only did the press give little or no heed to it, such was the reluctance of authority from judges downwards to enforce even the most blatant breaches of the rule, that there would appear to be no instances throughout the period under consideration. The press, local and national, were free not only to report all the stages of the ponderous Victorian progress to a trial, it freely, and often imaginatively, embroidered evidential fact with local gossip. In particular, if the accused had any previous bad character this was paraded to the public. Letters written by the accused and others were published before appearances in court. Totally false reports of confessions by the accused even in notorious cases for fraud and murder were left unpunished.

What has been shown in a series of recent books and studies is the sinister and biased role of *The Times* of London newspaper in creating bigotry and panic amongst its readers by inaccurate reporting and intemperate opinion pieces. Here, the damage being done by the establishment paper of record was to the thinking of the entire legal profession from solicitors and barristers to the judiciary, civil servants and government ministers. The study of the role of the 'Thunderer' (this nickname denoting its tone in influencing the establishment dates back to the 1830s) is detailed below as part of the general background to the myth of the Essex poison ring.

In fairness, it should be noted that on occasion influential regional newspapers came to the rescue of the unfairly convicted, as in the Ann Merritt case.

Chapter 3

The Justice System 1840–1890

The Police

The County Police Bill introduced to Parliament in 1839 was a voluntary one; each group of county justices of the peace could take the decision whether to adopt it. If they decided to do so they could appoint a chief constable and decide on the number of constables. A superintendent was to head each division and a deputy chief constable was to be appointed from amongst them. This was under general supervision of the Home Secretary, who framed the rules.

The chief constable had to report to the Quarter Sessions, the divisional superintendents to their local Petty Sessions. The system was tightly controlled by the local magistracy.

We are fortunate that Maureen Scollan[1], an ex-serving officer with the Essex police, has written an excellent history of the police in that county (*Sworn to Serve: Police in Essex*) since that local police force is the one most intimately connected with the arsenic poison investigations. Police constables were expected to be able to read and write, and were generally paid about three times as much as an agricultural labourer. An analysis of the first intake in 1840 showed a slight preponderance in the 20 to 30 age group over the 30 to 40 age groups. Those recruited over 40 were appointed superintendents and tended to come from the military. Few labourers were accepted, an effect of the literacy requirement. Most of the recruits were skilled: previously butchers, bakers and even a couple of silversmiths. There were half a dozen who had previously been police from other areas. Only about 30 per cent had been born locally. Since the first census was the year afterwards there is no information on the numbers already living locally but in all probability the great majority of recruits were from Essex.

Promotional exams were instituted in 1861 and the system introduced was in Lincolnshire (the other poison hotspot) where constables were examined in writing, spelling and arithmetic; sergeants took another examination in the higher rules of arithmetic, making up pay, charge sheets and summons returns, and the classification of different crimes under appropriate headings.

During the early part of the period superintendents were responsible for detection. Superintendent John Clarke from Newport was involved in the

Sarah Chesham case. Throughout the period the police force was male and they were reliant on their wives for dealing with women. A deposition from Mrs Clarke who was brought in to search Sarah, gave evidence that Sarah had said 'I have no more to do in poisoning my husband then you have ma'm. Dr Brown told me he had no more arsenic in his body than had been given to him by his medicine.'

The right of suspects to refuse to answer questions before trial was not codified as Judges' Rules until 1912. Prior to 1912, while torture had been banned, the mistreatment of silent suspects to induce a confession was common and the refusal to answer questions was used as evidence against them. The intermingling of the investigative and judicial roles was not formally divided until 1848, when the interrogation of suspects was made solely a police matter, with the establishment of the modern police forces. In effect, the working class illiterate, especially females, were at the mercy of the unskilled police until late into the nineteenth century.

Inquests

> For a modern painter there is a fine picture begging for canvas about this old judicial ceremony: the Knight and his jury on an untenanted plain holding their inquisition over the dead or retiring a few paces from the killed or slain to choose their verdict under the High Court of heaven. But beyond the picture the idea is obsolete. The stately Knight is now, by common consent, a doctor or a lawyer; the High Court of heaven has dwindled into 4 walls within a tavern, where elbow room is at a premium and air filtered clear of tobacco is a luxury; while the Constable or Beadle, once so overpowering in his magnificent attire, has become a sport for the solemnity of the past. Of the original design of the coroner's court the jury alone remains as a primitive feature to be retained, and still longer tried under a reformed administration.
> *The Lancet* (1874)

The Lancet's polemic was well justified. By the nineteenth century coroners had been investigating sudden or unexplained deaths for over six centuries. In a legal inquiry known as an inquest, the prompt investigation of unexplained deaths, originally a secondary purpose, had by the opening of the Victorian period become its main function.

A coroner and jury viewed the body of the deceased, examined witnesses, and reached conclusions about the cause and manner of death – whether natural, accident, suicide or homicide. But, as Cassie Watson[2] pointed out in a web posting, there were relatively few coroners in England and Wales: about 330 served a fast-growing national population in which several hundred thousand people died annually. How did they decide which deaths to investigate?

It depended on circumstances. Inquests were supposed to be held in cases of death from obvious violence or which occurred in prison, but other potentially criminal cases were distinguished from the mundane at a local level – coroners could not act until formally notified by a member of the public. To function effectively, the system required popular opinion to reveal evidence of foul play, and came to rely on parish officers to act as middlemen between local inhabitants and coroners who might live many miles away. Once the necessary notification, 'which regularly ought to be from the proper or peace officer of the parish, place, or precinct where the body lies dead' had been made, the coroner was legally obligated to hold an inquest. Inquests incurred costs which it fell to the counties to reimburse.

The coroner, usually a local lawyer, was paid per inquest until 1860, when coroners became salaried officials. They were paid per inquest (£1.6s.8d in 1837) plus travel expenses of nine pence per mile (one way only). Parish officers were paid for notifications, summoning witnesses and jurors, renting premises and arranging inquests. Some costs were easily eliminated. In particular, inquests were almost invariably held in a local tavern. The landlord regarded the free availability of their largest room as excellent business: jury witnesses and spectators found inquests thirsty work and strong ale flowed freely. In 1836 the Medical Witnesses Act authorised coroners to pay a doctor up to £2.2s to perform a post-mortem and give evidence, while the introduction of civil registration in 1837 led to increased numbers of inquests because causes of death had to be certified. By 1840 there was a reaction by magistrates. See 'The mysterious poisonings in Norfolk' (*The Times* below, reporting on Happisburgh debacle):

The inquest jury were, throughout the period, male and ratepayers, middle-class shopkeepers, farmers and proprietors of small businesses. The mantra supplied by the local press to describe an inquest was that it was held before the coroner and 'a respectable jury'. This respectability is best illustrated again by the observations of the foreman of the jury in the Happisburgh case.

> It is lamentable to perceive in what a state of wilful wickedness and ignorance many of the lower order of society still remained. He said wilful for were some parish churches better attended, they would there learn their duty to both God and men...

Clearly, the lower orders had to be kept in their place by the church.

But there were other problems with inquest juries, as shown in the inquest on Sarah Chesham's children:

> The Coroner, addressing a witness, said, 'It is very evident to me that you have been tampered with in the most unjustifiable manner, and it is confidently stated that your master is the person who has thus interfered with you. It appears that your master is a person named Wisbey.'
>
> Wisbey, who is one of the jury, declared that he had done nothing with the boy further than counselling him to tell the truth. Mr. Stevens, a juryman, said, 'Mr. Wisbey, it seems to me that you allow your servants to take a liberty with you which no servant of mine would dare to take with me. When that boy, John Chesham, left this room on last inquiry, he touched you on the arm, looked in your face, and smiled. You then said, "Well done, boy, you did it very well."'
>
> The Coroner (to Wisbey), 'I have no doubt you made that remark to the boy, and that could not have been done without an object. It was a strong remark to make, because was the conviction of all present that the boy had committed perjury. Has anyone mentioned the subject to you?' Wisbey, 'No.' The Coroner, 'Not either of the Newports?' Wisbey, 'No, I never spoke to them on the subject.' The Coroner, 'Have you not been there occasionally of the evening to talk about this subject?' Wisbey, 'Yes, I may have been there to talk about it sometimes.'
>
> The Coroner, 'Was anything said about the boy?' Wisbey, 'No, not that I recollect.' A Juror, 'Did Thomas Newport say anything about arsenic?' Wisbey, 'Yes, he said something about it, but I forgot what it was.' Mr. Stevens, juryman, expressed his conviction that the conduct of Wisbey had been disgraceful, and that his criminality had been increased by the fact that, as a juror he had sworn to do justice.'

No action was taken

Magistrates

The next stage in the progress of a capital case was a hearing before the local magistrates. Justices of the peace were appointed by the Crown for each county and for some boroughs. London was different: the City had its own system whereby the Lord Mayor and aldermen were *ex-officio* justices and outside the City there were nine police stations to which professional lawyers – stipendiary magistrates – were attached. By an 1839 statute they had to be barristers of at least seven years standing, had the powers of a bench of two or more lay magistrates, worked long hours (10 a.m. to 8 p.m.) and were paid £400 a year. Over the period the hours were reduced and the salaries increased (by 1900 the salary was £1400 a year). Some towns had a stipendiary magistrate: Salford and Manchester were early creators of the local office, but again, since the boroughs had to bear the cost, there were still only a handful of stipendiary magistrates outside London by 1890.

Commissioners of the peace were selected by the Lord Lieutenant of the County and appointed by the Lord Chancellor. By an act of 1723 county justices with certain exceptions had to own or occupy land in the county worth a hundred pounds per annum: as a consequence the county magistracy was the preserve of the landed classes. The appointments were often political and favoured Conservatives.

The Grand Jury

Proceedings at assize, since all capital cases were reserved for a High Court judge or a commissioner specially appointed with the powers of the High Court judge, always began with consideration of a bill of indictment (formal charges to be considered against the defendant). As David Bentley (*English Criminal Justice in the Nineteenth Century*) put it: 'The Grand Jury was the filter whose purpose was to throw out weak and baseless cases. Only a Grand Jury could find a bill of indictment and a prosecutor seeking a bill had to lay his evidence before it for its scrutiny.'

It consisted of not less than 12 and not more than 23 jurors and reached its decision by majority vote. The Assize Grand Jury was drawn in the main from the county magistracy and they were indeed grand – in the Biggadike case everyone on the jury was entitled to the title 'Esq'. It included the local MP and the foreman was a Baronet.

At the start of the session for which they had been summoned, grand jurors would be sworn and the judge would then deliver his charge to them, in which he would give them legal directions about any case likely to give difficulty. In the Biggadike case the judge not only had made up his mind about Biggadike, but virtually directed the Grand Jury to discharge Proctor so that he could give prosecution evidence against Biggadike.

The witnesses in the various cases would then be sworn in batches in open court, and sent to the Grand Jury room to wait their turn to be examined by the jury. Examination was conducted in private and in the accused's absence. If in the case the jury was satisfied that there was *prima facie* evidence of guilt, they would endorse the bill 'true bill' and it would be carried into court to be tried. If they were not satisfied, it would be endorsed 'no true bill' and the accused would be discharged, though they could be rearrested and brought before the next assizes session.

Throughout the period there was a growing demand to do away with the Grand Jury since it was an expensive and unnecessary procedure. Numerous attempts were made originating in the House of Commons and House of Lords but it was not until the twentieth century when Grand Juries were finally abolished in England and Wales. As all fans of American legal dramas on television are aware, the stage of the Grand Jury lingers on in the United States, but at least it's not presided over by the trial judge.

The right to counsel

In 1830 if you were charged with treason, or you were impeached you had a right to counsel. If you were charged with a lesser offence triable in the magistrate's court such as a misdemeanour you also had the right to counsel by Common Law. But you had no such right other than at the judge's discretion, if you were charged with murder or attempted murder or any other felony until the prisoner's consul act of 1836, which gave the right to counsel provided you could pay for him. But the act did not give the defendant's counsel the right to have the last word – they could only examine and cross-examine witnesses. It took 10 years battering in vain against majorities, firstly in the House of Commons and eventually in the House of Lords, to achieve this position. The reason the basic anomaly of the right to counsel took so long to mitigate was essentially the hostility of the judiciary and the bar to such a change. The arguments against change were that innocent prisoners had no difficulty in explaining themselves in court and in any case the judge acted as counsel for unrepresented prisoners. How a judge could do this when he had no means of taking statements from defendant's witnesses or even finding out who they were went unanswered.

Legal representation of poor defendants at trial

For the vast majority of defendants on capital charges the act was irrelevant since they could not afford counsel. According to *The Times* of 26 July 1841, the 1841 Summer Assizes contained 12 cases and in only one did the prisoner have counsel.

Assigning counsel was a practice developed by judges as a means of ensuring that prisoners facing grave charges did not go undefended for want of means. The judge would ask one of the counsel present in court to undertake the prisoner's defence, a request never in practice refused. By 1870 it would appear rare for counsel not to be assigned in a capital case.

However, last-minute assignment of counsel made for poor defences. He had generally to pick the case up as he went along, there being no brief. Access to the depositions in a few minutes before he was due to confer with the client was all that were allowed and he could not get enquiries if they were needed to be made because he had no attorney to make them.

The cases under discussion here varied

Mary Ball was defended by two barristers, Millar and Denison, who were paid from public funds.

Sarah Chesham, for her first three trials, was defended by Sgt Jones and paid for out of public funds. She was unrepresented in the final trial where she was convicted of attempting to murder her husband.

Lizzie Pearson, had no counsel engaged for the defence of prisoner, but at the request of the judge, Mr Ridley agreed to conduct the case on her behalf.

Mary Lefley was properly defended by QC and solicitor.

Ann Merritt (London), was unrepresented.

Sarah Barber had last-minute counsel.

Florence Maybrick was represented by Sir Charles Russell QC and a top legal team.

The judges

At the start of the century the 12 common-law judges essentially presided over all capital trials. Outside London from 1840 onwards only judges who held full-time appointments presided and it is notable that they were principally civil judges. By the end of the century the number of common-law judges still stood at 15.

They were recruited from the practising bar. The power of appointment was split between the Prime Minister and the Lord Chancellor. The former appointed the Lord Chief Justice and the Chief Justice of the Common Pleas, the latter all the other common-law judges. Under the Act of Settlement of 1701 a judge once appointed was only removable on a joint address by both Houses of Parliament. No English High Court judge has ever been removed. A judge could go mad in office, as Mr Justice Stephen did (Maybrick case) and was still allowed to try important cases until he could be persuaded by his colleagues to retire.

Without any form of appeal from their decisions, and a Home Office that disregarded any recommendation from juries in favour of the trying judges opinion, they were on the whole living examples of Lord Acton's dictum 'Power tends to corrupt and absolute power corrupts absolutely.'

Whilst there were honourable exceptions, as illustrated by Lord Denman's behaviour in the first of Sarah Chesham's trials, the judges' behaviour in the cases under examination here demonstrate the problems this created for the entire Victorian criminal justice system.

In Sarah Chesham's second trial, having been tried for attempted murder, the most recent penalty was a maximum of life imprisonment. The judge abandoned the basics of legal construction, where a newer act dealing with the same offence supersedes older legislation, to sentence her to death. He also took into account two previous charges of murder upon which she had been tried and acquitted. No one corrected this blatant abuse of the law.

Again, the judge's behaviour in the Priscilla Biggadike case has already been discussed (see Grand Jury description above).

Referring to the Maybrick case the *New York Times* wrote the following verdict on the English judiciary:

> The character... Of all English Judges has been almost incredibly hardened by the influence of this autocratic power. As a class they are the most conceited, dogmatic body of men probably existing in the whole English-speaking world. From habitually dealing with the whole criminal class as vermin, they come to regard the jury as a sort of servile race. Out of this has grown a monstrous abuse of the institution known as the charge to the jury...

The Americans at this time were entitled to feel superior. There, judges were constrained to stick to explaining the law, and were not entitled to give a summing up of the facts.

PART 2

The Myth of the Victorian Arsenic 'Poison Rings'

Chapter 4

The Nature of Poison Rings

Poison rings are essentially conspiracies. It is useful to understand two basic large-scale conspiracy organisational formats: wheel and chain conspiracies.

A wheel conspiracy consists of a single conspirator, generally the ringleader, who is interconnected to every other co-conspirator. The ringleader is the hub; the other co-conspirators are the spokes of the wheel. An example of a wheel conspiracy would be a mob boss linked to individual members of the mob following his or her commands. A chain conspiracy consists of co-conspirators connected to each other like links in a chain but to a central interconnected ringleader. An example of a chain conspiracy is a conspiracy to manufacture and distribute a controlled substance, with the manufacturer linked to the transporter, who sells to a large-quantity dealer, who thereafter sells to a smaller-quantity dealer, who sells to a customer. Whether the conspiracy is wheel, chain, or otherwise, the co-conspirators may be criminally responsible for the conspiracy and the crime(s) it furthers.

A classic wheel conspiracy

The Angel Makers of Nagyrév[1] were a group of women living in the village of Nagyrév, Hungary, who between 1914 and 1929 poisoned to death at least 45 people, though some estimates put the number as high as 300. They were supplied arsenic and encouraged to use it for the purpose by a midwife or 'wise woman' named Julia Fazekas.

Mrs Fazekas was a middle-aged midwife who arrived in Nagyrév in 1911 with her husband already missing without explanation. Between 1911 and 1921 she was imprisoned 10 times for performing illegal abortions, but was consistently acquitted by judges supporting abortion.

In Hungarian society at that time, the future husband of a teenage bride was selected by her family and she was forced to accept her parents' choice. Divorce was not allowed socially. During the First World War, when able-bodied men were sent to fight for Austria-Hungary, rural Nagyrév was an ideal location for holding Allied prisoners of war. With the limited freedom of POWs about the village, the women living there often had one or more foreign lovers while their husbands were away. When the men returned, many of them rejected their wives' affairs and wished to return to their previous way of life. At this time Fazekas began secretly persuading women who wished to escape this situation to poison their husbands using arsenic made by boiling flypaper and skimming off the lethal residue.

After the initial killing of their husbands, some of the women went on to poison parents who had become a burden to them, or to get hold of their inheritance. Others poisoned their lovers, some even their sons; as the midwife allegedly told the poisoners, 'Why put up with them?'

The poisoning became a fad, and by the mid-1920s, Nagyrév earned the nickname 'the murder district.' There were an estimated 45–50 murders over the 18 years that Mrs Fazekas lived in the district. She was the closest thing to a doctor the village had and her cousin was the clerk who filed all the death certificates, allowing the murders to go undetected.

The Angel Makers were eventually detected, according to Béla Bodó[2], a Hungarian–American historian and author of the first scholarly book on the subject, in 1929, when an anonymous letter to the editor of a small local newspaper accused women from the Tiszazug region of the country of poisoning family members.

The authorities exhumed dozens of corpses from the local cemetery. Thirty-four women and one man were indicted. Afterwards, 26 of the Angel Makers were tried. Eight were sentenced to death but only two were executed. Another 12 received prison sentences.

The twentieth century Hungarian Angel Makers flypaper poisoning ring is a typical wheel conspiracy, the ringleader being in this case Mrs Fazekas. It is important to note even in that case, with its abundance of proof, the role of rumour and press reports in exaggerating the magnitude of the problem. Whilst Prof Béla Bodó made a full estimate of 45 to 50 murders, the press magnified this number to 200 or 300 poisonings.

A classic non-conspiracy

Witchcraft trials, baseless accusations made by those, often in authority, with an interest in their own long-term aims, died out in the eighteenth-century. Contemporary with the Victorian fear of the poison rings was the French Civil War of 1871 after the defeat of France by Germany. Pétroleuses were, according to popular rumours at the time, female supporters of the Paris Commune, accused of burning down much of Paris during the last days of the Commune in May 1871. During May, when Paris was being recaptured by loyalist Versaillais troops, rumours circulated that lower-class women were committing arson against private property and public buildings, using bottles full of petroleum or paraffin (similar to modern-day

Molotov cocktails) which they threw into cellar windows, in a deliberate act of spite against the government. Many Parisian buildings, including the Hôtel de Ville, the Tuileries Palace, the Palais de Justice and many other government buildings were in fact set afire by the soldiers of the Commune during the last days of the Commune, prompting the press and Parisian public opinion to blame the pétroleuses. Recent research by historians of the Paris Commune, including Robert Tombs and Gay Gullickson[3], concluded that there were no incidents of deliberate arson by pétroleuses. Of the thousands of suspected pro-Communard women tried in Versailles after the Commune ended, only a handful were convicted of any crimes, and their convictions were based on activity such as shooting at loyalist troops. Official trial records show that no women were ever convicted of arson. Despite this, the myth of pétroleuses was widely believed until the twentieth century. In Paris itself, the sale of flammable liquids was banned for several months after the end of the Commune.

Chapter 5

The Victorian Evidence

There were two rural communities where there was allegedly a concentration of women executed for poisoning. The following is a list of the cases with the places where the women lived when the crimes were committed:

Boston
Eliza Joyce, 1844, Boston town.
Catherine Wilson, 1862, in London, native of Boston and probably committed one or more murders there.
Priscilla Biggadike, 1868, Stickney, seven miles from Boston.
Mary Lefley, 1884, Wrangle, seven miles from Boston.

The Essex group
Mary Shaming, 1844, Martlesham, six miles from Ipswich.
Catherine Foster, 1847, Acton, 20 miles from Ipswich.
Mary May, 1848, Wix, 10 miles from Ipswich.
Mary Reeder, 1850, Castle Camps, 25 miles from Ipswich.
Sarah Chesham, 1851, Clavering, 37 miles from Ipswich.
Mary Emily Cage, 1851, Stonham, Apsal, 10 miles from Ipswich.

Was it a witchhunt?

As Patrick Wilson remarked:

> One fifth of the women executed for poisoning in England and half the country women (as opposed to urban) hung for poisoning came from the neighbourhood of two market towns of no great size. The 'Ipswich murders' took place within a decade in very small villages isolated from the tide of progress. This might be a coincidence, but, if it is not, a cause must be sought. There were numerous witch trials in Essex, and it would be interesting to compare the witch trials of Suffolk and Essex in Lincolnshire with the trials of women for poisoning. The geography and economics of the agricultural districts surrounding the two East Coast towns may have had some influence in keeping alive pre-Christian traditions.

In all my research for the cases involving East Anglia and Lincolnshire, I came across just one remark (relating to the magistrates' court hearing of Sarah Chesham for attempted murder of her husband) which supports this theory:

> Chelmsford Chronicle – Friday 27 September 1850
> On being now informed in the usual way that she might state what she pleased the prisoner said she was innocent and she wished they would take her before a witch and then they would know who poisoned her husband.

Even superficial research at Wikipedia level demonstrates Essex as a centre of witchcraft during the witch hunt days of the seventeenth century and early Victorian times.

Matthew Hopkins (c.1620 – 12 August 1647) was an English witchhunter whose career flourished during the English Civil War. He claimed to hold the office of Witch-finder General, although that title was never bestowed by Parliament. He lived in Manningtree, Essex. His witch-hunts mainly took place in East Anglia; Essex being the hardest hit. He is believed to have been responsible for the deaths of 300 women between the years 1644 and 1646. In the 14 months of his crusade Hopkins sent to the gallows more people than all the other witch-hunters in England of the previous 160 years.

The village of Canewdon, on the Crouch estuary was reputed to be the centre of magic in early Victorian times.

'Three of cotton and three of silk.' One saying referring to Canewdon states that there will always be six witches in Canewdon: three of cotton (lower classes) and three of silk (upper classes). The use of the word cotton does help to date the saying as cotton only become widely available in Britain in the first half of the nineteenth century during the Industrial Revolution.

The 'Cunning Man' of Hadleigh was a man whose powerful personality and reputation brought the village and surrounding area to the attention of the outside world. James Murrell was born the seventh son of a seventh son in Rochford in 1780. In 1812 Murrell moved to Hadleigh, and set up business as a shoemaker. His natural skill in the art led him to give up shoe making and become a full-time 'cunning man'. His fame grew as a cunning man of unequalled ability and he was sought out by both local people and wealthy aristocrats from further afield. It was said that he would always ask people if their problem was 'high or low' i.e. did they need material or magic help. To tackle supernatural forces, Murrell would summon good spirits or angels to fight the bad ones. He was consulted on a wide range of issues including finding lost objects, clairvoyance and his ability to cast and break other witches' spells. Stories about Murrell were passed down by word of mouth and storytelling creating a legend around a man who was said to be the greatest witch/cunning man whom England had ever seen. His connection with Canewdon was also a strong one. The villages lie about nine miles from each other. Many educated figures criticised what they saw as his role in encouraging superstition among the local population; his death certificate recorded his profession as that of a 'quack doctor'.

There were others such as Harriet Hart (1814–1897) – the Witch of Snoreham village, Essex, England.

The Boston ring

Without going into the details of the crimes and trials of the individuals the evidence of any connecting link between any of the 'Boston ring' is very slim. Mary Lefley came from the same village as Priscilla Biggadike and guilt by association played a prominent part in her trial.

PART 3

The Essex Ring

Time Line - The Essex Poison Ring

January 1845
Joseph and James Chesham become ill and die in Clavering.

August 1846
Sarah Chesham arrested for poisoning Solomon Taylor. Inquest opens on Joseph and James as well.

21 September
Times article.

October
Inquest finds Sarah Chesham murdered both sons as well as Solomon Taylor.

11 to 13 March 1847
Trial of Sarah Chesham who is acquitted of all three murders.

April
Catherine Foster executed in Bury St Edmunds for murder of husband with arsenic. Thomas Ham dies in Tendring.

July
John Southgate marries Hannah, widow of Thomas Ham in Tendring.

June 1848
Death of William Constable (Spratty Watts) in Wix. Inquest opens.

July
Mary May found guilty at Chelmsford of murdering William Constable.

August
Mary May executed. Inquest into death of Thomas Ham in Tendring.

September
Nathanial Button exhumed. Inquest in Ramsay finds arsenic but no crime.

September 21
Second *Times* article

March 1849
Trial of Hannah Southgate for murder of Thomas Ham. Acquitted.

Summer and Autumn
A major cholera epidemic rages throughout Britain, with symptoms exactly the same as arsenic poisoning.

August
Mary Ann Geering convicted of murder by poisoning several members of her family.

May 1850
Roger Chesham dies in Clavering. Inquest on him opens.

September
Sarah Chesham arrested.

14/15 March 1851
Trial of Sarah Chesham for attempted murder of Roger. Found guilty of attempted murder and sentenced to hang.

24 March 1850 to 24 March 1851
Bill on sale of arsenic debated and passed by House of Lords.

25 March
Sarah Chesham executed.

Chapter 6

The Role of *The Times*

In 1959 the historian of journalism Allan Nevins[1] analysed the importance of *The Times* in shaping the views of events of London's elite:

> For much more than a century *The Times* has been an integral and important part of the political structure of Great Britain. Its news and its editorial comment have in general been carefully coordinated, and have at most times been handled with an earnest sense of responsibility. While the paper has admitted some trivia to its columns, its whole emphasis has been on important public affairs treated with an eye to the best interests of Britain. To guide this treatment, the editors have for long periods been in close touch with 10 Downing Street.

From the 1830s, 'The Thunderer' became the nickname of *The Times* newspaper, initially with reference to the writing of the journalist Edward Sterling (1773–1847).

The Happisburgh poisonings

The Times Monday June the 1st 1846

THE POISONINGS IN NORFOLK
HAPPISBURGH, SATURDAY NIGHT

Great as the excitement was throughout this part of the county on the discovery of the recent horrible cases of poisoning, it has been renewed and increased considerably by the fact of the Secretary of State, Sir James Graham, having expressed his intention to reinvestigate the circumstances attending the mysterious affair. A government officer has already arrived, and, assisted by Mr Superintendent Smith, of the Leedham division of the Norfolk police force, and Col Oakes, the chief constable of the county, having been making private enquiry; the result of which not only confirms what was stated at the coroner's investigation, but goes far to clear up the matter and point out the perpetrator of the diabolical crimes. It seems that the cases of poisoning which have occurred in this village and neighbourhood are no doubt more numerous and appalling than was at first imagined ... The deceased man, Balls, and he only, was the guilty agent in this murderous traffic. His object may be seen in disposing of his wife, who was an old bedridden woman, and who now and then occasioned him some trouble, but it is difficult to imagine a motive getting rid of the children, whom he had not to maintain, and to whom he invariably showed much kindness. The government officer is busily employed in this and the neighbouring villages in tracing out suspicious facts relating to the affair; upon the report of that gentleman will depend any further investigation.

The cases of poisoning are far more numerous than was at first imagined, and the report of the inquests before the county coroner will give but a faint idea of what has been done on this dreadful system. Suspicion, not stronger than that which now exists with reference to the cause of death of many others, led to the exhumation of the bodies of four persons and that of old Balls. The evidence at the inquest proved that four out of the five had been poisoned, and the probability Balls intentionally administered it. In addition to these deaths, there were several other grandchildren of Balls whose deaths were as suspicious; and hence arises the supposition, that if a strict enquiry were made respecting their fate, they would be found to have perished by similar horrible means. Within ten years no fewer than twelve grandchildren of the deceased Jonathan Balls, eight belonging to one daughter, Mrs Green, and four to the other daughter Mrs Pestle, the subject of the recent proceedings before the coroner, have died after being attacked with similar symptoms. To this list may be added Balls and his wife, both clearly ascertained to have perished from arsenic; and yet in all these very suspicious deaths, only one inquest was held, until the enquiry consequent on the shocking discovery. All these children were in the habit of visiting their grandfather's house frequently ... By several persons it has been proved that old Balls was in the habit of buying arsenic for years past ... There are a few persons residing in the vicinity of the village that remember Balls's father and mother dying suddenly and in a very suspicious way, similar to the other deaths; twenty-two years ago they came to live with him, and shortly afterwards perished as before stated. It also ought to be stated that during the last few years many labouring men who were in the habit of mixing greatly in Balls's society, and visiting him at his house, have died after two or three days illness, and from a cause far from being satisfactorily explained. These numerous deaths, all of a similar character, coupled with the circumstances of Balls having been known to have been guilty of several wicked acts, have naturally given rise to a general opinion throughout the district they have been unfairly disclosed of; in fact, they have been poisoned in the same way as the children whose bodies have been exhumed. As has been mentioned,

Balls was in the habit of perpetrating disgusting offences, and according to a statement made to us by one of the heads of police, has been twice charged with the offence of arson and was generally termed in the village a mischievous old man.

One fact shows very clearly that Balls was alone implicated in this dreadful affair, which unfortunately was lost sight of by the coroner and jury. When the last child of his daughter, Mrs Pestle, died, the mother became alarmed, and said she would preserve the piece of membrane which the child threw up and give it to the surgeon, Mr Hewett, to be examined. This circumstance was stated at the coroner's inquest; but it did not come out in the medical testimony that the piece of membrane in question been examined. On Mrs Pestle stating her determination, the old man replied 'Oh don't do that' but, she still declaring her intention to do so, he must have taken the poison immediately afterwards, for he was a corpse within a few hours... There is no doubt that if an enquiry had been instituted in the first and second death, the dreadful system would have been detected and the other diabolical murders prevented ... It is anticipated that the preliminary enquiry will terminate about Monday night, and a report of the result will probably be forwarded to the Home Office on Tuesday.

Enter rumour, many tongued.

Notes on the Happisburgh case

A Home Office enquiry was launched. The Home Office file[2] contains the following information.

1. From the Register who is a surgeon 3 May1846

The report becoming so prevalent in the district that a number of persons have died exhibiting similar symptoms to the deceased Jonathan Balls I wrote to the registrar and again to the parish offices and Minister of Happisburgh stating I was not satisfied and that I considered they gave me a hasty certificate without making due enquiry. The following are the answers received:

2. William Clawes 4 May 1846

The overseers of Happisburgh came to me yesterday to say that you had written to them to make enquiries about the case of Balls and wish me to write to you. I have not been able to ascertain anything more about it than when I saw you before he was buried that I took the actual care to see the guardians of the parish and they express themselves quite satisfied, indeed I registered the death on the information of one of them, so that I can say no more about it.

I am dear Sir,

Yours truly

3. From the parish offices of Happisburgh

Sir

In reply to yours and as you require an immediate attention, we did give you a hasty certificate, but it was a correct one so far as we were able to ascertain, we have since been to Walham and enquired of different persons and there is no such report prevalent as you state. We would feel obliged if you would give us the persons named who called upon you to know the reason you were so quiet? As we cannot give any further information than that which we have already done.

I am so your very humble servant,
Clarke overseer and constable,
sincerely, George Vincent (and two churchwardens).

PS myself and churchwardens called on Mr Clowes on Saturday and he says no doubt Balls died from the effects of poison but further information we cannot give you.

4. Norwich 21 May 1846

In consequence of these replies I made the journey to Happisburgh to obtain information where I was quite satisfied that there were reasonable grounds for supposing deceased died from the effects of poison and that a great number of persons have died under similar suspicious circumstances, I immediately issued my warrant for the Disinterment of 5 bodies and proceeded with the investigation I ordered the bodies to be analysed and 3 very skilful surgeons and chemists attended to whom great praise is due for the care and attention they gave to the case. The result of the investigation was that 4 of the bodies disinterred appeared to have died from the effects of poison; the other body was so decomposed it was impossible to be sure. I then issued my warrant for the exhumation of 5 more bodies and a very long investigation took place on analysis it was clearly proved that 2 had died from the effects of poison and the opinion of the surgeons was that the other died from the same cause but the consequence of the bad state of the bodies there was a difficulty in drawing a conclusion.

From the general mass of evidence I have taken in these cases I am clearly of the opinion that the deceased Jonathan Balls was the party who committed these numerous murders and that being some reason causing him to suspect that the discovery would take place put an end to his own existence in a similar way. I am bound to remark that I believe the cause of the parish officers not sending for a coroner, in the first instance to be the result of the circular issued by the magistrates of Norfolk and sent by them into every parish in this county of which the following is a copy:

'…resolved that it be, and is accordingly a recommendation in this court that every coroner acting in this county when requested to hold an inquest should require a certificate from the magistrate or from the Minister or a churchwarden overseer or guardian of the parish stating the necessity to his opinion of its being held and that the coroner for said should deliver such certificate with his bill and that in case said certificate should not be produced the coroner should make strict enquiry as to the necessary of an inquest by the court'.

In consequence of this order of magistrates duties of coroners are much fettered and I take the personal opportunity of submitting that some more reflective mood than the present board to be resorted to for giving information to the coroner in all cases of sudden death. In this county there are police officers in every part … it would be desirable they should receive instructions to communicate with the coroners in all cases of sudden death. They are for the most part a more active set of men than the local authorities … Present case was 1st investigated by the parochial authorities.

I take the liberty of sending a copy of the remarks of the foreman on delivering in the verdict of the jury in this case and I also heartily concur with him that some better regulation ought to be made.

I have the honour to be your very humble servant
J Pilgrim, coroner for Norfolk.

5. The Foreman's remarks as appended

The jury retired to agree upon their verdict and after a lapse of about half an hour returned when Atkinson, Esq, the foreman requested on the part of himself and Jury to make a few observations.

He said no one could agree more than they, that such an occurrence should have disgraced this peaceable neighbourhood, or that such mysterious and horrible cases of poisoning should ever have taken place in a civilised country but it is lamentable to perceive in what a state of wilful wickedness and ignorance many of the lower order of society still remained. He said wilful for were some parish churches better attended, they would there learn their duty to both God and men, and then the jury and those present would be spared the witnessing such horrible scenes as those which had been brought them together on the present occasion. The jury did not think that blame could be imputed to any of the ministers of parishes where these melancholy investigations had taken place, they thought that Sir James Graham had taken proper measures but searching out the author of these continued murders the such they must be called he said that they were of the opinion that inquests are not held oftentimes where they ought to be in cases of sudden death – it frequently, said the foreman, the parish officers in consequence of instructions given scenes are unravelling for the coroner (and in many cases police), it is of importance but attempts to investigate the matter themselves are naturally sought to keep down county expenses, but not to sacrifice of human life, and we think that these cases must operate as a caution to the parishes generally as to the necessity of investigating before coroners and surgeons where there is the least suspicion that all is not right. Doing so in the 1st instance. A great many lives might have been saved by the speedy recommendation of justices and its punishment of the perpetrator of the deed we could suggest that some further collaborations should be made for giving notice to the coroner in cases of sudden death, that post-mortem examinations should be made wherever required by the coroner or jury, and that to that end the payments incidental should be paid without so much dispute, it is also highly necessary that the state of all poisonous drugs should be better regulated and that no other but a chemist should be allowed to dispense them, and that with great caution to whom they are supplied. They wished also to say that they thought the investigation was highly necessary and had been satisfactory to the district to the public generally and that ought to be fairly remunerated the medical gentleman had had a very disagreeable and difficult examination to make, they had given the intense attention for which they merited the acknowledgement of the jury.

6. J. Pilgrim, coroner for Norfolk to J.M. Philipps Esq. Secretary of State's office, Whitehall

Sir, in answer to your enquiry respecting the propriety of an investigation by an experienced member of the detective police into the deaths of Jonathan Balls, Elizabeth Bowles, Samuel Postle and Elizabeth Postle

I beg to state that in my own experience the only guilty party is the deceased Jonathan Balls, but really excitement in the neighbourhood of Happisburgh is very great in consequence of its being strongly suspected that there are other parties implicated and other deaths from a similar cause. I think therefore for public satisfaction it will be desirable that no means been left untried to discover the authors of the crime. Should it be determined that an efficient person be sent to investigate I shall be happy to render every assistance in my power.

7. Home Office note (OS 1386) 24/05/1846

As to sending down the detective police officer in this case of poisoning at Happisburgh the letter should be forwarded to Chief Constable of Norfolk.

8. Norwich. J. Pilgrim coroner for Norfolk to J.M. Philipps Esq, Secretary of State's office, Whitehall 18 July1846

The recent cases of poisoning at Happisburgh in Norfolk.

In compliance with the request of the late Secretary of State Sir James Graham to supply general information upon the subject of this case and to communicate the results of the enquiry I beg to state that in the latter part of April last I incidentally heard that a man by the name of Jonathan Balls residing at Happisburgh had died suddenly under suspicious circumstances.

I wrote a letter to the Minister and parochial authorities of that parish and also saw the registrar of the district. Not receiving any reply I wrote a 2nd letter and received an answer as follows: –

'We the churchwardens and overseers of the parish of Happisburgh are satisfied that Jonathan Balls of this parish died from old age (79) and he had for the last 8 days being obliged to go to bed in the course of the daytime and have every reason to believe that he died of old age.'

Andrew Siely and George Vincent, churchwardens, Theo Clark and Mrs Siely overseers.

Was Jonathan Balls guilty?

Our attention is drawn to the following pieces of evidence from the Home Office file. There is in fact no reason to doubt the evidence of the parish officials that they indeed attended Jonathan Balls who had, in their opinion, been on his deathbed for eight days and was incapable of getting out and about. During this time he was being attended by his daughter, Mrs Pestle. Since he could not have a quantity of arsenic available to him without her knowledge, how could he have poisoned himself? Further, how could the poison have acted as quickly as she said it had, and before the Jonathan Balls autopsy, we only have her word that she accosted him and he did away with himself.

The coroner and local gossip were of the suspicion that this senile old man could not have accomplished these mass poisonings by himself, the motive was almost non-existent. The Home Office could not be bothered to get a proper investigator sent from London, but as the matter rests it reminds me of a case I was involved in where an Essex housewife in complete ignorance that she had been accused and charged with being a member of the Mafia had returned home, was tried in her absence, and the other seven defendants all blamed her as leader of the gang. Here the old man was conveniently dead so everyone could blame him. On what evidence we have today, Mrs Pestle is surely the prime suspect.

Chapter 7

The Times

Extracts from *The Times* 21 September 21 1846:

When we directed public attention three months ago to the frightful case of wholesale and indiscriminate poisoning in a remote Norfolk village… In our last paper, however, we reported the proceedings of an adjourned inquest in Essex, which threatened to supply materials for a conclusion almost as terrible as that resulting from the discoveries in Norfolk…

The following are the circumstances of the case, as sworn to in the evidence adduced … in the beginning of August a farmer, named NEWPORT was bought before the magistrates in Saffron Walden for the affiliation to him of the illegitimate child of LYDIA TAYLOR … suspicions were accidentally created that this child's life had been tampered with, and the enquiry was sufficiently pushed at the time to warrant the apprehension of SARAH CHESHAM, the prisoner, and she was committed to take her trial … Rumours were current the prisoner's own children have died by poison … The coroner issued his warrant for the exhumation of the bodies of her two sons – aged 10 and 8 years … their bodies were found to contain arsenic enough to kill a whole family. An inquest was accordingly held upon them … now again stands adjourned for a period of 5 weeks … promising to lead to evidence of a very important and conclusive character.

What the circumstances may be we cannot venture to conjecture [*But they did! At length*]. Crimes of the blackest dye, which the whole neighbourhood appear to have long known, or believed, are casually brought out apropos of some ordinary topic …When she is once in custody, of course every tongue is loose.

Though this case, according to its alleged particulars, is wanting in some of the outrageous enormities of the other, yet it exhibits features which are scarcely less strange or revolting. Murder was not committed murders' sake, but it was committed higher. As the facts are sworn to, in an ignorant and secluded village of Essex lived a reputed poisoner – a woman … who could put any expensive or disagreeable object out of the way, and who, as it was understood, practised her infamous trade upon her own children. Deeds which the imagination connects are seen at this moment naturalised in an uneducated English county. In the house of this Essex woman was actually found by the police an assortment of poisons & ointments, powders, and the like, such as was discovered by CLAUDIUS in the private cabinet of CALIGULA ... Whether SARAH CHESHAM was guilty of murder or not remains to be decided by a jury of her countrymen. That much is said to be held doubtful. But there is no doubt whatsoever ... It is beyond question that an accepted and reputed murderess walked abroad in the village unchallenged and unaccused and that all the inhabitants had seen her children buried without remark or outcry, though they were clearly convinced that there had been foul play. It is impossible not to infer from such facts as these, coupled with the disclosures in the previous case above alluded to, that our regulations for registering and scrutinising tests and their causes are yet most futile and ineffective, and that the ill-advised and shapeless suspicions occasionally found current respecting frequency of these frightful practices amongst the lower classes of society rest upon grounds which are neither unsubstantial nor insufficient. In the Norfolk case the matter was very justly thought worthy of government interference...

We cannot close these observations without remarking on the spirit displayed by some parties during the inquest, which would argue depravity beyond even the ignorant unconcern which passes over murder is a thing of no moment. Not only the mother of the accused, but other persons, On Friday, as will be found in our last paper, it actually turned out that one of the jury may be tampering with an undescribed child of the prisoner, who was a principal witness in the case. What is to be said of a district where cold-blooded murder meets with all the popular favour which is shown to smuggling in Sussex, or agrarian assassinations in Tipperary?

The Times, 22 September 1848

In the observations which we offered some two years ago upon the practice of wholesale poisoning, which are then come to light in the counties of Norfolk and Essex, and to which we regret that we have been recently compelled to return, we drew attention to a particular circumstance disclosed in the investigation which appeared to us calculated to create more real terror and to call for more prompt interference and even the very enormity of the deeds themselves.

No room was left doubting but the practice of secret poisoning, whether really carried on to any great extent or no, was at least supposed to be so; and in this case more is to be inferred from the supposition than from an actual disclosure of the fact ... Persons, believed by everybody to have made away with their husbands and children, were yet received into the common society of the village without any other regard ...

For a terrible confirmation of the views we then expressed, we can now point to the facts which are daily struggling to light in the investigations at this moment pending in the same county ... Witnesses admit with perfect naiveté that they were always convinced that certain persons, either men or children, have been quietly poisoned.

There was also, a woman generally reputed to be skilled in the conduct of these affairs, and whose agency for instruction was held at the disposal of any applicants. By an unusual piece of fortune ... MARY MAY paid the penalty of her crimes before the system of which she had been the head and chief was fairly disclosed. For it is not the least horrible feature about these catastrophes, that murder, as pursued and practised, seems to acquire a zest of its own, killing for killings sake becomes a frightful kind of gratification. Thus at Happisburgh, in Norfolk, it was proved that the old man whose conduct was the subject of enquiry had been known to poison passers-by and (Mary May) was at last detected by being observed to slip something into the mouth of a little child who she accidentally met in the fields. At Thorpe, where the inquest is still pending, it turns out that the witnesses are one day the prisoners of the next, and that those who give evidence against others are liable to equal suspicion themselves.

Indeed, the mere fact of an intimacy with a woman is now considered as affording *prima facie* grounds of suspicion...

We have not introduced the topic to our readers without the intention of indicating, as far as is practicable, the precautions immediately within our reach against a moral epidemic far more formidable than any plague which we are likely to see imported from the East. We are really hardly bold enough to hazard any specification of the number of victims to this diabolical practice but the graphics, by those best competent to judge, would appear to them either incredible or horrifying. To begin with, it is certainly competent to the authorities to check the present facilities for obtaining poison, and this is a point of more consequence than might at first be thought, for our modern LOCASTAS have fortunately no extensive acquaintance with the properties of deadly drugs. In every single case which has been investigated we believe that arsenic in its commonest form as being the agent of death, By stopping therefore, the indiscriminate sale of arsenic according to one or other of the numerous regulations which had been recommended for this purpose, the chief, if not the sole instrument of mischief, would be removed from the reach of the criminal. In the next place, though it may seem unnaturally cruel to add a single ounce to the burden of the Parish surgeon, yet the peculiar opportunities of that officer enable him, to cooperate most effectually with the local authorities in the detection of this hideous crime. But, beyond all other measures, it is imperatively necessary that the security supplied by the common law of the land against foul play with human life, should be so long negatived by the criminal parsimony of county officers. We mean that the duties of the coroner should not be circumscribed by the economy of his paymasters.

What apprehensions, indeed, could be entertained of law or justice by a woman who had been already left to the undisturbed perpetration of six successive homicides?

The last two articles have been deliberately edited to emphasise how much *The Times*' 'thundering' has been fuelled by rumour and gossip. Proof is in short supply.

PART 4

Sarah Chesham

Chapter 8

The Trials of March 1847

Morning Chronicle 12 March 1847

ASSIZE INTELLIGENCE. HOME CIRCUIT. – Chelmsford, March 11. Crown Side. (Before Lord Chief Justice Denman.)

Cases of Poisoning at Clavering. – Sarah Chesham, 36, a good-looking woman, the wife of a labourer, was indicted for the wilful murder of Joseph Chesham, her son, by administering to him a large quantity of arsenic. There were two other indictments for murder by the same means against the prisoner, one for the murder of James Chesham, another of her children, and another for murdering Solomon Taylor. The case appeared to create very great interest, and the Court was crowded during the trial. Mr. Montagu Chambers, with Mr. Wordsworth and Mr. T. Chambers appeared for the Crown, and the prisoner was defended by Mr. Serjeant C. Jones and Mr. Charnock. The Learned Counsel for the prosecution having stated at some length the facts of the case to the Jury, the following evidence was adduced.

Margaret Vines deposed that she lived at Clavering, and was acquainted with the prisoner. She remembered a short time before her son Joseph died that the prisoner asked her to buy her two pennyworth of arsenic when she went to Newport. The deceased shortly afterwards applied to her for the arsenic, and said he had been sent by his mother, but she told him she had not bought the poison, and returned the money. Cross-examined – The prisoner had several other children, and she always appeared to be very kind to them. She complained of being overrun with rats when she wanted her to get the poison.

William Law, a ratcatcher, deposed that the prisoner about the same time also made an application to him to get some arsenic, but he did not do so. She said she wanted to buy it for rats. Cross-examined – He believed there were a great many rats in the prisoner's cottage. Evidence was then produced to show that on that day and Saturday prior to the 9th of January, 1845, on which day the deceased child died, he was in perfect health, and made no complaint of any illness whatever.

Thomas Davids deposed that he occupied a cottage adjoining that of the prisoner and her family, and the floor of their bedroom was over the room in which he and his wife lived. He knew the prisoner's children, Joseph and James, and remembered their both dying suddenly in January, 1845. On the Friday before that day he saw Joseph and he seemed perfectly well. The next morning he saw the prisoner, and she told him Joseph was very ill – very bad indeed. Witness asked her what was the matter with him, and she said that as he was coming home on Friday, Mr. Thomas Newport, his late master, had met him, and struck him with a stick, and being frightened, he jumped on one side, and she thought he must have hurt something in his inside. Witness said if that was the case she had better apply to Mr. Hawkes, the parish doctor; and she replied that she would do so as soon as she could get an order. During a considerable part of that night he heard the sound of two persons groaning and vomiting in the prisoner's bedroom, and he had no doubt it was the prisoner's children whom he heard. He met the prisoner on the following morning, and told her that her children appeared very ill, and she said that she would go home and make that all right. On the Sunday night the prisoner knocked him up after he had gone to bed, and told her her child was dying. He then went into the cottage and found the boy Joseph was just dead, and he assisted to lay him out, but did not observe any marks of violence upon his person. The witness further stated that the liquid vomited by the children came through the floor of the room and on to the table where he and his wife were at breakfast. Cross-examined – The prisoner's husband was in the house at the time. The prisoner appeared to be crying, and held a handkerchief to her face. James, the other child, who afterwards died, was then alive. He did not examine the body of the child very particularly, because at that time he had no suspicion that there had been any foul play towards it.

By the Lord Chief Justice – The prisoner is a married woman, and lived with her husband. They had no other children besides Joseph and James.

Elizabeth Davids, wife of the last witness, confirmed the testimony with regard to the children groaning and vomiting during the night, and also spoke to the fact of the liquid coming through the ceiling. She likewise said that when the prisoner was taken into custody upon this charge she asked her to take care of her remaining boy, and she said she did not know whether she should ever come back again. The witness also said that upon one occasion, before the prisoner was apprehended, she told her that she dared say she should be hung on a gallows at the top of Chelmsford gaol, and that she should be burned underneath it.

By Sergeant Jones – She was very deaf. The prisoner might in reality have said that she counted that those who died of hard work would be buried under the gallows.

Mr. Stephen Hawkes, the union surgeon at Clavering, deposed that upon receiving information of the death he went to the prisoner's cottage, and he said, upon hearing the circumstances, that as the death from such a cause was very extraordinary at that season of the year, it might be necessary to open the body. The prisoner made no objection, and nothing further passed upon the subject. He attributed the death to cholera.

By Sergeant Jones – The symptoms that were described to him appeared to be those of cholera, and he certified to the registrar of the district that that was the cause of the deaths.

By Mr. M. Chambers – I did not see Joseph Chesham until after he was dead. The Lord Chief Justice – And did you feel yourself justified in certifying to the registrar that the death was occasioned by cholera when you had not had any opportunity of observing the symptoms of the disorder previous to death? Witness – I had no other cause of death to give from the symptoms.

The Lord Chief Justice – You knew nothing about the symptoms of your own knowledge, and you had no right to certify that the child died of cholera. You were aware that the Coroner had the power to order an examination of the body in order to discover accurately the cause of death.

The Rev. Mr. Brookes, the vicar of Newport, deposed that upon hearing of the death of the children he went to the prisoner's cottage to console her upon what was considered her sudden bereavement. The prisoner told him that Joseph had been ill for some time before he died, and that on Friday, when he came home, he complained of having been beaten by Mr. Newport, and when she asked him to have his supper he would not have any, and said he should never want any more supper. She spoke in bitter terms of Mr. Newport and his family, and said that her son Joseph was very much hurt at being dismissed from his service for stealing eggs, and said just before he died that he was innocent of the charge. The witness added that he remembered the coffin containing the two bodies being exhumed, and, although they were perfectly black, he could recognise the features of both the children, and pointed out which of the two was Joseph. Cross examined – When he went to the prisoner's cottage he had not the slightest suspicion that there had been any foul play, and he went away under the same impression. He had had opportunities of observing the conduct of the prisoner to her children, and never saw her act in any manner unlike a kind mother.

Mary Pudding said she remembered the prisoner coming to her house at Clavering shortly after the children died, and she kept on talking about them, and said that Tom Newport had turned her boy Joseph away and she did not know what to do with him. She then repeated the story about Newport striking him, and said that she and her child were always in the way, and it would be a good thing if they were both in the churchyard together. She also said that there had been some talk about a Coroner's inquest, but she would not have had one for the world, because her child would have been cut about.

Cross-examined – She had known the prisoner more than twenty-years, and she always looked upon her as a kind and affectionate mother. When she saw her on this occasion, she exhibited all the appearance of the grief of a Mother who had suddenly lost two children.

Mary Chesham, the prisoner's mother-in-law, proved that the bodies of the two children were buried in one coffin, and that it was the same coffin that was afterwards taken up. The prisoner described the illness of her children to her, and said that they were taken with pain in their body and continually wanting drink.

Mary Hall, the matron of Chelmsford gaol, deposed that while the prisoner was committed upon this charge, she expressed a desire for her to write a letter on her behalf. She at first took down what she wished to be stated in pencil, and afterwards wrote it in ink. She subsequently handed that letter to the governor of the prison, and it was the same now produced.

Cross-examined – she is sure she read it over to the prisoner. The governor told her to give him the letter, and she acted during the proceeding under the authority of the governor. She did not know whether the prisoner was aware that there was no intention to send the letter to the person to whom it was addressed. Was not aware that it was the intention of the governor not to send the letter.

Sergeant Jones – In point of fact, did you not know that the letter was to be made use of as evidence against the prisoner at her trial?

Witness – I did not know it at the time I wrote it nor did the prisoner.

Sergeant Jones – Did you not believe that the object was to make the letter evidence?

Witness – I do not know.

Sergeant Jones – Did you give her any caution?

Witness – I did not.

Sergeant Jones – I suppose you know now that the letter was never sent to the person to whom it was addressed?

Witness – Yes.

Sergeant Jones – Do you not know that it was immediately sent to Lord Braybrooke, the committing magistrate?

Witness – Yes.

Sergeant Jones – And was then sent to the Home Office, and afterwards to counsel to consult upon it?

Witness – I heard so afterwards.

By the Lord Chief Justice – I took the statement down from the prisoner's mouth – she wanted to add more.

Chief Justice – And why did you not write more for her?

Witness – Because it was a long story she wanted to tell me. The letter in question was then put in.

The following is a copy –

'Chelmsford Old Gaol, Dec. 22. 1846.

'Mr. Thomas Newport,

'Sir – Mr. Bowker informed me when I saw him last, that my friends would keep me with money to board myself, he left me a half sovereign. Mr. Bowker said he would call again by the time that money was spent, but I have not seen him since. I know it is not in my own friends' power to keep me, therefore you must; for, Mr. Newport, you well know you promised me, when we stood against Pondfield Gate together, that I should want for nothing – that what I wanted I was not to stand for any expense, for you would pay it. You told me not to speak of it, but now, I must, for you won't send to me, nor let my own relations come to see me – for 'tis you and you only that keep them from me – you know you ruined me and brought me to all this trouble, and you know it is true, and my friends know the same – I wish I told all about it when I was at Newport station, for if I had spoke the truth there, you must have been in prison as well as myself. You deserve to be here more than I do, for you did it and not me, and you know I have told you that I would speak of it, times and times, and you told me not to be a fool; for I told you I would have a letter wrote and keep it by me for fear anything should happen to me; for I always told you you would be the death of me, and so I say now. It is your money keeps you out of prison; you deserve to be here more than me. Mr. Newport, you shall support me. for I am suffering for the crime you did. You caused the death of my poor children. I am wretched, and always shall be, for you know what I have upon my mind, and I cannot never be happy any more, and if you do not suffer in this world, you will in the next. You know this is all true, and much more if I could be allowed to send it.

'From the unhappy Sarah Chesham.

'PS. I hear I am going to be brought in fault about Sarah Parker, at Wigett's, but you know it was yourself did that.'

Mr. Henry Brookes, surgeon at Newport, deposed that he removed the contents of the stomachs from the bodies of both the infants, and having carefully placed them in separate bladders, and marked them, he transmitted them to London to undergo chemical analysis.

Mr. Taylor, surgeon, and lecturer on medical jurisprudence at Guy's Hospital, deposed that he received the bladders and analysed their contents. The one marked No. 2 which contained the stomach of Joseph Chesham, he found to contain a large quantity of arsenic, and he produced some copper plates covered with the arsenic that was obtained from the stomach, 'there must have been at least eight or ten grains of arsenic, and there was certainly sufficient to have destroyed life'. He should say in this case that, beyond all question, the death was occasioned by arsenic.

Cross-examined – He was decidedly of opinion that a less quantity than eight grains could not have occasioned the appearances he found in the stomach of the deceased.

Re-examined – He had not the slightest doubt of the cause of death. He found arsenic in powder in the stomach, and every part of the stomach contained poison.

By the Lord Chief Justice – He discovered enough poison to have destroyed two persons. This was the case for the prosecution.

Mr. Sergeant Jones then addressed the Jury for the prisoner, and in the course of his speech he urged that there was an entire absence of anything like positive proof against the prisoner, and also an absence of any direct evidence that she had ever had any arsenic in her possession. The Lord Chief Justice having summed up, the Jury, after deliberating for a quarter of an hour, returned a verdict of Not Guilty.

* * *

Indictment

Owing to the number of challenges it was difficult to get a jury for the trial of the second indictment against the prisoner, for poisoning, with arsenic, the other child James, on the same day, 10 January. A jury having at last been empanelled and sworn, Mr Chambers stated the facts of the case, which were very similar to those in the last. Lord Denman proceeded to sum up the evidence, observing that 'he did not remember a second criminal trial being brought where a formal acquittal had taken place on the same facts, and those facts certainly stronger but the history of all the case was most extraordinary, such we had never heard before. These two children were suddenly taken ill, and suddenly removed from this world by the operation of deadly poison; and it was not wonderful that counsel should take the opportunity of asking the opinion of second jury upon it.' The jury, after a consultation of 20 minutes, returned a verdict of Not Guilty.

Chapter 9

Sarah Chesham Trial For Murder
Of Husband

Essex Standard Friday 7 March 1851.

THE CLAVERING MURDER.

The trial of Sarah Chesham, charged with administering poison to her husband, with intent to murder him, at Clavering, having been fixed for Thursday morning, an immense crowd gathered round the entries to the Court, anxious to hear the investigation into the case of one who had become notorious by her previous trial in 1847. Mr. Bodkin and Mr. Clark conducted the prosecution; prisoner was undefended. The Prisoner having been arraigned, and pleaded not guilty.

Mr. Bodkin opened the case for the prosecution. They had, he said, heard the indictment read, which charged the woman at the bar with a most serious offence, and he had to bespeak their earnest attention to the very solemn enquiry about to be made into circumstances in themselves so extraordinary that it had been thought right, under the authority of the Home Office, to lay this case before them. In the outset he had to request them to dismiss from their minds everything respecting the former transactions of this wretched woman, and to decide upon the particular charge now before* them upon the evidence which should be adduced, and upon that and that alone to found their verdict. He was the more anxious to press this upon them because it would be impossible in this inquiry to avoid references to other transactions of a similar character to that about to be brought under their notice, and as far as he could he would dismiss them from his mind, but in the course of conversations between the prisoner and others allusions to those former transactions were so palpably made that it would be a species of false delicacy in him not to allude to them. In 1847 she was tried for a similar offence in the poisoning of her two children, upon which she was acquitted, and he alluded to this only to impress upon them the importance of not allowing this to prejudice their minds. The learned counsel then gave an outline of the facts as deposed in evidence, and said if it was proved that she administered the poison it would be for them to say whether there could be a doubt of her intention in its administration.

Sarah Chesham deposed – Deceased was my son-in-law, and husband of the prisoner, he was about 45 years of age at the time of his decease, and had been ill from the winter time, and died in May, 1860. During the latter part of his illness I resided with the deceased eight or nine days: prisoner's father, named Parker, and a daughter and three sons of the prisoner, were also at home. During the last six days I was in the house the deceased was unable to feed himself, and the prisoner fed him. I never saw anyone else feeding him during the last six days. She gave him a mixture of honey and milk, but not any more for some time before his death. The last time she gave him anything to take was about two o'clock on the morning he died, when she gave him something in a tea-spoon. On Wednesday he received nothing but a portion of an orange. For the last few days of his life I was with him continually, but all that he had was fed by prisoner, who seemed willing to go. and I remained in the room. In answer to the prisoner, witness said she did not see Nathan Copperfield give the deceased anything, and that she (prisoner) always appeared kind to her husband.

The deposition of Mr. George Willing, relieving officer, who has died since the committal of the prisoner, was read. It set forth that on his visits to the deceased he found him suffering from great distension of body, with frequent attacks of vomiting and purging, and that for a short time before his death prisoner fed him with tea, milk, and flour.

Mr. Hawke, surgeon, of Saffron Walden, who attended the deceased by request of the relieving officer, found him labouring under violent cramping pain in the bowels and distension of the stomach, accompanied with sickness; suitable remedies were administered, but the symptoms returned at intervals, sometimes with increased violence; an irritant poison taken in small quantities, would produce those symptoms; he recommended his wife to get some further advice, but she said she was satisfied, saw the deceased two days before death; he was then rapidly sinking, and unable to help himself; from the post-mortem examination he concluded that the immediate cause of death was disease of the lungs; he took the stomach and portions of the large and small intestines (which were inflamed) and handed them to Professor Taylor.

Mr. Thomas Brown, surgeon, also of Saffron Waldon, who assisted at the post mortem examination, also deposed to inflammatory appearances, such as would be produced by an irritant poison.

Supt. Clark spoke to searching the prisoner's house. She made no objection till he took a bag of rice from the kneading trough, when she said, 'I hope you ain't going to take that away as it is my father's, and I have used some of it for my husband.' The rice was handed to Professor Taylor.

Mr. Lewis, the coroner, stated that at the inquest, there being no charge against the prisoner, she was examined as a witness. Mr. Bodkin, as the prisoner had no counsel, hesitated to use her deposition. The Judge thought it was admissible, and it was subsequently put in and read. The prisoner therein described her husband's symptoms, and denied that she had ever fed him with rice or milk.

Professor Taylor detailed the results of his analysis: there was no trace of food in the stomach; in the fluid which it contained there was a small quantity of arsenic and also upon the coals; the intestines bore the appearance of the action of arsenic; the whole quantity found was about the 20th part of a grain; that would not have been sufficient to destroy life; it might have been the residue of a much larger dose taken some days before; he should attribute the symptoms described by the medical witnesses to the repetition of small doses of arsenic: in the bag of rice (about one lb.) he found 16 grams of arsenic; every grain of rice was coated with it.

James Parker, the prisoner's father, proved buying the rice; he had eaten some of it several times, and it took no effect whatever upon him.

Hannah Phillips detailed conversations with the prisoner, in which the latter spoke of how her children were poisoned by another party – how she had poisoned the child of Lydia Taylor, and suggesting how she (the witness) might make a pie to get rid of her husband.

After the evidence. The learned Judge summed up. It was, he said, an offence which still remained capital under the 1st ACT Victoria; and although it was said she had acted with uniform kindness to the deceased, and that consequently no motive could be assigned for the deed; yet if the evidence brought the charge home to the prisoner, it would be their duty, however painful, to find the prisoner guilty. Before, however, they come to that decision, he begged them to have the proof of guilt brought home irresistibly to their minds. After a few minutes' consultation, the Jury returned a verdict of Guilty. His Lordship, having assumed the awful symbol of death addressed the prisoner in terms of the usual Homily and observed:

...According to the evidence which has been given you confessed that you have murdered your own children, and although you may have escaped justice, at least for a time, you have at last been overtaken.

Was Sarah Chesham guilty of murder?

The most thorough analysis of the Essex murders and Sarah's innocence is to be found in the Master's thesis by adult Canadian student Jill Ainsley[1]. Her telling analysis of the general press clamour surrounding the accusations of poisoning and the escalations of convictions of Mary May and indeed Sarah Chesham into mass hysteria and wholesale poisonings terrorising the villages deserves detailed study. Her hypothesis that the prevailing agricultural use of arsenic referred to in the letter to *The Lancet* (see Part 1) coupled with the accusation of theft of eggs might well have resulted in Sarah's two sons poisoning themselves by accident, is the most sensible explanation of their undoubted deaths by arsenic I have encountered. As for the death of her husband we have the following evidence with regard to the bag of rice.

Yes it was true that she tried to prevent the police taking away the bag of rice but it was on the grounds that her father had rice prepared for him regularly and he would miss it. (The Cheshams were in penury, and it would have been a burden to replace it.) This was coupled with the uncontested evidence of her father that she regularly prepared rice for him and there had been no ill effects. Dr Taylor's evidence was that 'the bag contained enough rice to kill six people', that 'every grain of rice was covered and the whole appeared to have been carefully mixed up together so that every part of the rice was poisoned and the interior of the bag containing the rice was likewise covered with arsenic'.

So how did the idea of Dr Taylor's that the poisoning had occurred with little doses over a period of time square up with the large quantity of arsenic carefully spread through the rice? And why on earth did Sarah Chesham not get rid of the rice immediately her husband died if she had indeed put so much arsenic in it? One is driven to the probable conclusion that when the rice was taken by the police from her house it did not contain arsenic. She was also open with both the doctor and her mother-in-law about the feeding of milk and rice to her husband.

Then there was the evidence of the testimony of Hannah Phillips. In the formal evidence she made allegations that adultery formed part of Chesham's motive for ridding herself of her husband. It was Ainsley who noticed in her voluminous research that Phillips did not explain why she failed to report Chesham's confessions about having poisoned Solomon Taylor and her intention to poison Lydia Taylor, or why she didn't disclose Chesham's threats about her husband while he was still alive and she might have spared him the results of eating one of Chesham's seasoned pies. There were also quite extraordinary statements by her markedly different evidence in the magistrate's court and assize, but there was no one acting on Sarah's behalf to cross examine this dubious witness, so willingly accepted by the trial judge as proof of the previous murders. Her husband gave evidence that he had no idea his wife was so close to Sarah, and she had never talked to him about these conversations until after the inquest.

In my experience of miscarriages of justice abroad I came across a number of instances of police 'improving' evidence when they were quite sure that those they had in custody were guilty of the crime. The most ridiculous cases I was involved with were due to the planting of spare weapons on innocent demonstrators in Italy and Belgium, proved by international press video footage to have taken place.

Superintendent Clarke was in charge of all the cases brought against Sarah; he must have smarted over the criticisms of the conduct of the investigations of the first three cases. He must have been quite sure that she was guilty of poisoning her husband as soon as he died and well before Dr Taylor's examination. If Sarah was unlikely to be responsible for the arsenic in the rice then he was probably responsible for 'improving' the evidence after its confiscation. I do not believe poor Sarah Chesham was guilty of killing or trying to kill anyone.

PART 5

Mary Ball

Mary Ball Timeline

28 June 1818
Mary Wright (later Mary Ball), daughter of Isaac Ellis Wright, christened in Nuneaton.

22 November 1819
Birth of Mary Ann Evans, later known as George Eliot, born at Griff, near Nuneaton.

22 April 1838
Mary Wright and Thomas Paul married at Mancetter church. Both give their ages incorrectly.

20 January 1847
Mary Ann Ball born in Back Lane, Nuneaton, daughter and only surviving child of Thomas and Mary Ball.

The crime

4 May 1849
Mary Ball buys one pennyworth of arsenic from Illife's Chemist shop in Nuneaton marketplace. Her neighbour, Elizabeth Richardson, signs as witness to the purchase.

18 May
Thomas Paul goes fishing with friends Joseph Petty and Thomas Watts. Returns home, feeling 'out of sorts', eats gruel and goes to bed at 6 p.m.

19 May
In the early hours of the morning Thomas is in great pain, refuses to have Dr called. Later that day, Mary acquires order parish and has Dr Prouse examine Thomas at 2 p.m. Later the same day Dr Prouse refuses to visit Thomas again when asked to do so by Mary.

20 May
In the early hours of the morning Thomas dies. Dr Prouse is called that morning and diagnoses death by natural causes – inflammation of the stomach.

21 May
Constable Vernon suspects foul play and interrogates Mary. He wants to know what Mary did with the arsenic she had bought some two weeks earlier. He checks Mary's version, finds contradictions and, together with constable Haddon, arrests Mary on suspicion of murder.

22 May
Post mortem carried out by Dr Prouse and Prof George Shaw at Birmingham University confirms presence of arsenic in Thomas's stomach. Mary charged with murder and taken to Coventry jail to await trial.

The trial

28 July 1849
Mary is tried for the murder at the County Hall Summer Assizes, Cuckoo Lane, Coventry. The judge is Mr Justice Coleridge: after a trial lasting more than six hours she is eventually found guilty of wilful murder and sentenced to death.

Events between trial and execution

31 July 1849, Tuesday
The Reverent Bellairs, Vicar at Bedworth and visiting magistrate Coventry prison visits Mary.

1 August
Bellairs falsely claims to have visited Mary on Wednesday not Tuesday.

2 August
Mary visited by her daughter Mary Ann with Mary's sister and mother.

Bellairs visits Nuneaton. The Rev Savage, Rector at St Nicholas Church, Nuneaton – Mary's parish – writes a letter on Mary's behalf to Home Secretary.

Memorial submitted on Mary's behalf by her lawyers pleading for a pardon.

3 August

Bellairs visits Mary for the second time in three days.

Bellairs writes letter to Home Secretary against a show of mercy for Mary.

Mary has something to say but only to Stanley the prison governor.

4 August

Mary tortured by Chapman the prison chaplain but still refuses to confess; Coleridge writes report on the Memorial on Mary's behalf.

Warrington passes on report with note.

5 August

Chapman suspended provisionally.

Stanley reads to Mary.

Mary confesses to Stanley?

Bellairs preaches condemnation sermon on his own insistence.

6 August

Grey turns down plea for mercy.

Mary visited by friends.

7 August

Hearing suspends Chapman permanently from duties as prison chaplain.

Plea papers returned to Coleridge.

Mary hears of unsuccessful results of the Memorial on her behalf from her solicitor.

Execution

9 August

Mary Ball becomes the last woman to be publicly hanged in Coventry. The execution takes place on scaffolding erected against the exterior of the prison wall, adjacent to the county jail. Around 20,000 people witnessed the spectacle.

Chapter 10

Background

On 13 October 1817 Isaac Wright and Alice Ward married in Nuneaton. On 28 June 1818 Mary Wright (later Mary Ball) was christened – probably born at the end of May or very early June.

Mary Ball's whole life was spent in Nuneaton, then a small town of approximately 6,000 inhabitants, the main industry being ribbon weaving, an industry based mainly on home workers and in depression since the end of the Napoleonic wars and, at the time of her birth, due to competition from the technically advanced French. A trade agreement with France allowed cheaper ribbon, a major consumer commodity, to flood the English market.

We know a lot about the life of the town in the 1820s and 30s, Mary's formative years, through Robert Muscutt's pioneering work based essentially on John Astley's diaries[1], a meticulous record of life in Nuneaton from 1810 until the mid 40s providing a comprehensive and lively portrayal of the town's social, economic and intellectual activity.

For example Astley notes on ribbon weaving:

> December 1831 – the year 1831 was a year of great distress to the dependence on the ribbon trade. Unemployment and poverty was the lot of hundreds in this town. The poor rate doubled. 700 gallons of soup were given away weekly (the soup kitchen had been opened the previous month). In November 2,700 people have been receiving parochial relief and soup from the charitable fund.

Astley calculated that of a total of 4,219 looms in Nuneaton, 3,482 were unemployed, leaving fewer than 20 per cent working. Mary Wright would then have been 12 and helping her father, Isaac, with the Inn he ran.

Astley records the turmoil caused in October 1830 by the coming into operation of:

> The ministerial acts of throwing the beer trade open taking off of the whole beer duty (about 2 shillings and 8p per barrel) it excited great interest amongst the people and was anticipated... Drinking and enjoyment was the order of the day...'

It is typical of Astley that he lists the names of all the old public houses and new beersellers in Nuneaton … There were 44 existing pubs and 33 new ones, a total of 77 for an adult population of approximately 4,000; a ratio of 1 Inn to 80 adults during a depression. Innkeepers' earnings must have suffered with the rest.

Amongst other things it is clear that Mary probably had no schooling and never learnt how to read or write. On the documents that exist signed by her, the signature is a cross not a name. As shall be seen this was a matter of life and death for Mary after her conviction.

Marriage

Thomas Ball and Mary Wright were married on 22 April 1838 at Mancetter church. Thomas had been christened at 10 years on 15 May 1831, which made him at best 17 years old on his wedding day, but the marriage certificate gives his age as 20, whereas Mary's age on that certificate was given as 21, a slight exaggeration. James Ball, their first child, was christened on 4 January 1839 and died four days later in his first year of life. The 1841 census finds Mary, Thomas, and their living child William Paul, living in Abbey Street in the same house as Mary's parents and her two sisters, Sarah and Elizabeth, aged 14 and 12 respectively.

On 17 September 1843 John Bacon married Jane Ball, older sister of Thomas. Sometime in the mid-1840s John and Jane Bacon became next door neighbours to Thomas and Mary. In addition to the married couples, there was John Bacon's younger brother, William Bacon, who was still in his teens when the new residents arrived at some time after 1843. It was young William, or 'flitch' Bacon as he was nicknamed who later allegedly became Mary's lover.

In the ensuing 12 years Mary gave birth to six children, only one of whom survived infancy. Mary Anne born on 20 January 1847 was the only child destined to survive, again as Muscutt remarked, Mary had probably begun an affair with William Bacon and maybe it was his genes that donated the child a sturdy constitution that kept her alive until 1927.

Chapter 11

The Trial 27 July 1849

From the *Coventry Herald*, 3 August 1849

CHARGE OF MURDER

MARY BALL, aged 31, was charged with the wilful murder of her husband, Thomas Ball, at Nuneaton. Mr. Hayes and Mr. Mellor appeared for the prosecution; attorney, Mr. Craddock. Counsel for defence, Messrs. Millar and Denistoun; attorney, Mr. Cowdell.

Joseph Petty deposed that he is a ribbon weaver, living at Nuneaton; had known Thomas Ball, husband of the prisoner, for some years; on the morning of the 18th of May, witness, with Thomas Watts and Ball, went fishing in the Little Burton Canal; they left home about 9 o'clock the morning, and returned about five minutes past 4; they all came to Nuneaton together; Ball went straight home, and witness went home; when they were out, Ball appeared to be well; the same evening he saw the prisoner; all deceased had, while out with witness, was a little cold water from a pump; prisoner came about 9 o'clock to witness's house, and said 'Tom is very bad a-bed; I want him to have a doctor, and he won't listen' She then left; prisoner again came over on the following morning about 11 o'clock, and said. 'Go and see Tom, he's very bad;' witness went, and found deceased in bed; prisoner was there; deceased said he could make no water, complained of his belly and being very sick, threw up, and said he should die; witness remained with him about a quarter of an hour; prisoner was walking about the room crying; saw deceased at 7 o'clock at night, when he appeared to be in the same state and made the same complaint as in the morning; witness remained with him quarter of an hour; saw him again at 12 o'clock that night; deceased said 'Look, feel my arms, they are quite benumbed – rub them;' the prisoner was by at the time; witness rubbed deceased's arms, and told the prisoner to call him up if Ball was worse; witness then left; about 2 o'clock in the morning, prisoner called him up, and said Tom's dead;' witness then went over, and prisoner had a fit, cried, and tumbled down; she was in the fit about ten minutes; witness went up and laid deceased out, and asked prisoner to go to deceased's sister's to have a cup of tea; at the time witness saw deceased, when he was alive, he complained of thirst; had known him for 16 years; he had been married 12 years;

deceased had six children, and had buried five of them; he was a healthy man; when witness went in the morning, and found him dead, he did not see anything hanging by the fire.

Cross-examined by Mr. Miller – It was just after Nuneaton Fair, which lasted three days; deceased's father-in law kept a public-house, and deceased assisted him for two or three days during the Fair; prisoner was not at home when deceased came home from fishing, she called at the house of witness after they returned, to know if her husband was come back; the prisoner was subject to fainting away, and had a very bad memory.

Re-examined – She could not retain things long at a time.

By the Judge – Had lived near them for two years, and during that time he knew prisoner to be subject to fainting fits, when she was put about she would faint away; witness had seen her faint away when she was put about; it was out ten minutes before she came to herself; witness thought her memory got worse; she did not have a doctor for her fainting fits; she never fainted away excepting she was what witness called put about.

Selina Ryland is the wife of Edward Ryland; knew Ball, husband of the prisoner, for four years; lived next door to him for two years and a half, and within about 140 yards during the latter part of his life; they had four children, and one alive at his death; never knew them to have any dispute but once, and that was about six weeks before Ball's death; on that occasion prisoner came down and said her husband had beaten her on account of some lies his sister Jane had told him; prisoner cried, and said before he should serve her in that way, by heavens she would poison him. She had never seen them quarrel but twice; witness went with prisoner to her own house; they quarrelled and had a few angry words; prisoner then said the words about poisoning; witness asked why did he beat her; deceased replied he saw enough through the chamber boards yesterday with Bill; one other time of their quarrelling was when deceased went to Macclesfield; they came to her house to breakfast, and witness, after breakfast, gave deceased some pork; he took his handkerchief to tie it in, and asked his wife to fetch him another; she had replied she would see him first; deceased said he would fetch it himself, and as he was going prisoner said she hoped that as he set the first step on the railway, a gang wagon would run over him, and heaven, if he ever returned, she would poison him; this was in March or April, 1848.

Mary Bishop, wife of Samuel Bishop, lives at Nuneaton; the father (deceased) lived two doors from them; prisoner came to their house with her cousin, a man named Ward, who went away and left them alone; witness said she wondered what Ball would say at her coming there; prisoner said she wished they were all in hell, and the next time there was anything said about it, she would murder her husband; witness then said that would be end to both of them; prisoner said she would do it if she went to hell.

Elizabeth Richardson, wife of Joseph Richardson, lives at Nuneaton, near to prisoner, on the other side of the road; recollected Ball dying; had some conversation with prisoner on the 4th of May; she came to witness about half-past 10 o'clock the first time, then about 12, and again about 2; prisoner asked witness to go with her to buy pennyworth of arsenic; witness asked what it was for; prisoner said for bugs; witness agreed to go; this was at half-past 2 o'clock; they went to Mr. Illiffe's; when they got to the door, prisoner said she did not like to ask for it, and gave witness the penny to pay for it; they both went into the shop together; Mr. Illiffe's elder shop man, a younger one, and two men whitewashing, were present; witness asked the elder for a pennyworth of arsenic; she did not like to say bugs, but said vermin; the shop man gave her the arsenic wrapped up in paper, and then in another paper; there was the word 'Poison' on the paper; witness is no scholar, but could tell that word; the man who gave it said 'Is she come for a witness?' witness replied 'It's for her, and I have come for a witness for her;' witness gave it to prisoner, who said, as they were going home, 'Don't say anything about it, as you know what a set of devils I live among;' prisoner carried it in her hand, and said 'You think such a bit as this would poison anybody?' witness replied that half that quantity would; they got home about 3 o'clock; witness went into the house again about half-past 3, called prisoner down stairs, and said 'Mary, if I were you I would tie a handkerchief over my mouth, for it might damage your inside;' prisoner replied that she had thought of that herself; prisoner gave witness a penny farthing to buy half-a-pint of ale, for her trouble in going to fetch the arsenic; she had tea cup in her hand; in about 20 minutes afterwards prisoner came into witness's house and said she had done them; on the day prisoner's husband died, witness went into her house; prisoner afterwards came into witness's house at breakfast; witness said 'Mary, it a bad job your poor husband going off suddenly;' prisoner replied 'It is a good job he's gone' this was said at witness's house, while she was at breakfast; she seemed better than anyone would the loss of a husband; witness had seen prisoner and her husband often quarrel; they lived very unhappy life; had heard deceased call prisoner whore, when she answered him that if she was not one she would be; had seen them quarrel about a quarter of a year before his death; had seen prisoner in presence of Vernon, the constable, when witness told the latter about going for the arsenic; prisoner told Vernon she had mixed it up in the cup, and after mixing it up she had thrown the cup away, and asked witness if she had not seen her throw the cup away; witness said how could she, without looking through the wall?

Cross-examined – Prisoner inquired of witness what would destroy bugs; witness said she had used arsenic for the same purpose herself, and found it succeeded; she asked witness not to say anything about it, as her husband's friends would think she was a dirty woman, his sister having said that those who were clean need not have them; when she came down with the cup she had the feather in the other hand.

By the Judge – She had used it herself in mixing water with it: when prisoner came down she had something in the cup looking like paste; the feather did not look wet, as she had not begun.

Philip Morris is an assistant to Mr. Illiffe, chemist, at Nuneaton; the prisoner and last witness came in and asked for arsenic; he inquired what they wanted it for; they said for bugs; he cautioned them, labelled it 'Arsenic – poison,' and they left.

Abel Vernon deposed that on hearing of Ball's death he went to the house, and on seeing the prisoner, said 'This is a bad job, your husband going off in this way;' witness then said 'Mary, have they been informed you have been buying poison;' she did not deny it, and said she had been with Mrs. Richardson to buy it, that she had mixed it in cup, used it all, thrown the cup away, and burnt the paper, for fear her child should get hold of it; that was all the conversation; prisoner said she had thrown it in Richardson's dirt-hole; he searched the dirt-hole on Monday, but could not find it; witness then went with Haddon to Richardson's house; Haddon asked her about buying the poison; she said the same as she had said before; on the 21st of May witness went to the prisoner's house, and found her at home; he said Mary, I have been informed that you have been giving your husband poison she denied this, but said she had taken little of the arsenic out the paper, put it in sugar-paper on the pantry shelf, where there were some salts, and he must have taken it in mistake; she did not know where the paper was; she had taken the salts upstairs; when they went to the pantry he could neither find the paper nor the salts, and prisoner then said she had taken the salts upstairs, and she would give them to him; she went upstairs, witness following, and from behind an old teapot on the chimney she took out a paper with some salts, which she said had been bought at Illiffe's; there were about nine drams; prisoner said she wished she had told witness and Haddon first, in consequence of which he fetched Haddon, and she repeated in the presence of Haddon what she had told witness; witness examined the bed's head, which was anointed with something white in two places; witness then took prisoner into custody.

Cross-examined – Prisoner said she wished she had told him and Haddon, as she was afraid she should be taken into custody.

Ann Hopkins is the wife of John Hopkins, of Nuneaton; had known deceased from a child; heard of his death on the Monday; went to his house and asked his wife to let witness see him; prisoner took her upstairs to see him; when witness was going out prisoner asked her to sit down, and she would tell her all about it; she said she had had Abel Vernon and Mr. Haddon, who asked her where she bought the stuff, and she told them at Mr. Illiffe's; they asked her what she had bought it for, and she told them to do the bedsteads for the purpose of killing the bugs; that she had burnt the paper, and thrown the cup away; she wished she had told them the truth, as it would perhaps be better for her, for if they opened her husband she should be hung; witness said, 'Oh Mary! Do not say it, before the jury, or you will be done'; prisoner then said, 'I am done, for I had a bit of arsenic in a paper, which I put in his gruel and gave to him, made some gruel and gave him some all the day, and very sick and bad he was;' that was the last prisoner said to her; a man named Blunt came in about some tickets, which she gave him, and said what was she to about some cloth to make her husband some trousers; he said he would pay the use of them (meaning interest); she then called him back said, 'Do you think he has thrown it up?' Blunt said, 'Thrown what up? you G–d–d fool; if he has not thrown it up, when they cut him open it will be seen on his stomach, for his stomach will be like a piece of beef;' then the prisoner said, 'I shall be hanged.'

Cross-examined – Blunt was before the Coroner; she was put out of the room while he was examined; did not hear the evidence read; did not hear her say he had gruel to make him throw it up; she gave him gruel; he threw all the day, and he was very sick and bad.

Thomas Watts is a weaver, and lives at Nuneaton; went with Ball and Petty on a fishing excursion on the 18th of May; they came home together in the afternoon; deceased passed witness's door, and he never saw him afterwards alive; when they were out deceased complained of being very dry, and had some water from a pump; the last day of Nuneaton fair was on the Wednesday as the deceased died on the Sunday; saw prisoner and said, 'Mary, I understand they are going to open your husband, and if they do and find any poison, you will be taken up. Prisoner then cried bitterly, and said she was sure to hang; this was on the Monday; she then told him that after dressing the bedstead to poison the bugs, she had a bit of the stuff left, which she put on the shelf in a paper; witness replied, 'Good Lord, Mary I hope William Bacon had nothing to do with it?' prisoner said he was as innocent as a lamb; a man named Kean then came up and said Bacon wanted to speak to her at Peacock Lane; prisoner left witness and went to Bacon; witness went up to him and said, 'William, if you stand talking here you will be taken up he never saw any quarrelling between the prisoner and her husband; witness and deceased were shopmates; prisoner used to come to the shop, in which Bacon worked, to help her husband; when witness and deceased were out fishing he told witness he had had a sup too much at the fair, and his inside was very queer.

The Judge – Had nothing to eat all the time they were out fishing. John Woodhouse was about twenty yards from prisoner; on the Sunday her husband died he went to the house, and saw the prisoner and another person named Wright; prisoner said she was troubled at the tale they had got about; witness said that need not trouble her if she knew she was innocent; she then asked if they would cut him open; witness told her they would; she asked if she could stop them, and he said he thought not; she said she would if she could; on the Monday he saw Jane Watts and Elizabeth Wright, and he said, Mary, how came you to do this?' she said she could that and hundred times more.

Mr. Prouse recalled – He should say from two to three grains arsenic would produce death was quite certain from twelve to fourteen grains would produce death; had he heard nothing about the poisoning, the appearances he observed in opening the body would not have led him to any other conclusion than that he had given a correct certificate of the cause of death. This closed the case for the prosecution.

Mr. Millar, in addressing the jury on behalf of the prisoner, expressed his deep sense of the solemn duty he had to perform. He asked them to give a verdict strictly in accordance with the evidence, and he was certain if they did so they would acquit the prisoner. He then called their attention to the station of life in which both the prisoner and her husband moved, so that they might form a proper estimate of the foul language imputed to her in the course of the quarrels which had been mentioned. This language did not necessarily imply the existence of feelings more vicious, or more vindictive, than prevailed in the higher classes of society. Notwithstanding these quarrels, there was no evidence to warrant the belief that they did not, upon the whole, live on good terms together, therefore there was the absence of any adequate motive to the commission of the dreadful crime with which the prisoner was charged. With respect the expressions made use of by the accused, and which were looked upon as confessions of guilt, such expressions might be attributed to the agitated state of mind in which she appeared in consequence of the suspicions cast upon, and the insinuations that had been thrown out against, her. He then called the attention of the jury to the evidence, endeavouring to explain it away, or making it speak in her favour. There was no concealment as to having obtained the arsenic, which had been purchased three weeks before the murder. There had been no quarrel, even when they went to the fishing. The surgeon had acknowledged that the deceased had taken the cold water in consequence of his stomach being out of order; and as to the circumstance of his having taken an aperient draught, was anything more likely than that a person in his station would do so, thinking would ease his stomach, having had nothing to eat? Besides, he complained to one of the witnesses on the Friday that he had had more drink than usual during the previous three days, and felt very queer in his inside. Was it not likely, this being the case, he would take salts? The man going to look for the salts, where he supposed they were, took the arsenic, by mistake; as prisoner was out when deceased returned, and finding himself no better, he went to bed. When she returned he was in bed, the salts having been previously removed upstairs, where they were found as she stated. When the arsenic was placed in the pantry there was no doubt she intended take it away again, but being a woman of a forgetful habit had not removed it, and this had led to such fatal consequences. As to the fact of having burnt the paper, a good reason had been given for that because her child should not come to any harm. He contended that by placing the paper on the shelf, when she knew it was a dangerous poison, would amount to no more than manslaughter, and instanced the case of a confectioner at Northampton, who had suffered his apprentice to sell some emerald green, by which some persons came by their death: he was found guilty of manslaughter. Her culpable negligence in placing the paper of arsenic on the pantry shelf, and finding it gone, had been the cause of this alarm in her mind, and, through the agitation, not being able to give a correct or satisfactory account of it; therefore, at the most, she was only guilty of manslaughter. Had she intended to murder her husband she would have been satisfied, to save appearances, in going once to the surgeon, as he, being one the poor law union surgeons, had so many persons to attend he had no time to pay that attention (being a pauper) which the case demanded. With the specimen they had had from the surgeon and others they could not place much credit on conversations; because, if it had been true of her having admitted giving him the poison, and that it would have been better for her had she told the truth at first, she meant it would have been better had she told them of the poison being taken, so that proper remedies might have been made use of. She said she had kept back a portion of the arsenic to dress the holes in the bed sacking. He thought they would not be justified in returning a verdict of guilty to the charge of murder from the evidence. That they would come to the conclusion that he died from the effects of arsenic, he did not think there would be much doubt. However, into that part of the case he should not go. Trying the case its real merits they would discharge their duty as reasonable men, which he was sure they would do, if they were satisfied without any reasonable doubt. Could they say the woman was guilty? Was sure they would weigh the facts cautiously before they arrived at that conclusion, because there would be no remedying such a mistake in a case this kind. In cases of a lighter kind there might be a remedy, but in this there would be none. (The learned gentleman occupied about two hours and a quarter in his address to the jury.)

The Judge, in summing up the case to the jury, remarked that the prisoner at the bar was charged with the wilful murder of her husband, administering arsenic to him in some gruel. It had been suggested by the prisoner's counsel that the deceased had taken it by mistake in some gruel; but if they did not come to this conclusion they might come to a verdict of not guilty, because according to the law the prosecutor was bound to prove the guilt of the prisoner: the prisoner was not called upon to prove her innocence. He was not saying they would come to this conclusion. They might suggest a third, which would answer the case of the prisoner well as the one suggested by the prisoner's counsel. The question was, did the prisoner administer the poison? Prove this it must be shown she had it in her possession, else without this the case would be weak. To show she had it in her possession, his lordship called the attention of the jury to the circumstance of her going to buy the poison; and her mixing a portion of it in a cup, with a feather in her hand, proved she set to work immediately, and that arsenic was in the house when this crime was committed. The coarse expressions she had made use of were no proof of her guilt, and he cautioned them against being led away by them. After this caution, he would call their attention to the evidence of the witnesses who spoke to this fact. His lordship then went very carefully and minutely through the whole of this part of the evidence, and then said the first question for them to consider was, whether the prisoner was in possession of the arsenic at the time, on which point he considered there could be no doubt. The next question was, did she administer it to her husband? They had heard the whole of the evidence; and after a full and impartial consideration, giving each part its due weight, if they were satisfied there was no guilty intention, they would return a verdict of not guilty, or if they bad the least doubt, they would give the prisoner the benefit of it. But if, under all the circumstances, and after they had carefully considered the whole, they came to the conclusion that she was guilty, they would give a verdict accordingly. The summing up occupied one hour and twenty-five minutes. The jury retired at twenty-five minutes to seven. At ten minutes past eight they returned into court, when the foreman said they had agreed to a verdict of guilty, with recommendation to mercy. His lordship asked, upon what grounds? The foreman replied that some of the jury were not quite satisfied with part of the evidence. The judge told them they must reconsider their verdict. They then turned round, and immediately returned a verdict of guilty. The judge then put on the black cap, upon seeing which the prisoner shrieked out, begged for mercy, and declared she was innocent. His lordship, after dwelling upon the enormity of the crime, and the cause thereof, said he could not hold out the slightest hope of mercy. He then sentenced her to be taken to the place from whence she came, and (after a convenient time) thence to the place of execution, there to be hung by the neck till she was dead, her body to be then buried within the precincts of the prison. May the Lord have mercy on your soul. The Court was crowded. The prisoner had on a black shawl, and manifested throughout the whole of the trial as much indifference as if she was merely a spectator.

Chapter 12

The Fight for Mercy

The key documents were:

2 August
The humble memorial of Mary Ball prisoner under the sentence of death now lying in her Majesty's jail at Coventry – a legal document drawn up by Mary's lawyers.

A letter from the Rev Savage, Vicar at St Nicholas, Mary's parish church, pleading for mercy.

3 August
Letter from Henry Bellairs, clergyman and magistrate, in effect dealing with the Rev Savage's letter.

4 August
The trial judge Coleridge receives the above documents and writes to the Home Office. The lawyers' petition uses the following arguments:

> That your petitioner is a woman of mean education, defective eyesight, imperfect memory and subject to epileptic fits.
>
> That your petitioner is advised that the learning and venerable judge who presided on the trial of me your miserable petitioner as far as my distracted memory will afford said: 'that was not the time or place for him to make any observations which might lay the foundation of the hope of mercy.'
>
> And that your petitioner further show that the jury who passed (judgement) upon the trial of your petitioner were greatly divided in opinion, and that they retired and were closeted together for upward of three hours, and the date of such jury were of the opinion when they retired from the jury box in court that your humble and miserable petitioner was not guilty to the last and fatal moment the said jury never were agreed to find her guilty save upon the promise that she should be recommended to mercy and that in pursuance of such bargain your petitioner was as she had advised improperly and unconstitutionally convicted of an offence which she now knows solemnly asserts her innocence...

Mary's eyesight and memory both had a bearing on the trial. The defective eyesight may have caused confusion between the arsenic and salts, and the possible lie about the disposal of the excess arsenic could have been genuine lapse of imperfect memory.

The Rev Savage's letter stresses the fact that Mary herself fetched the doctor and showed her anxiety about her husband's health by going to a second medical man when the first refused to attend the dying man. Mary's depth and level of intelligence and ignorance also featured.

Coleridge's letter commences: 'I do not doubt her guilt at all nor do I see any effect stated by the petitioners that bring it into question.' He then recounts the sequences of the events as he saw them. Her husband went out and came home apparently quite well, she reports him ill at about two hours after and says she wanted him to have a doctor but in fact (that being 6 p.m.) no doctor was applying to until 2 p.m. the next day. He died 12 hours later.'

Some facts are omitted. A witness testified that Thomas had not been feeling well before going home. He also implies that Mary was reluctant to call a doctor and she deliberately delayed the visit. He totally ignores the evidence that she needed a poor law order to get a doctor.

What we have here is that Coleridge is convinced of Mary's guilt regardless of the jury men's opinion, who he seems to feel were unduly influenced by some evidence in favour of Mary. Both during the trial and in his report Coleridge deliberately steered events, both of the jury's decision and now the outcome of the appeal, to an outcome he deemed desirable.

He concludes: 'However … Nor do I think such bargains ought to be encouraged at the same time it is not satisfactory as could be desired in a case of life or death'.

Waddington, the Home Office official responsible to the Home Secretary, ends his report to the Home Secretary: 'The compromise, then, was a breach of duty on the part of the jury and might not, strictly speaking, have any weight at all on the decision of the case. You will see, however, by the last sentence in Coleridge's letter that he is not quite satisfied.'

On the above evidence, there was surely a reasonable expectation that Mary would receive mercy and probably be sentenced to transportation for life.

However, the same day, the Home Office received a letter from Bellair.

> Sir
> The governor of the Coventry jail having informed me as one of the visiting justices of the said jail that a prisoner under the sentence of death, Mary Ball, signed a petition to your ex and said, in which amongst other things it was set for that eyesight wanted, I deem it my duty to acquaint

you that any proper mercy on those grounds is false. Those at the jail assured me that she can read small print without the aid of spectacles.

I beg to add that the said prisoner's request I visited her on Wednesday last (1st August) and in consequence of a statement then made to me, but yesterday went to Nuneaton and examined several persons. I am sorry to say that I elicited nothing from them which would justify any application by me on her behalf. This case has naturally created a strong sensation and I was hopeful that I might have been able to address you differently.

I have the honour to be so,
Your faithful servant.

Bellair's statement is wrong as to the date he visited Mary, perhaps not too much should be read into that. What is surprising is that he should visit Mary at her own request when there were other magistrates and clergyman already involved in her case: in that respect this suggestion he visited her on Wednesday could have been deliberate.

What is totally astonishing is the assertion based on the alleged testimony of the prison governor that Mary was able to read small print without the aid of spectacles. In that one sentence we have the risible claim that Mary was not only of good eyesight but also literate. From her marriage certificate of 1838 to the memorial presented she always signed with her mark. Further, Bellair was resident in Bedworth and travelled the 10 miles to Coventry and back on horseback or by coach and then he made the 6 mile return journey to Nuneaton where he examined 'several persons' (all in 48 hours). We do not know who they are but he could not have consulted his colleague the vicar in Mary's parish.

As Robert Muscutt remarks, the clue to this vicious and dishonest letter may partially be found in this minister's domineering and self-opinionated character. It is generally accepted that the character Mr Fellowes in George Eliot's *Amos Barton* is based upon him.

> At the other end of the table ... Sits Mr Fellowes, rector and magistrate, a man of imposing appearance with a mellifluous voice and the readiest of time. Mr Fellowes once obtained a living by the persuasive charms of his conversation, and the fluency with which he interpreted the opinions of an obese and stuttering baronet, so as to give that gentleman a very pleasing perception of his own wisdom. Mr Fellowes is a very successful man, and has the highest character everywhere except in his own parish where, doubtless because his parishioners happened to be quarrelsome people, is always at fierce feud with a farmer or two, culinary proprietor,

a grocer, who was once churchwarden, and Taylor who formerly officiated as clerk.

As Muscutt observes 'the terse betrayal, for all its gentle irony, is of a self-seeking smooth talking cantankerous sycophant.'

In his research note *'Arsenic and the gallows in Mary Ball's Coventry'* Dr Norwood Adams, researcher at the Centre for the History of Medicine, University of Warwick, writes that:

> The murder trial – in which Mary sat silently while witnesses, advocates, jury and judge established an authoritative version of corrections in their appropriate consequences – reflects various crosscurrents, one of which was a then emerging gendered construction of poisoning, not merely as a familiar type of crime but also as a particular social threat.

Did she confess?

A handbill, was also published.

> THE CONFESSION OF MARY BALL AS MADE TO MR STANLEY, GOVERNOR OF THE JAIL, TO WHICH IS ADDED AN ACCOUNT OF HER EXECUTION.
>
> She said, 'I want to tell you something!' I said, 'What is it Ball?' She answered me, 'I did not like to tell anyone else but you! I told Mr Bellair, on Tuesday, a lie.' I said 'What was that?' She said 'I told him I knew nothing about it myself but that is false. I put the arsenic on the mantle shelf told him there was some salts on the shelf – he might take them, they were doing good: I knew at the time it was not salts but I thought if he'd taken it himself I should not get into any scrap about it, that people would think he took it by mistake.' I then said to her 'For God's sake Ball what made you do it?' She answered me and said 'Why, my husband was in the habit of going with other women, and use me so well: no one knows what I have suffered, but I had I known as much as I do now I would not have done it for I would rather have left him and gone to the work house: but I hope God will forgive me.' I asked 'If anyone else knew anything about it?' And she said 'No one'. I asked her how she came to say anything about salts to her husband? She said 'The complaint he was not very well: I thought I would then tell him there was salts on the shelf, but I knew it was not.'

While it reads well, could it be true? Surely not, because there is a lack of a Holmesian dog bark: the first thing the governor would do would be to rush this confession to the Home Office. No such document exists.

The woman, who in Coventry on 9 August 1849 was hanged before a crowd of 20,000, was at worst, cause of a spur of the moment self-poisoning which could have been prevented, and at best, instigator of a straightforward accident.

Mary Ball and George Eliot

In 1849 Mary Anne Evans (who wrote under the pen-name George Eliot) was living in Coventry. She was a close friend of the Brays, and Charles Bray was the proprietor of the *Coventry Herald*. Her father, Robert, died on 31 May and was buried on 6 June. On 12 June she left England with the Brays for a long tour of the continent. There is some evidence that she was kept informed of the sensational events in Coventry during July and August 1849. The Brays had returned on 3 August, back in time for Mary Ball's execution. What remains of Mary Anne's correspondence of the period (largely destroyed by her husband on her death in 1880) speaks of her being starved of news from Coventry and requesting copies of the Herald from the Brays.

Whilst we are aware that Hetty Sorrel as a character in *Adam Bede* was based on the condemnation of Mary Voce for infanticide two generations earlier, it is quite clear that Hetty's trial is set in St Mary's Guildhall Coventry. The description in Adam Bede:

> The place fitted out that day as a court of justice was a grand old Hall, now destroyed by fire … Grim dusty armour and in high relief in front of the dark oak and gallery the further air; and under the broad arch of the great mullioned window opposite was spread a curtain of old tapestry, covered with dim melancholy figures, like a dosing indistinct dream of the past. It was a place that through the rest of the year was haunted with the shadowy memories of old kings and queens, unhappy, this crown, imprisoned…

As Muscutt remarks:

> Both the physical features in the historical associations fit perfectly in the Guildhall. And it provides the ideal scenario for the fictional drama. *Adam Bede* was written less than 10 years after the real trial of Mary Ball in the County Hall. Was her reading of the reports of this event present in the great novelist's mind when she penned the witness statements, the jury's verdict and the judge's solemn pronouncement of the death penalty?

PART 6

Priscilla Biggadike

Chapter 13

Prelude: The 'Boston Murders'

Mary Ann Milner, 1847

At the time of the crimes, 27-year-old Mary Ann lived with her husband in the north Lincolnshire village of Barnetby le Wold where he was a farm labourer. According to contemporary reports she was an attractive woman. She was a serial poisoner who had, in all, four victims, three of whom died and one, her father in law, who survived but was paralysed. Her parents in law had become ill and were ordered to eat sago which Mary Ann prepared for them. When Mary, her mother in law, died it caused suspicion and her body was subsequently exhumed and found to contain arsenic.

Mary Ann was tried in a packed courthouse before Mr. Justice Rolfe at Lincoln on 20 July 1847 on three separate indictments. These were the murders of Mary Milner on 5 June, her sister in law, Hannah Tickels, on 26 June and her niece Ellen Tickels on the 15 June, to all of which Mary Ann pleaded not guilty. The prosecution was handled by Messrs. Wildman and Dennison and the defence by Mr. Miller. The murder of Mary Milner was tried first and Mr. Wildman presented the bare facts of the cases and asserted that the motive was purely to obtain money from the burial society. Mr. Miller highlighted the deficiencies in the evidence and maintained that Mary Ann had no motive for wanting her mother in law dead. Mr. Justice Rolfe summed up favourably to Mary Ann and the jury quickly bought in a not guilty verdict. The second indictment was therefore heard. The jury heard that Hannah Tickels had been poisoned by arsenic in a pancake on 26 June and that the arsenic had been purchased from the village grocer, William Percival, on the pretext of poisoning rats.

Hannah had eaten the pancake at breakfast with Mary Ann and quickly became ill and started vomiting. However she was able to tell her friend, Mary Winter, about the pancake. Another of her neighbours gave evidence that Hannah had told her about the pancake and she had mentioned this to Mary Ann who turned pale and was almost unable to walk. Mary Ann went to Hannah's house and reportedly asked her 'O Hannah, do you think the pancake has caused you to be so?' Hannah survived until around 6 p.m. that night. As the death was suspicious a post-mortem was held by James Moxon and the presence of arsenic in Hannah's body was confirmed by Mr. Patterson, a surgeon from nearby Brigg. Thus Mary Ann was arrested and charged with the crime. In his second summing up Mr. Justice Rolfe told the jury that there could be little doubt that Hannah's death was caused by eating the pancake with arsenic in it, but the real point that they had to determine was whether the arsenic was knowingly or accidentally mixed into it.

The jury took 20 minutes to convict Mary Ann and as she received the mandatory death sentence, the third indictment was not proceeded with.

Aftermath

From 1817 on, the gallows at Lincoln was erected for each execution on the roof of Cobb Hall, a large tower forming the north east bastion of the castle and visible from the street below. It was accessed by the prisoner and officials via a spiral stone staircase within the tower leading up to the roof level. William Calcraft had travelled up from London to execute Mary Ann, since she was due to go to the gallows atop the Cobb Tower of Lincoln Castle at noon on Friday 30 July 1847.

Mary Ann made a written confession to all three murders but asked that it not be made public until after her death.

At about 7.45 on the Friday morning a matron discovered Mary Ann hanging from a metal staple in her cell; she had hanged herself with a silk scarf that she had worn at her trial. It was reported that she was naked and that her clothes were neatly folded up. She had last been seen alive around 9 p.m. the previous evening by the prison chaplain. An inquest was held the following day and returned a verdict of felo-de-se (suicide).

As a result all prisoners under sentence of death were never left alone in their cells between sentence and execution.

* * *

Catherine Wilson 1862

From *Bad Companions* by Kate Clarke[1]

> Catherine Wilson, *nee* Crane, sometimes known as Constance Wilson
> or Catherine Taylor, was born in Surfleet near Spalding Lincolnshire.

Crimes

> Wilson worked as a nurse first in Spalding, Lincolnshire, and then
> moved to Kirkby, Cumbria. She married a man called Dixon but her
> husband soon died, probably poisoned with colchicum, a bottle of which

was found in his room. The doctor recommended an autopsy but Wilson begged him not to perform it, and he backed down.

In 1862 Wilson worked as a live-in nurse, nursing a Mrs Sarah Carnell, who rewrote her will in favour of Wilson; soon afterwards, Wilson brought her a 'soothing draught', saying 'Drink it down, love, it will warm you.' Carnell took a mouthful and spat it out, complaining that it had burned her mouth. Later it was noticed that a hole had been burned in the bed clothes by the liquid. Wilson then fled to London, but was arrested a couple of days later.

First trial

The drink she had given to Carnell turned out to contain sulphuric acid – enough to kill fifty people. Wilson claimed that the acid had been mistakenly given to her by the pharmacist who prepared the medicine. She was tried for attempted murder but acquitted. The judge, Mr Baron Bramwell, in the words of Wilson's lawyer Montagu Williams, QC, 'pointed out that the theory of the defence was an untenable one, as, had the bottle contained the poison when the prisoner received it, it would have become red-hot or would have burst, before she arrived at the invalid's bedside. However, there is no accounting for juries and, at the end of the Judge's summing-up, to the astonishment probably of almost everybody in Court' she was found not guilty.

When Wilson left the dock, she was immediately rearrested, as the police had continued their investigations into Wilson and had exhumed the bodies of some former patients. She was charged with the murder of seven former patients, but tried on just one, Mrs. Maria Soames, who died in 1856. Wilson denied all the charges.

Second trial

Wilson was tried on 25 September 1862 before Mr Justice Byles, again defended by Montague Williams. During the trial it was alleged that seven people whom Wilson had lived with as nurse had died after rewriting their wills to leave her some money, but this evidence was not admitted. Almost all though had suffered from gout. Evidence of colchicine poisoning was given by toxicologist Alfred Swaine Taylor, the defence being that the poison could not be reliably detected after so long. In summing up the judge said to the jury: 'Gentlemen, if such a state of things as this were allowed to exist no living person could sit down to a meal in safety.' Wilson was found guilty and sentenced to hang. A crowd of 20,000 turned out to see her execution at Newgate Gaol on 20 October 1862. She was the last woman to be publicly hanged in London.

The Boston connection

There were Boston victims. The *Boston Chronicle* of 26 July 1862 recorded the following inquest:

> The jury again assembled at the Peacock Inn to receive Prof Taylor's report of the analysis of the viscera of the deceased (Peter Mawer), evidence was given to the effect that the body of the deceased was exhumed on 3 July and that the lungs heart et cetera were sent to Dr Taylor for analysis.
>
> The coroner then addressed the jury as follows:
>
> 'Gentlemen, several witnesses are in attendance who could give the most circumstantial evidence with reference to the death of Peter Mawer. I do not think it is necessary to call them for this reason, that although their evidence aggravate previous suspicions, and prove almost a certainty that Peter Mawer was poisoned, yet chemical analysis has entirely failed to prove the presence of poison in the remains.
>
> 'It is now my duty to explain to you the circumstances which led to the exhumation of the body eight years after burial. He died on 17 October 1854, having previously made a will in favour of Mrs Wilson, his housekeeper; it is known that he was paid a large sum of money in cash a few days before his death, which money has never yet in any way been accounted for. The whole neighbourhood believed that he was poisoned and that this suspicion had been a matter of conversation for eight years. After the death of Mawer, the female, then called Catherine Wilson, but now called Constance Wilson, left the town for a time after disposing of a life interest in Mawer's estate. Two or three years afterwards, we find her in the house of a Mrs Jackson, near Bargate Bridge, Boston. She introduced herself as a nurse, companion, and confidential friend, Mr Jackson being from home in his business as a painter at Spalding.
>
> In a few days Mrs Jackson died with all the symptoms of poisoning and it was then found that Mrs Wilson, in the name of the dead woman, had withdrawn money to the amount of nearly £300, from Mr Grant's bank, the hard earnings of the husband. With the money she got clear, bidding defiance to the coroner, doctors and chemists. I pass over various rumours with reference to similar cases, because they have not come, at present, before the public, but there need be no delicacy in reminding you that this woman is now under remand charged with having poisoned Mrs Atkinson... They prove this fact – that wherever this woman introduced herself as a friend and a sister of mercy she proved a messenger of death.

The ensuing events from trials to execution were faithfully chronicled in the local press and became an enduring sensation.

Chapter 14

Death Watch

Transcript of prison officials

We are extremely fortunate in that, uniquely, the diaries and journals of the top officials in Lincoln prison for the year 1868 have survived. The relevant extracts cited here are those from the Governor of the prison, John Foster. (G), the chaplain H.W. Richter (C) the surgeon Mr Broadbent (S) and the Matron (M).

This transcript is as accurate as I can make it. Some of the handwriting is hard to decipher. The best handwriting of these diaries is that of the surgeon. The most sparse diary is that of the matron which accounts for the relatively few entries attributed to her.

October 1868

24 Saturday

(G) Priscilla Biggadike and Thomas Proctor committed by the magistrates at Stickley for trial at the Assizes charged with murder received today. The female having a female child with her 10-month-old. When the surgeon visits the prison attention will be called to prisoners. (Marginal note: surgeon's attention is called to Priscilla Biggadike and her child)

(M) Priscilla Biggadike received the trial at the next Assizes she has a baby with her and cannot attend chapel she has an allowance of 1 pint of milk and 6 ounces of bread daily this child.

25 Sunday

(G) Allowed Priscilla Biggadike 1 pint of milk and 6 ounces of bread daily for her child until seen by the surgeon… Priscilla Biggadike already attending to her child.

29 Thursday

(G) Priscilla Biggadike is in bed and complains of violent pain in her side to see the surgeon today. (Marginal note. Priscilla Biggadike to see surgeon.)

(M) Priscilla Biggadike very poorly and sick. Unable to look after her daughter.

30 Friday

(G) Biggadike still in bed (Marginal note Biggadike unable to leave bed.)

(M) Priscilla Biggadike rather better.

31st Saturday

(G) Priscilla Biggadike better … Priscilla Biggadike's child (Mabel?) Removed to the union workhouse at Lincoln at 10 a.m. today (Marginal notes Biggadike better,
    Biggadike's child removed to the union.)

November 1868

1 Sunday

(G) Priscilla Biggadike is in bed complains of real pain all over. Sent for the surgeon at 9 a.m. (Marginal note Biggadike in bed, to see surgeon.)

(M) Priscilla Biggadike very poorly.

2 Monday

(G) Biggadike was saying and allowed tea not milk in morning by order of the surgeon.

(M) Priscilla Biggadike no better.

3 Tuesday

(G) (Marginal note governor absent on duty.)

Priscilla Biggadike better today

4 Wednesday

(G) Priscilla Biggadike is somewhat better but still in bed. (Marginal note Biggadike a little better.)

5 Thursday

(G) Biggadike better and able to attend chapel (Marginal note Biggadike better.)

9 Monday

(M) Priscilla Biggadike likes to have ordinary prison food instead of tea.

10 Tuesday

(G) Priscilla Biggadike ordinary diet breakfast surgeons order see 2nd (Marginal note Biggadike better ordinary diet and infusion.)

December 1868

11 Friday

(G) Priscilla Biggadike convicted of the murder of her husband by poison today and sentenced to be executed; has been placed in C2 rooms in charge of Hannah Dowse warden. And strong instructions given in accordance with the prison rules. (Marginal note Priscilla Biggadike under sentence of death.)

(M) Priscilla Biggadike has been convicted of murder and sentenced to be executed placed in charge of Hannah placed in cell 6 B corridor.

12 Saturday

(G) Priscilla Biggadike allowed tea in place of Grual by order of the surgeon (Marginal note Priscilla Biggadike to have tea.)

(C) Visited Priscilla Biggadike convicted death.

(S) Visited Priscilla Biggadike a prisoner under sentence of death she has spent a restless night and refused all her food. She may be allowed tea and sugar and bread and butter in place of the ordinary prison diet.

13 Sunday

(C) Patricia Biggadike visited her in the afternoon found her much distressed and thoughtful of her situation.

(S) Visited Priscilla Biggadike. She has had some sleep during the night. Her appetite is very indifferent and her spirits are very much depressed.

(M) The surgeon has ordered Priscilla Biggadike to have a glass of wine before going to bed.

14 Monday

(G) Priscilla Biggadike under sentence of death has been told this morning that the date fixed is Monday the 28th day of December next. She appeared very much distressed and said is that all that is left for me. (Marginal note Priscilla Biggadike told the date fixed for her execution.)

Copy to the Right Honourable A Price. Secretary of State at the home department

Sir – I beg leave to report that at the Assizes held at Lincoln for the County of Lincoln on the 9th day of December 1868 Priscilla Biggadike was convicted of the wilful murder of her husband and sentenced to be executed also that the date fixed by her execution is Monday the 28th day of December 1868 at the hour of 9 o'clock in the morning.

I have the honour to be, Sir, your obedient servant,
J. Foster Governor
(Marginal note Priscilla Biggadike reported to Home Office.)

The accounts of money and other articles handed over to the Sheriff of the County of Lincoln by James Foster of Lincoln Castle belonging to the convicts of felony at the Assizes held on the 9th day of December.

Priscilla Biggadike two earrings and one gold ring, 3 shillings and 3pence

(S) Priscilla Biggadike is much in the same state as yesterday.

15 Tuesday

(G) Priscilla Biggadike allowed one glass of wine and going to bed, daily, by order of the surgeon. (Marginal note Priscilla Biggadike to have wine.)

(C) Visited Biggadike who still continued to deny her guilt saying it was Preston who did et cetera.

(S) Visited Priscilla Biggadike who is extremely depressed. She may be allowed a glass of wine every [evening].

16 Wednesday

(C) Visited Priscilla Biggadike steadfast in denying her guilt.

(S) Priscilla Biggadike complains of a rheumatic pain in the shoulder.

17 Thursday

(C) 3 o'clock visited Biggadike who surprisingly thought something with would be done for her. Cautioned her about delaying confession not to entertain such an idea ... Have written to the Minister of her parish requesting him to use his interest for her.

(S) Priscilla Biggadike is more composed.

18 Friday

(C) Visited Biggadike.

(S) Priscilla Biggadike is much as usual.

19 Saturday

(S) Priscilla Biggadike is in a better state of health than she has been since she received her sentence.

20 Sunday

(G) Priscilla Biggadike reported by the matron for attempting to ... One of her pocket handkerchief is ongoing to bed last night caution. (Marginal note Biggadike cautioned for attempting to conceal ... handkerchief.)

(C) Biggadike visited her both morning and afternoon.

(S) Priscilla Biggadike in better spirits.

21 Monday

(G) Priscilla Biggadike complains of being poorly and unable to leave her bed, to see surgeon today. (Marginal note Biggadike poorly to see surgeon.)

(C) Saw Priscilla Biggadike in the infirmary suffering both in body and mind read a letter to her received today in answer to one sent to the Minister Mister Cottermore in reference to some statements that she had made in a letter to him to her statements in it (he says) what importance can be attached? Even if true she assisted at the deed and attempted to conceal it by Mister Cottermore's wish I read the letter to her she denied passionately that having either assisted the murder for attempting to conceal it what can be held out to her of happiness?

(S) Priscilla Biggadike is in bed and very much depressed.

(M) Priscilla Biggadike very poorly and unable to get up and go to chapel.

22 Tuesday

(G) Priscilla Biggadike is better unable to attend chapel. (Marginal note Biggadike better.)

(C) Visited Biggadike warned her solemnly of dying unrepentant and unforgiven reminded her that everybody even her friends and relations considered her guilty … and then asked her whether she still denied being guilty she said (without hesitation) yes.

(S) Priscilla Biggadike is better.

(M) Priscilla Biggadike better this morning.

23 Wednesday

(G) Priscilla Biggadike appears very much depressed and has not taken anything this morning (Marginal note Biggadike depressed cannot take food.)

(C) Visited Biggadike: the governor made her acquainted this morning with the day of her execution she was greatly disturbed.

3 o'clock visited Biggadike hoping she would feel able to make confession of the crime…

(S) 3:30 p.m. Priscilla Biggadike is much depressed.

24 Thursday

(G) Priscilla Biggadike is somewhat better but very much depressed.

(C) Visited Priscilla Biggadike read and prayed with her.

(S) Priscilla Biggadike is much the same she sleeps well.

25 Friday

(G) Biggadike appears more composed this morning but taken very little food.

(C) Visited Biggadike.

(S) Priscilla Biggadike is much as usual.

26 Saturday

(G) Priscilla Biggadike visited by her sisters and brother, Rachel Taylor, Susan Hinckley, Susanna Reed and George Wylie at 11 a.m. until 1:30 p.m. and Biggadike... Visiting magistrate came back at 2.30 p.m.

(Marginal note Biggadike visited by her sisters and brother and visiting Justice.)

(C) Visited Biggadike... Exhorted her to take advantage of seeing her friends... Today to make full and truthful confession.

(S) Priscilla Biggadike is much depressed having been visited by her friends.

27 Sunday

(G) Priscilla Biggadike appeared very much depressed nothing to say.

(C) Visited her after service... Left her with the Hope that she...

(S) 5.30 visited Priscilla Biggadike she is in a low depressed state of mind. But sleeps well. May be allowed brandy at the discretion of the matron.

28 Monday

Priscilla Biggadike executed by order of the court appears very frightened to be executed.

Doctor Hutchinson, County coroner, Held inquest on the body of Priscilla Biggadike and 3 p.m. verdict that she died by hanging according to law.

(C) Priscilla Biggadike executed this morning at 9 o'clock was with her for half an hour previous and spent prayer exhorted her to make confession she said she had nothing to do with the death. At the foot of the scaffold I dressed her solemnly to her… Do you still say you are not guilty of crime for which you are about to suffer? She answered without hesitation I do.

(S) I have this morning witnessed the execution of Priscilla Biggadike. Her death was somewhat lingering.

Comment: An unhappy record of an increasingly desperate woman, her mood swings and adamant refusal to admit guilt in the face of enormous pressure. Her death, was laconically described by the surgeon as 'somewhat lingering'.

Background and early life

Priscilla was born Priscilla Whiley in the Lincolnshire village of Getney and lived there all her life until arrested for the murder of which she stood accused.

Getney in 1861 was a parish of around 400 inhabitants. Most of the adult males were either farmers or agricultural labourers.

Chapter 15

The Trial

Extracts from the *Stamford Mercury*:

FRIDAY, 11th of December 1868 LINCOLN WINTER ASSIZES

The commissions for the trial of prisoners for the city and County of Lincoln were opened on Wednesday afternoon by Mr Justice Byles, who arrived in Lincoln by the midday train at the Midlands station... Yesterday morning the trial of prisoners in the County Hall commenced...

The Grand Jury

Sir Charles Anderson, Bart., Foreman
18 members including Col Amcotts MP all of them local magistrates.

The Charge

His Lordship, in his address, confined his remarks exclusively to the indictment for murder ... but that was one for them to investigate, involving the most serious charges, and it was a case at all events so far as was respected prisoner, in which the greatest care was required on there, for the proper administration or the failure of justice might depend on the way in which they were disposed of the important facts before them. They were aware that the case was that of Priscilla Biggadike, aged 29, residing at Stickney, and Thomas Proctor, also a young man, only 31, who were jointly charged with the wilful murder of Richard Biggadike at Stickney on 1 October 1868. No doubt they were well acquainted with the facts, much better, probably, than he was ... The deceased and his wife, the female prisoner, did not live happily together; but that there would be abundant evidence. They quarrelled frequently, and loudly and passionately. ...They were in the house, when Proctor beckoned her to come out for he wanted to speak to; and then he said 'Mind what you say' to which she replied 'You take me for a fool! Don't tell me more than I know.' About a week after Proctor was in the house of a neighbour somewhat 'on in beer' when he got up and laid his hands on the table, saying 'I have something on my mind that would make anybody's blood run cold, and it does mine' then he laid his face in his hands and burst out crying, and said he had lost his best friend. Justice Pyles said he would not dictate to or even advise the grand jury what to do, but probably they would think it right to send in a bill against her: as to Proctor there was considerable difficulty in his case, for if they send down a bill on insufficient evidence he must be acquitted and discharged with perfect immunity, but if, believing the evidence insufficient they threw out the bill, then he might be rearrested at any future time, should further evidence be forthcoming and be put on his trial on the same charge.

Stamford Mercury Friday 18 December 1868

The bill against Thomas Proctor committed for the murder of Richard Biggadike was also thrown out, but a true bill was found against Priscilla Biggadike for the same offence

Friday, December 11

THE MURDER AT STICKNEY

Priscilla Biggadike was charged with the wilful murder of her husband, Richard Biggadike, by poisoning on 30 September at Stickney – Mr Bristow conduct of the prosecution, and Mr Lawrence, at the request of the judge, watched the case on behalf of the prisoner. The learned counsel for the prosecution opened the case, and addressed the jury at considerable length. He said it was impossible to exaggerate in any terms the serious nature of the enquiry to be laid before them for consideration. Whether they merely considered the nature of the offence it was serious enough, but when they remembered that the prisoner was charged with the murder of her husband, and that by the most atrocious means known to the law – poisoning, the aspects of the case assume the most serious complexion. He therefore solemnly urged them to get their most serious attention to every detail of the evidence to be laid before them, to dismiss from their minds any rumours or statements they may have heard of the case outside the jury box, and after carefully weighing all the facts adduced before them, to give a verdict is in their conscience they should think right. The facts of the case, he said, would not require a very lengthy statement at his hands, because so far as the prisoner was concerned they laid in a very narrow compass, but he would confine them to that as much as he possibly could. The learned Counsel then proceeded to give an outline of the facts of the case. He said the person whose death the enquiry was about lived at the village of Stickney, near Boston, and was by trade a Wells sinker, well-to-do, and earning good wages. In the house where he lived resided his wife and three children, and two lodgers, named Ironmonger and the man Proctor, who had also been committed for trial on the charge of murdering the deceased, but discharged, grand jury annulled the bill against. The deceased, his wife, and the three children and the two lodgers all slept in one room (the only sleeping apartment in the house), into separate beds, and it frequently happens that the deceased man had to get up and go to his work in the morning leaving the lodgers in there. In the course of time, the husband became jealous and accused his wife of being too intimate with the man Proctor, this gave rise to serious quarrels between Biggadike and his wife, and on several occasions when they have been having words, the woman was heard to say that 'She wished he might be brought home dead and stiff someday' and that 'she wished he was dead.' This state of things continued for some months, the breach between the prisoner and her murdered husband becoming wider and wider, and expressions of loathing and disgust for husband frequently escape the prisoner.

On 30 September the deceased man went to his work (sinking a well) in his usual good health, and when he returned in the evening he was likewise in excellent. He made a hearty meal of mutton, shortcake (made by the prisoner) and tea and he then lit his pipe and sat down by the fire; but in the course of 10 minutes he was seized with violent sickness and purging which continued to increase in violence all through the night until the morning, when he died. At the request of the deceased, Dr Maxwell was sent for, and he at once saw that the man was suffering from some irritant poisons. He prescribed for him, but of course without any hope of saving him, and after the death of the unfortunate man he held a post-mortem examination on the body, and then his suspicions were confirmed. The contents of the stomach were sent to Prof Taylor, and the result of his investigation with the discovery of arsenic in large quantities. In the meantime the female prisoner being taken into custody, she made statements at one time attribute in the death of her husband to suicide, and at another, accusing Proctor of having committed the crime, declaring she saw him put the arsenic in the tea and medicine. The learning counsel, in the course of his remarks, commented on the different important points in the evidence, and concluded by gaining pressing on the jury duty of necessity of banishing from their minds anything that they might have heard out of the jury box, and to decide upon the enquiry from the testimony of the witness produced before them.

The first witness called was Jas. Turner a joiner of Stickney who deposed to the deceased Biggadike having been in his usual excellent good health on 30 September last, when he left off work at about 5 o'clock at night. Deceased could not write at all.

George Ironmonger said he lodged at the house of Biggadike about half a year, but to the time of the death of the deceased, Proctor also lodged there. On the day of the poisoning Proctor went out fishing, and returned home to tea at about quarter past 5 o'clock. Mrs. Biggadike prepared the tea and she and her children had theirs at the same time. They had some shortcake, and one was put away for the deceased, who had not got home. He and Proctor went fishing again after tea: he went out of the house first and Proctor followed him after about half an hour. They returned home again between 5 and 6 and when they got there the deceased had just finished his tea. He went into the yard and began retching when he came into the house again, he appeared in great pain. About five minutes afterwards he went out again, was sick and purged when he returned the second time he said 'I can't live long this how; you must fetch the doctor.' His wife asked him if she was to go, and he replied 'no let George (meaning the witness) go; he will go the quickest' he (witness) went to Mr Maxwell's and when he returned, Biggadike was upstairs. The next time he saw the deceased was about 6 o'clock in the morning, lying across the foot of the bed. His wife seemed rather down, but did not complain of being sick. The prisoner prepared the food for all in the house. Deceased could neither read nor write.

By Mr Lawrence: Proctor remained behind in the house, when I went to fish, from a quarter to half an hour. I never heard deceased and his wife fall out: they always appeared on friendly terms: they had a few words sometimes.

By Mr Bristow: I am a boatman, often away from home for months. By the judge: I never saw any poison in the house. I don't know it when I do see it.

Mr Peter Maxwell surgeon, Stickney, said he was called to the deceased about 7 o'clock in the evening. He found him in bed, in great pain, violently sick and purged. The prisoner said her husband had been ill since about teatime, and on being asked what he had tea, she said 'he had nothing but what we had ourselves.' He (witness) asked what it was, and she told him cake and mutton. He got a bottle and poured some of the vomit into it, and took it away. Prisoner asked what was the matter with the deceased, and he (Mr M) told her he had taken something but not agreed with him. He told her to come for some medicine, and she did, bringing with her a piece of shortcake. She said as he (Mr M) did not appear very satisfied what the deceased had had tea, she had brought a piece of the cake for him to look at. He told her he did not want it. About 11 o'clock he went to the deceased again, and found him worse, vomiting large quantities of blood, and he was in a state of collapse. When he heard that the deceased was dead, he sent for a policeman. He made a post-mortem examination of the body, and found the internal parts of it in a very inflamed state. He removed the stomach and coats, a portion of the small intestines, the liver, spleen and kidneys, and sent them sealed in jars and bottles, with the vomit, by Superintendent Wright, to Professor Taylor, in London. He came to the conclusion, from the examination he had made, the deceased died from the effects of some irritant poison.

Superintendent Wright deposed to taking the jars and bottles with their contents to London, and delivering them to Professor Taylor. He also said, 'I apprehended the prisoner at the enquiry before the coroner, charged her with the murder of her husband at the same time cautioning her not to say anything that was at all likely to convict herself, as I should have to give in evidence whatever she said.' She replied 'It's hard work I should bear all the blame: I am innocent.' On our way to Spilsby, when near the railway station, I said 'We have not been long coming from Stickney: the last train is not in yet.' She replied 'I was not thinking about the train: I was thinking about what should I say and I haven't said. I found a piece of paper in his pocket, wrote above, saying that he had done it himself, and the reason was stated, he was so much in debt.' I said 'I understand from someone that your husband could neither read nor write himself.' I said, what have you done with the paper?' She replied 'I burnt it: Will you tell the gentleman?' I said 'I will.'

Doctor Alfred Swayne Taylor deposed to receiving the jar and bottles brought by Superintendent Wright, and related the result of his examinations of the contents, he stated he found large quantities of arsenic in the intestine and another parts. And also in the vomit. Not the slightest doubt that the deceased was poisoned by arsenic.

Mary Ann Clark deposed: On the 30th of September, about 8:30 o'clock, the prisoner came and asked me if I would go to the doctors with her. She had a piece of cake in her hand, and said the doctor had said she had been putting something in the cake she ought not, that she was going to take it to him. When we came back, I went upstairs to see the deceased, he was bleeding from the mouth and nose, and exclaimed, 'Lord, have mercy on me.' The next morning about 6 o'clock, Proctor called me, and said 'Dix worse; he's dying: Will you come in?' I went upstairs: Mrs Ironmonger and the prisoner were there. Mrs Biggadike said deceased had thrown a cup at her, and that he kicked her off the foot of the bed, and afterwards got out of bed and threw his arm backwards and knocked her down. The prisoner did not fret whilst we chatted: she appeared as usual.

Mr Lawrence: Prisoner said when she brought the bread to me, 'The doctor says I have put something in the cake, but I have not.'

Jane Ironmonger widow, deposed: I live under the same roof as the Biggadikes. The deceased and his wife lived on bad terms. They frequently quarrelled. I once heard Mrs Biggadike say she wished he might be brought home dead, and at another time that he might come home stiff. On Monday, 28 September, a day or two before the deceased was taken ill, Mrs Biggadike came into my house, and after talking about a dog and that is being poisoned last winter, asked me how those Garners got on about poisoning. I told her I did not know. She replied that she thought they were transported. She also said she understood the doctors and police could not find poison in the meal or sago. Biggadike has often told me he could not read or write.

By Mister Lawrence: When prisoner made those threats she was always in a great passion; and the deceased was rather deaf. Prisoner is quite excitable, and a woman who uses strong language.

Susan Everington said: I was passing the prisoner's door on 26 September, and seeing her standing there, I said 'Mrs B, I am very sorry that you and your husband have got to live very uncomfortable together. I understand you disagreed when you went to Boston the other day, and he has put you out of doors. I hope it's not true, He's a good-looking man, and a kind good husband and father I hope.' She replied 'It does not matter, I cannot abide him.' She was suckling her child and I asked if the deceased made any fuss with his children. She said, 'No he never does when they are little.' She said sometimes when he was in drink he would say the child was not his, and she used to reply, 'Never mind whose it is, I know it's mine.'

Eliza Fenwick said: I am sister-in-law to the female prisoner, and was accustomed to call at the deceased's house. About three or four months ago my husband and I called as we were going to the shop, when I drew Mrs Biggadike's attention to the mice having eaten a hole in my flour bag. She replied 'If you like, I will give you a little "white mercury" to kill them,' and got up intending to fetch some. My husband stopped her by saying he would not have any of that old stuff in the house, as the children could be poisoned by it. The deceased was not at home on this occasion. I called him again one day about a month before the deceased died and the prisoner asked me if I had seen her new dress. I said no; and she fetched it down. The deceased said 'That's been bought with my money' and the prisoner replied 'No, it's not been bought with your money; he is a fine gentleman when he gets dressed up in his dark cloth.' I went to the house. Proctor, one of the lodgers, went out of doors as soon as I got in, and said 'Here, I want you.' I said 'do you mean me?' He replied 'No, I want Mrs Biggadike.' Mrs B went to him, and I heard him say to her, 'Now, mind what you say.' She replied, 'Do you think I'm a fool: don't tell me no more than I know.' When I came downstairs I said to Mrs Biggadike 'They say you poisoned him.' She replied 'Yes, I know they do; it was that Doctor Maxwell, but I'll give the devil to it.'

By Mr Lawrence: It was the deceased who said 'He's a fine man when he is dressed in his black cloth,' and not the prisoner.

By the judge: I said they say you poisoned your husband the prisoner answered 'Yes, I know they do but they tell lies. I know who it was gave it out; it was old Maxwell, but I'll let the devil have it.'

Edwin Fenwick husband of the last witness, confirmed her evidence as to the offer of 'white mercury' by Mrs Biggadike to poison mice with.

J. Farr. Phillips, Governor of the house of correction at Spilsby, deposed on 14th October: The prisoner (who was in my custody) applied to see me: she came into my office, accompanied by the matron, and said she wished to make some statement, and tell all about her husband's death. I cautioned her in the usual way, that whatever she said I should be obliged to take down in writing, and produce against her at her trial. She then made the following statement:

"On the last day of September, on Wednesday, I was standing against the tea table and saw Thomas Proctor put a white powder of some sort in a teacup, and then poured some milk (which stood on the table) into it. My husband at that time was in the dairy, washing himself: my husband came into the room directly after, sat down to the table, and then I put his tea out: he drank it, and more besides that. About half an hour afterwards he was taken ill: he went out of doors and was sick, then came in again, and sat about 10 minutes, and went out and was sick again, and then went to bed and he asked me to send for the doctor which I did. The doctor was an hour before he came. I went to the doctor's about a quarter of an hour after he left, and he gave me some medicine and ordered me how to give it to him: Two tablespoonfuls every half-hour, and I was to put a mustard plaster on the stomach, and he came no more till 11 o'clock that night. I came downstairs to go out of doors, and asked Thomas Proctor to go upstairs and sit with my husband. When I went upstairs into the room, as I was going up I saw Proctor putting some white powder into the medicine bottle with a spoon and he then went downstairs and left me in the room with my husband. As soon as he had left the room, I poured some medicine into the cup and gave it to my husband, and I tasted it myself. In an hour afterwards I was sick, and so I was two days after. What I have stated about the medicine took place about 2 in the morning, and after the doctor had gone. I wish you to send a copy of what I have said to the coroner, and I wish to be present at the inquest to state the case before them as it is the truth.

Priscilla Biggadike, X her Mark

Thomas Proctor, the man who had also been committed with the prisoner on this charge said: I lodged at the house of Biggadike on 30 September, I went home to tea between 4 and 5 o'clock, and afterwards went out fishing again. Ironmonger went out about 10 minutes or a quarter of an hour before me. Mrs Biggadike and I were the only persons left in the house. The tea things were on the table when I went out. I did not put any white powder into a teacup that day or at any other time: I had not any in my possession. When deceased was upstairs, Mrs Biggadike asked me if I would sit with him, and I did. I did not put any white powder into the medicine bottle. I did not see the prisoner sick or in pain. I saw deceased going on in his garden gate as I was going back to fish.

Dr Clegg, of Boston, coroner produced the depositions taken at the inquest, and the evidence given by the prisoner at her own request and against his will. She then gave the same account about tea as the other witnesses, and added that she was sure there was no poison could have got into the cake or anything else by accident or otherwise. She declared there never was any poison kept in the house for destroying vermin that she knew of. She took the piece of cake left by her husband to the doctor for his satisfaction, she thought he did not seem satisfied. He would not examine it, and she and her children ate it the next day. This concluded the evidence.

Mr Bristowe, in summing up the evidence, observed that from the testimony of Mr Maxwell and of Dr Taylor, was the highest living authority, that the deceased died from the effects of arsenic, and there was nothing in the evidence to lead to the conclusion that he administered it to himself. He had no desire to press the case unduly against the unfortunate prisoner, but he must say that the evidence as to the unhappy terms in which she and her husband lived pointed to the motive which might have induced her to poison him to get him out of the way. Mr Bristow also commented on the other points of the evidence, but as his Lordship dwelt upon them also it is not necessary to give them in this place.

Mr Lawrence in addressing the jury for the prisoner said he need not remind them of the momentous issue at stake, and of the solemn duty devolving on them as well as himself. He begged them, if possible to dismiss from their minds everything they had heard of this case before coming into court and to bring their mind is a perfect blank to the evidence alone as adduced before them that day. No doubt deceased died from poisoning, and the great and all important question was whether it was given to him by the prisoner. It must've struck them that the first part of the case was entirely wanting in evidence, for the prosecution failed to show that there was poison in the house at the time it was said she gave it to them. Not only could they not prove she had poison at the time, but they could not come nearer than four months before this occurrence, and even then, 'White Mercury' was only mentioned; it was never seen, and further, generally cases of this kind, the person charged was found dealing with boys not at the time of the death of the murdered person. Then again, as to the motive, he submitted that nothing approaching adequate motive had been proved. For though witnesses had said that they lived on unfriendly terms, yet, when asked what sort of language she habitually used, they admitted that she used very strong language on the most ordinary occasions. But every single word she had said been raised up against her to support the prosecution, and things which in themselves would be perfectly harmless, were raised up after this lapse of time to show she had a bad feeling towards her husband. He submitted there was not a single word uttered by her before this occurrence to show sufficient motive, or that they were anything but idle words which she was in the habit of using. Then as to her being the first to mention poison, that was easily accounted for, and when Mr Maxwell found the man very ill he asked her what he had had for tea, and it was evident her suspicions were aroused by his question, and being thus put on the defensive she did all she could to avert suspicion from herself, but that was no proof she knew poison had been given to her husband. This accounted for taking the remainder of the cake to Mr Maxwell, who, for some unknown reason, would not keep it. Then, as for the other replies, whenever it was put to her that she had poisoned him, she always denied it, telling one of them she knew they said she had poisoned him, but they had told lies. It was evident, too, from Dr Taylor's evidence that the poison must've been taken before, as he said in evidence that it generally was some hours before arsenic took effect; whereas if it was taken at tea its effect showed in less than half an hour, there was no evidence that it was given at that time, and no one indeed ever saw the poison. It was not for him to suggest that any other person administered the poison; it was enough for him to show that it was not necessary – according to the evidence, that she must've given it. Then as to the statements made by her to persons in authority: was there anything to fix the crime on her without the statements? And expression was whether these statements could not be accounted for in a reasonable man? They could not believe them all as they were not consistent, and why then should they fix on that which told most against her. The first, made by the coroner, a sum account of the matter, but implicated no one; then she made a statement to Superintendent Wright, in which she said she had found the paper in her husband's pocket which contain the statement that he took the poison himself; and the third statement was on 15 October in which she attempted to throw the whole blame on Proctor. What did all this tend to show question why that she, finding suspicion growing stronger every day against, tried to free herself from it by every means. But did that bring to their minds the conviction she was guilty? And again, if she was capable of giving poison to her husband, would she not also have the strength of mind sufficient to lead her to tell the same tale? Instead of this they found a weak woman labouring under suspicion, on every occasion told a different story, and that was to be accounted for from the horror she naturally felt, to free herself from suspicion. There was no proof that she did it – only that it was possible she might have done it. He had no wish to frighten them from doing their duty, but it was a matter of life or death, and were they to find her guilty without sufficient evidence a life would pay the forfeit. He implored them to take the whole circumstances into consideration, to scrutinise the evidence most carefully, and then see whether they could say they have no doubt whatsoever about guilt, remembering that although they might have a little doubt, yet the slightest doubt sufficient to turn the scale in favour; if the scales were so fairly balanced as to leave some lingering doubt in the minds, then he would say that mercy be extended to the prisoner even as they hoped from mercy themselves.

Justice Byles in commencing the summing up, remarked that they had been reminded by the Counsel on both sides that this was a matter involving the life of a fellow creature; which induced him to observe that if murders of this kind were not found out, the lives of the community were involved in it. The crime was a secret one, and therefore they could not expect that such a case should be proved by direct evidence, and when such was brought home to the perpetrator it was generally by indirect and circumstantial evidence; but when that consisted of a number of circumstances, all converging to one point, without one fact being brought forward inconsistent therewith, then it was good evidence to decide upon, and such as was being daily accepted as satisfactory and the question for them now was whether the evidence laid before them, being only circumstantial, was such as to produce conviction in their minds as to the guilt of the prisoner. His Lordship then went over the evidence of each witness, making observations thereon as he proceeded. As to the husband and wife not living comfortably together ... If they believe that evidence, there was strong evidence that they did not live together on good terms, that she did not stand high in his opinion, and that she knew she did not. A joiner named Turner deposed that Biggadike could neither read nor write, and that was important evidence; nor did it stand alone ... and as to Procter, they had seen him, and therefore had the opportunity of judging whether such was probable in his case, he thought that the prosecution had shown a wise distraction in calling him. They had heard his evidence, and would see whether there was any ground at all from imputation on him; though that was not the question they had to try, for if she saw him put the powder once into the tea, and then into his medicine, it would not absolve her. Coming to the evidence of Mr Maxwell ... she believed the suspicions were aroused, though when she asked him what was the matter with her husband, he merely replied that something had disagreed with him, which was a very prudent answer, and one of itself not calculated to arouse suspicion. He said nothing about poisoning, and yet she, before anything of the kind was mentioned, took him a piece of the cake they had for tea, but there was nothing to lead to the conclusion that the cake was poisoned. Having read the evidence of Dr Taylor, his Lordship passed on to consider the various statements made by the prisoner – when she insisted on telling her own story, and when she began by declaring she wanted to tell 'all she knew;' the first point to be observed was this that she said nothing then about the paper she afterward said she found in her husband, and nothing that implicated Proctor, though she said she wanted to tell all she knew, and after the inquest when she was in custody she made another statement to Superintendent Wright (who appeared to be a very intelligent officer) in which he first mentioned the paper; but that he could not help saying was a very strange story as Biggadike could neither read nor write. He was sorry to have to make such an observation. Then she made another statement on 15 October, putting in what she had omitted in the two former statements that implicated Proctor, and even if it were true that he did with the arsenic in, she saw the white powder put in, and yet admitted that she afterwards gave the medicine to her husband. That was the most extraordinary story.

His Lordship, concluding said 'Now, I believe that I've gone over the whole of the evidence, or at least the most material parts, and if it be desired I will read what has been omitted, and this is the first question. Did the unfortunate man die from poison? If not, of what did he die? If he died from poison, and that was arsenic, was it administered to him by accident, or did he take it accidentally? Such things have happened; the prisoner says it could not have been an accident because there was no poison in the house; but it might have been an accident for all that, without knowing anything about it. If you think he took it himself, and not by accident, was it suicide? An attempt is being made to show that it was, but the evidence makes that extremely improbable. If he did die from arsenic, but did not take it by accident, normal for the purpose of committing suicide, and who did give it to him? There were three persons in the house – prisoner, Proctor and Ironmonger, but suspicion had been thrown on Proctor, but you will see whether any suspicion rests on him, and if you do not think her statement true, then who did give it him? It is said that she had a motive from the unhappy terms on which they lived together; it was also stated in evidence that she had poison in the house not long before, for she offered it to some neighbours; and then there is the fabrication of exculpation evidence which an innocent person may make, which a guilty one is more likely to attempt. These are the facts, and as I began so I end, by telling you that such cases approved by surrounding circumstances; but I must say to you that the responsibility is not mine and I beg you to be guided by nothing I have said, and I thank God the responsibility is not mine. If you are satisfied that the evidence that the prisoner poisoned her husband, it will be your duty to find her guilty; but if you're not satisfied, then you will have to give her the benefit of any doubt you have.

After some short consultation in the box, the foreman rose, and amid the breathless stillness of the court, in reply to the question of the clerk of the court, 'What say you; is the prisoner guilty or not guilty of the crime with which she is charged?' The foreman said 'Guilty' and after a pause, 'but we recommend her to mercy'. The judge: 'On what grounds?' This plain question was evidently unexpected and the foreman look for instructions from his fellows during and after some whispering and prompting he said 'Only because it is circumstantial evidence.' The judge: 'Your verdict is guilty?' 'Yes'.

The judge (having assumed the black cap) said 'Priscilla Biggadike, though the evidence is only circumstantial, yet more satisfactory evidence I've never heard. You must now prepare for your impending fate by attending to the religious instruction which you will receive, and which, if you had given heed, you never would have stood in this unhappy position. The sentence of the court is that you be taken from whence you came, and then to a place of execution and that there be hanged by the neck till you are dead, and may the Lord have mercy on your soul.'

FRIDAY 1ST OF JANUARY 1868
EXECUTION OF A WOMAN AT LINCOLN

The particulars of the murder of Richard Biggadike by Priscilla his wife have been laid before the public so recently and so fully in this paper but no lengthened recapitulation is now demanded.

On Friday George Ironmonger, one of the lodgers, applied for permission to see her, but was refused, she having expressed no desire to see him. On Saturday her three sisters and a brother were with her two hours and they exhorted her, if guilty, confessed the crime, but she did not.

... In reply to a letter from Ironmonger's employer, she dictated an answer in which she said she had found peace with God, but made no mention of her crime. She also implored George Ironmonger to seek forgiveness...

... Monday, the day appointed for the execution, broke forth bright though cold... The sad procession emerged from a side door in the prison wall ... It came to the south end of the County Hall, where, in a corner the new scaffold was erected … The doomed woman moaning and leaning for support on the warders on each side of her. The distance was about 200 yards, and when half was got over, the culprit asked, amid sobs 'How much longer is it?'. And, on being told 'Not far' she said 'My troubles are nearly over' … The procession altered by a sign from the chaplain, who addressed her 'I want was once more with you still persist in your declaration of innocence? Do you still say you had nothing to do with it, either in thought word or deed?' She immediately answered 'I do so.' At the foot of the drop, she sat down in a chair provided for her … The chaplain again addressed her as follows 'I have spent half an hour with you this morning in the endeavour to impress upon you a proper sense of your condition; you are soon to pass from this world into another, to stand before he to whom the secrets of all hearts are revealed; and I most earnestly implore you not pass away from this world without first confessing all your sins, including not only general sins, but also the one which you are about to suffer I had hoped you have made that confession and that enabled me as a minister of Christ, to have pronounced forgiveness of all your sins under the promise that he came into the world to save sinners, and it is grieved me very much find that you still declare you are not accountable for the death of your husband, that you still say you never gave the poison, nor saw any other person do it nor did not connive at it; and that you are entirely free from the crime. Do you say so now? The prisoner answered without the slightest hesitation 'Yes.' the chaplain resumed: 'There is only one hope left: and it is this, that you say you have confessed your sins to God but not your fellow creatures, but all I can say is that I leave you in God's hands, and may he have mercy on your soul. What a satisfaction it would be to your children, your friends and relations, to know you had passed from death to life (sic) under the promise that your sins were forgiven, and that you had been admitted into the blessing kingdom of God. I fear I can hold out no more hope – the matter is for you and your God. Had you made an open confession, I should have done what, as a minister of Christ, I am authorised to do, pronounced your sins, though many, forgiven. I am sorry I cannot exercise that authority at the present moment I must leave it to God'.

To this appeal no answer was made, and her moment having arrived the wretched woman ascended the steps of the drop … And was placed under the fatal noose; whilst this was being adjusted and her legs fastened together, she stood with great firmness but moaned and occasionally shouted the explanation 'My troubles are nearly all over; surely my troubles are ended: surely won't hang me' as the drop fell she gave a loud shriek then nothing was heard apart from a gurgling, it being four minutes before all was still and life quite extinct … Thus ended this melancholy affair.

Was Priscilla Biggadike guilty?

She did not think she was, she even applied for bail at the first hearing. The clue to her connection with her husband's death being the statement to the governor (above), a careful reading of that statement would simplify it to 'Yes I was present when Proctor gave the poison to my husband, but I didn't realise it was poison at the time and had some myself.'

As to Proctor, the only explanation why the judge took care to exclude him from the proceedings was that the judge must have been convinced before the trial started that Biggadike was guilty and it was useful to have Proctor as a prosecution witness. After all, there was clear other evidence against him apart from Priscilla's statement. He was also a ratcatcher, the only common occupation that had access to commercial quantities of poison under the poisons act. I wonder what everyone would have thought if his sentence to 18 months for actual bodily harm had occurred before the trial rather than 10 years later.

This case has overtones of the great eighteenth-century poison case involving Mary Blandy, daughter of a rich Oxford attorney. Doting on her father, and troubled by the bad relations between her father and her lover, a Captain Cranston, she was persuaded by her lover to feed her father with 'the Scottish Pebbles' to make him more amenable to a proposed marriage. The lovesick woman believed her lover but the Scottish pebbles were arsenic and she was convicted and executed for her father's death. I find it credible that at the time Priscilla Biggadike believed that her lover was giving something harmless to her husband.

PART 7

Ann Merritt

Chapter 16

The Official Record of her Trial
at the Old Bailey

ANN MERRITT, Killing > murder, 4th March 1850.

599. ANN MERRITT, was indicted for the wilful murder of James Merritt.

MESSRS. BODKIN and CLERK conducted the Prosecution.

SAMUEL KETHERIDGE. I am a labourer, living at Cold bath-lane, Hackney – the deceased, James Merritt, was a fellow-workman of mine for a fortnight before his death – he was a turncock to the East London Water-works Company. On Wednesday, 23rd Jan., I parted with him in the street at a quarter-past nine o'clock at night – he was then in his usual health, excepting a slight cold – he had been at his work that day – next morning, Thursday, the 24th, I called on him at his own house about eight – I saw the prisoner – she told me her husband was sick in the yard – he came into the room in a minute or two – he said, in the prisoner's presence, that he had been eating a basin of broth, and had taken a cup of hot tea upon that, and he expected it had turned on his stomach, and made him sick – the prisoner could hear that, but said nothing – I then left the house with Merritt to go to work, about a mile off – when we got to Clapton-Square, half a mile from Merritt's house, he said he felt very thirsty – we went into a public-house, and he had two-pennyworth of rum and a little warm water and sugar – we then went to work separate ways – I saw him next in Clapton-Square, about ten that morning, and left him there – there was nothing the matter with him then that I observed – I went to his house about a quarter after eleven – he had asked me at ten o'clock to come there – I saw the prisoner – the deceased was eating some gruel out of a basin – he did not eat it all, but handed the basin, with some in it, to the prisoner – she took it from him, and said she would keep it hot on the hob for him – he said, 'I don't care what you do with it' – directly afterwards we left the house together, and at twelve o'clock he left me – I saw him again from one to a quarter-past – he told me he felt very sick and very queer, and he should not be able to do his work, and wished me to do it for him – he then left me to go towards home – between five and six in the evening I went to his house, to leave his tools – the prisoner let me in, and told me to go up-stairs to Jim, as he was very ill, and wanted to see me – I went up, and she followed me – he was in bed, and said he was very sick in his stomach, and had cramp in his feet – he said, 'I don't wonder at it; the work we have had to do, and the weather we have had, it is enough to kill a horse' – the prisoner was standing at his bed-side – she said nothing – that was the last time I saw him alive.

THOMAS DENMAN. I am a plumber, living at Clapton-road – I knew the deceased. On Thursday morning, 24th Jan., at twenty minutes past twelve, I saw him near the reservoir at Stamford-hill – he was sick and vomiting, and complained to me – he went to a public-house, and drank a small glass of brandy – he walked down with me, and I left him – that was all I saw of him.

JAMES ASHBY. I live at Homerton. I was a turncock of the East London Waterworks in Jan. last – I knew James Merritt – I went to his house, in Pear-tree Place, Clapton, on Thursday, 24th Jan., about twenty minutes to eleven o'clock – I saw the prisoner – I asked where her husband was – she said he was in the back-yard, and she would call him – she did so – he came out of the back-yard – he looked very queer, as if suffering from a severe bilious attack – he told me he felt very queer – there was some hot beef and potatoes cooked on the table, and by their invitation I partook of it – I think it was the prisoner asked me – the deceased said he could not eat it – I sat down by the table, and did eat it, with my back to the door – he could not eat the lunch prepared for him, and preferred a basin of gruel – he did not ask for it, Mrs. Merritt said he might prefer it – I sat down to eat, and did not notice what was going on, but I don't think Mrs. Merritt went out of the room – I next saw her doing something at the table, as if she was mixing up the basin of gruel – I cannot say what she had in her hand – I saw a basin on the table, but what she was doing particularly I did not notice; I cannot account for what it was; I was rather short of time, and wished to get away – in the act of coming away, I saw Mrs. Merritt pouring out something into a basin, which I supposed to be gruel by the look of it – I did not see what was done with it – the deceased took none of it then – Merritt and me were both together, coming out of doors – at the end of Pear-tree Place I left him, and came back to my work, and I saw no more of him alive – I did not so much as look back after him.

Cross-examined by MR. CLARKSON. Q. Recollect yourself, and tell me whether the prisoner's husband did not say he should like to have some gruel, while the hot beef and potatoes were on the table? A. I think I must recollect that; he did say that – I do not recollect whether the prisoner left the room or not, at the same time; recollecting myself, I think she did go out of the house, because there is only one room to the house – she was not more than a minute away from me – I cannot say whether she returned with the oatmeal in a basin – my memory has not failed me since I was before the Magistrate – what she made was at the request of the husband – I will not be positive whether there is a cupboard in the room, there seldom is a room without one – I recollect that she went out of the room, or the house – she returned in a minute, and brought a basin, with what I thought was some oatmeal – she mixed it in my presence, as I sat at the corner of the table eating the beef and potatoes – he walked away with me, without touching it, to the corner of Pear-tree Place, and I do not know what became of him.

COURT. Q. You said at first that she was doing something at the table as if she was mixing up gruel, you say now she took oatmeal; should you know it to be oatmeal if you had not heard gruel mentioned? A. No; it was something representing oatmeal.

MARY GILLETT. I lived with my husband next door to the prisoner and the deceased – I knew him. On Thursday morning, 24th Jan., at half-past eight o'clock, the prisoner called me to her, and told me Merritt was very sick, and had got the bile – I said it served him right, he should not drink so, and went back to my house – there are three rooms to their house, and a wash-house – the door from the street opens into the sitting-room, the bed-room is over that – there are two rooms up-stairs – there is a cupboard in the front room – between ten and eleven o'clock I saw the deceased coming through the gate to his house – he seemed to be ill – he went into his house, and I lost sight of him – I passed by the house about half-past one – the door was open – I did not go in, only to the door – the prisoner was in the room, emptying some thick gruel out of a saucepan into a basin, and pouring some water to it – I asked her what she was doing – she said, 'I am thinning this gruel for Merritt to drink, he is so very thirsty' – the gruel was made of oatmeal, one of my little boys fetched it from the corn-chandler's, at her request, between ten and eleven in the morning, shortly after Merritt came home ill – I saw no more of either of them till ten minutes past nine at night when Mrs. Merritt came for me, I was in bed – I got up and dressed myself – I went with my husband and the prisoner into the deceased's bed-room, and found him in bed retching violently – he complained of a burning pain in his chest, and a violent pain in his stomach – I gave him water half a dozen times or more – he asked my husband to fetch Mr. Toulmin – he left for that purpose, and shortly afterwards Mr. Frederick and Mr. Francis Toulmin came – the prisoner had come to me window at five, and said she was going to ask Mr. Toulmin to send Merritt something for the bile, but Merritt did not wish to see him – she went away, and shortly after returned, and said Mr. Toulmin was not at home, he had gone to dine at the Manor-house – she then went into her house – she came twice to me in the evening; the first time was between six and seven – I asked her how Merritt was – she said he was very bad – I said, 'Have you not had any one to him?' – she said, 'No, I will wait a little longer, as Merritt does not wish to have a medical man' – one of the children came to say that the father was sick, and wished to get out of bed, and she left – at half-past eight she came again – I was not in bed then – she said, 'If I should want you during the night, Mrs. Gillett, will you come to me?' – I said, 'Is Merritt so bad, and have you not had any medical gentleman to him?' – she said, 'I have sent for Mr. Brooks, and he is out; I sent for Mr. Welch, and he refused to come, but sent two pills, which I gave to Merritt' – she said 'I sent Jemmy (meaning her little boy) to Mr. Toulmin, and they wanted to send the child with a note to the Manor-house, but the child said he did not know where it was, and came back again' – I went to bed, and she went home, and at half-past nine she came and called me up, and I went and remained at the house till half-past twelve, when he died – I and the prisoner were present when he died, no one else – she remained there about half-an-hour after he died – she said, 'How true Mr. Toulmin's words are! they always come to pass; because he always told me, if anything came to pass, he would go off like the snuff of a candle' – she went to the downstairs front-room – there is no bed there – she sat up the whole of the night – there was a fire in that room all night – I sat up there too – about eight in the morning Mr. Urrey was sent for – I do not know who sent for him; a person said it was me; I was ill that morning; I do not recollect doing it – two women, named Geary and Patten, were with the prisoner besides me – Mr. Urrey soon came – there was a conversation between him and the prisoner – I do not know what passed – they were in the front room – Mr. Toulmin was present – nothing was said about the Society that I heard – he had a conversation with the prisoner and left – I remember a few days before, being at Mrs. Merritt's, it was on the 22nd; a person named Bartholomew had died on the 20th, and I said what a pity it was that Mrs. Bartholomew was left with such a family, and so near her confinement, and only to receive 7l. 10s. – the prisoner said, 'If anything should happen to Merritt, I shall be entitled to the full benefit' – I was at the prisoner's house the day the surgeons opened the body – Mr. Toulmin was there – after it was opened, the prisoner asked me if I had asked Mr. Toulmin the cause of death – I said, 'From what has passed between Mr. Hacon and Mr. Toulmin, there is not the least doubt that he has been poisoned' – she clasped her hands together, and said, 'Do you think I am guilty, Mrs. Gillett?' – I said, 'I don't doubt you' – she walked about the room in a very agitated manner, and seemed to be suffering a great deal in her mind – on the morning of the 28th, before the Inquest sat the first time, I went in to Mrs. Merritt's, and she said, 'You know, Mrs. Gillett, that Annie and me (meaning her little girl)

Above: Florence Maybrick (q.v.) reading her statement in court – the only recorded incident of an accused being allowed to make a statement whilst on trial, before her case caused a change in the law.

Right: Contemporary *Punch* cartoon.: 'Guide to poisoning'.

PUNCH, OR THE LONDON CHARIVARI.—November 20, 1858.

THE GREAT LOZENGE-MAKER.

A Hint to Paterfamilias.

Above left: Victorian hypocrisy: William Morrris.

Above right: Early Victorian Essex Policeman.

Below: Early cartoon lampooning Inquests.

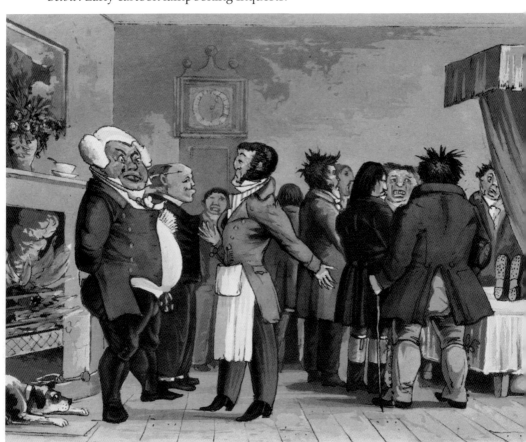

~ 1929 ~
FLYPAPER POISONER KILLED FOR PROFIT
~ Júlia Fazekas ~
~ HUNGARY ~

SERIAL   KILLER

An article   from 1955

N°35

La Commune.

Above left: Julia Fazekas: mastermind of the Angel Makers.

Above right: Contemporary cartoon of a Pétroleuse.

Right: Sarah Chesham: Execution Handbill.

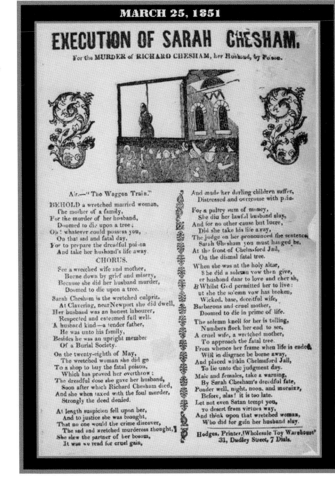

MARCH 25, 1851

EXECUTION OF SARAH CHESHAM.

For the MURDER of RICHARD CHESHAM, her Husband, by Poison.

Air.—"The Waggon Train."

BEHOLD a wretched married woman,
The mother of a family,
For the murder of her husband,
Doomed to die upon a tree;
Oh! whatever could possess you,
On that sad and fatal day,
For to prepare the dreadful poison
And take her husband's life away.

CHORUS.

See a wretched wife and mother,
Borne down by grief and misery,
Because she did her husband murder,
Doomed to die upon a tree.

Sarah Chesham is the wretched culprit,
At Clavering, near Newport she did dwell,
Her husband was an honest labourer,
Respected and esteemed full well.
A husband kind—a tender father,
He was unto his family,
Besides he was an upright member
Of a Burial Society.

On the twenty-eighth of May,
The wretched woman she did go
To a shop to buy the fatal poison,
Which has proved her overthrow;
The dreadful dose she gave her husband,
Soon after which Richard Chesham died,
And she when taxed with the foul murder,
Strongly the deed denied.

At length suspicion fell upon her,
And to justice she was brought,
That no one would the crime discover,
The sad and wretched murderess thought,
She slew the partner of her bosom,
It was we read for cruel gain,

And made her darling children suffer,
Distressed and overcome with pain.

For a paltry sum of money,
She did her lawful husband slay,
And for no other cause but lucre,
Did she take his life away,
The judge on her pronounced the sentence,
Sarah Chesham you must hanged be,
At the front of Chelmsford Jail,
On the dismal fatal tree.

When she was at the holy altar,
She did a solemn vow then give,
Her husband dear to love and cherish,
Whilst God permitted her to live;
But she the so'emn vow has broken,
Wicked, base, deceitful wife,
Barbarous and cruel mother,
Doomed to die in prime of life.

The solemn knell for her is tolling,
Numbers flock her end to see,
A cruel wife, a wretched mother,
To approach the fatal tree.
From whence her frame when life is ended
Will in disgrace be borne away,
And placed within Chelmsford Jail,
To lie unto the judgment day.

Male and females, take a warning,
By Sarah Chesham's dreadful fate,
Ponder well, night, noon, and morning,
Before, alas! it is too late.
Let not even Satan tempt you,
To desert from virtue's way,
And think upon that wretched woman,
Who did for gain her husband slay.

Hodges, Printer, (Wholesale Toy Warehouse)
31, Dudley Street, 7 Dials.

... Lessons in making poisoned mince pies ...

Above: Death mask of Mary Bell.

Left: Sarah Chesham caricature.

Below: The condemned cell at Lincoln.

Above: Cartoon on the Merritt case.

Right: Captain James Analby Legard RN, Sarah Barber's rescuer.

Below: Lizzie Pearson. This is Gainford church and green photographed around 1870. In the foreground is the village knife grinder, George Smith, who mysteriously disappeared shortly after James Watson was found dead.

Above: Mary Ann Cotton.

Below left: Mary Lefley.

Below right: James Maybrick.

Florence Maybrick.

Catherine Flannagan.

Margaret Higgins.

Left: Sir James Stephen, the judge in the Maybrick trial.

Below: Maybrick. The 'smoking gun' prescription.

ate the remains of the gruel' – I said, 'Don't say so, Mrs. Merritt, for I never saw any of you eat it' – she then said, 'If you did not, Ashby did, and he can clear me; and Ashby ought to be the first witness before the Jury' – she said Ashby and Andrews (the summoning-officer) had mixed it up between them, and that Ashby was not wanted; that he ought to have been the first witness – that conversation took place on different occasions – what she said about Ashby being the first witness, was before the Inquest; it was between eleven and twelve, and the Inquest sat at 12 – on the 31st. After the Inquest was adjourned, she came to my house, and asked me if I had heard that poison was found in Merritt's stomach – I said I had – she said, 'I am innocent; he was a dear, good husband, and it was not likely I should do such a thing' – she then said, 'Dear creature! if that is the case, he has done it by his own hand' – I said it was not very likely, as he had purchased a new pair of boots the night previous to his death – during the conversation Andrews came, and Mrs. Merritt said, 'Mr. Andrews, Mrs. Gillett knows I ate the remains of the gruel' – I said, 'I saw none of you eat it' – that was all that passed – I was there on Wednesday evening, 30th Jan., when she said, 'Do you think, if I had any hand in his death, I should not have let him live until after the day when I should have received the full benefit?'

Cross-examined. Q. How many times have you been examined? A. Four times, at Worship-street, as near as I can recollect – I have repeated several times that she asked if there had been poison found in his stomach, and that I said there had, and I am almost sure I did at Worship-street; I have also said she said, 'If so, it must have been by his own hand' – I said so at the Inquest – it was after the body had been opened, on the 28th, in the afternoon, that she put her hands together, and said, 'Mrs. Gillett, do you think I am guilty?' – my answer was, 'I do not doubt you,' or, 'I don't doubt you for a moment;' I am not certain to the very exact words – I did not think for a moment that it was Mrs. Merritt – that was my mode of expressing it – she told me on the Monday before she had sent to Mr. Welch, and he would not come; not that she said he refused to come on the Monday, but that he refused to come – these conversations ran over various times from the 22nd to the 31st – they were not connected with each other at all; and as far as the Benefit or Burial Society is concerned, I was the first person that referred to it, speaking of my regret about Mrs. Bartholomew – I said it served her husband right, for drinking so – he had been drinking during the last five or six weeks – I never knew him drunk until that time – I have known the prisoner twelve months exactly – she has had five children – she buried two in the summer – she always appeared to be a kind, affectionate mother, and always paid attention to her husband, as far as I am aware of.

Q. During the sickness, did it lead you to the conclusion that she was anxious and distressed at the state he was in? A. I did not notice it particularly – she was fretting at the time, but it is a thing not at all unusual to see her fret, for she was constantly crying – I have heard Merritt quarrel with her on account of the difficulties she had plunged him into – that was a few days before his death – they quarrelled on Monday, the 21st – that was during the six weeks he had been drinking.

FRANCIS TOULMIN. I am a surgeon, residing at Clapton. I was acquainted with the deceased several years prior to his death – I was in the habit, of seeing him occasionally, and on one occasion professionally – between half-past ten and eleven o'clock, on Thursday night, 24th Jan., I was sent for to go to his house – I was dining at the Manor-rooms, at Hackney – I went at once – I found him in bed – he complained greatly of pain in his stomach and cramps in his legs – he was sick; his pulse was very low, and his skin below the natural temperature – those were the leading symptoms – I went home, and sent him some medicine, some pills containing calomel and opium – I called again on Friday morning, the 25th, and saw him dead – I saw the prisoner, and said his death had been somewhat unusual, and it would be satisfactory to have a post-mortem examination – her answer was, that of herself she had no objection, but she had promised her husband that such an examination should not take place, as he had a great objection to it – I said, 'Under such circumstances I shall not press it.' – An Inquest was held on Monday morning, 28th Jan., at twelve o'clock – I was present, and was desired to make a post-mortem examination – I did so that day, assisted by my partner, Mr. Hacon – I commenced it as early as possible, about a quarter to two – Mr. Welch, a surgeon in the neighbourhood, was also present – the head was first examined, and the contents of the cranium found to be healthy, with the exception of some slight turgescence of the vessels – I opened the abdomen, and removed the stomach whole, with its contents, consisting of a thickish matter, slightly pink, which were poured into a glass stoppered bottle – I laid open the stomach itself, and examined it coats, upon which I found red spots, such as are observed in persons who have died of an irritant poison – I placed the stomach and intestines, and a portion of the liver, in an earthen jar, which I covered over and sealed – I then took the earthen jar and bottle, with their contents, to the London Hospital, and delivered them to Mr. Long, the assistant to Dr. Letheby, he not being there – I found nothing to account for death but what I have mentioned – the external symptoms, the sickness, and so on, which I observed on the 24th, were such as would be accounted for by the presence of an irritant poison – I have no recollection of any conversation with the prisoner on the subject of the probability of her husband's sudden death – I never saw any symptoms which would lead me to suppose he would be suddenly taken away – to the best of my belief, I never used such an expression as that he was likely, in my opinion, to go off like the snuff of a candle.

Cross-examined. Q. Had you been aware that he had been for six weeks a man given to drink? A. Not to my knowledge – to the best of my knowledge and belief I never used the expression about his going off like the snuff of a candle – there would have been some cause for my using the expression, and I never saw the cause – I attended him six weeks ago – I conversed with him on the subject of his ailment, which was strangulated rupture – that was the only time I attended him – the prisoner paid such attention to him as a wife would be expected to show – I knew the prisoner some years back, prior to her marriage, living in a family – I have reason to believe that at that time she was well thought of, as a relative of mine lived in the family – she has been married seven or eight years – I have heard nothing to her disparagement since, until this charge – I never saw anything to find fault with, in her conduct to her husband and children.

JOHN LONG. I act as assistant to Dr. Letheby, in the laboratory. On Monday, 28th Jan., I received from Mr. Toulmin, at the hospital, a glass bottle and an earthen jar – they were sealed up – I locked them up in the laboratory, and gave the key next morning to Dr. Letheby – I saw them then in the same state.

DR. HENRY LETHEBY. I am a bachelor of medicine and professor of chemistry, at the London Hospital. On 29th Jan. I received from Mr. Long a glass bottle and earthen jar – I entered on an analysis of their contents – I experimented on the contents of the bottle first, and detected eight grains and a half of white arsenic – by one course of experiments I reproduced the arsenic in a metallic form – it is in this tube (produced) – the earthen jar contained part of a human stomach – I noticed a peculiar appearance in it, which I have noticed in cases of poisoning by arsenic – there was a very small portion of a whitish powder adhering to the inner lining of the stomach, too small a quantity to ascertain what it consisted of – I then examined the intestines that were in the jar – I subjected them to a chemical analysis – the result was the detection of a very small quantity of arsenic – there was also in the jar part of a human liver – I subjected about a quarter of a pound of it to experiment – (I say that, that you may form a judgment of the quantity in the entire liver,) and obtained a quantity of metallic arsenic (produced) – it was too minute a quantity to weigh – that in the stomach was the only quantity I weighed – that would be quite sufficient to produce death – I had an opportunity of witnessing a case where two grains and a half killed – the general quantity would be eight grains – I look upon that as an average dose – it would generally be fatal – vomiting is almost invariably the consequence of arsenic introduced into the stomach – a person attacked in that way would be likely to throw up a portion of the arsenic – looking at the quantity I found, and the parts I found it in, in my judgment, the arsenic I found had been taken not more than two or three hours before death, but that is a matter of opinion; a dose might have been given before – it would depend on many circumstances how soon it would find its way to the liver.

Cross-examined. Q. About five grains of arsenic you say would cause death; do you mean taken together? A. Yes, or less; 2 1/2 grains have done so – I know nothing of this transaction, but from the examination – I found a very small portion in the liver; perhaps about 1/10th of a grain in a quarter of a pound of liver – a liver weighs about 5lbs. on an average – supposing it was equally diffused, there would be twenty times that quantity; that would be two grains – my observation in reference to the time it had been taken, has reference both to the stomach and liver.

Q. Is the data at all safe? A. Yes, I will tell you why; I found in the stomach 8 1/2 grains of arsenic, and there was not much in the intestines; I conclude, therefore, that there had not been time for it to have been passed into the intestines which would have been the case if it had been taken a long time before death; but there was only a trace in the intestines, so I conclude it was a very short time before death – that furnishes a data to me to form a judgment on the subject of hours – food remains in the stomach five hours before it passes into the intestines – I am able to say, that the contents of the stomach pass into the intestines within four, eight, or ten hours – from experiments which have been performed on living subjects, I have not the least doubt – I saw the intestines; they were in the jar; they did not appear to be influenced by arsenic; they were slightly red, and there were traces of arsenic; I have reduced something that was in the intestines into a metallic state – I experimented upon it, and found it was arsenic – it was destroyed in the experiment – I was obliged to submit it to experiment to prove it was arsenic – it is not likely I should find arsenic in the liver, without some being in the intestines – the time would not depend on the constitution of the person – digestion depends on the constitution, but I am speaking of the average – digestion is more or less rapid, according to the constitution of the person who has received the subject matter – I have heard of cases in which matters which would not digest have remained three or four days, but those were solid matters – I think liquids pass into the stomach under all circumstances within five hours, as they are imbibed – there is a valve, which prevents solid matters from passing into the stomach till they are digested – the arsenic was in a liquid state; all except a little white powder on the side of the stomach – I am obliged to have recourse to an average to form an opinion as to how long it would take – we have no means of dealing with an independent case, but by the average.

MR. BODKIN. Q. What did the contents of the stomach look like? A. Thick gruel; they were filtered, and I examined the filtered portion – my opinion is that the arsenic had been taken two or three hours.

ANN GEARY. I live at King's-road, Clapton. Early in the morning of Friday, 25th Jan., I was sent for to go to the house of James Merritt – I got there about twenty minutes to one o'clock – Merritt was dead – I assisted in laying out his body, and remained in the house till eight in the morning – the prisoner was weeping all night long – as I was going away, Mrs. Gillett asked me, in the prisoner's presence, to call on Mr. Urrey; I lived near him, and called to tell him to go up to Mrs. Merritt's house – he is Secretary to the Clapton Burial Society.

JAMES URREY. I act as Secretary to the Clapton Benefit Club. The deceased became a member two years ago – he was proposed on the first Wednesday in January, and admitted on the first Wednesday in February – the 2nd of Feb. – the two years would reckon from 2nd Feb. – in consequence of a message that was brought to me by Ann Gearey, on 25th Jan., I went to Mrs. Merritt's about half-past eight o'clock in the morning – I knocked at the door, and found the prisoner there – I said, 'Mrs. Merritt, I am sorry to hear of your loss' – her reply was, 'Oh, Mr. Urrey!' – she seemed absorbed in grief – Mr. Toulmin came in, and she and Mrs. Gillett went out of the room – I afterwards said to the prisoner, 'Mrs. Merritt, your husband, had he lived till the 2nd of Feb., you would have been entitled to 10l., but as it is, you will only be entitled to 7l. 10s.' – she said nothing to that – when the deceased was admitted a member, a copy of the rules was given him – this is one of the printed copies of the rules of the club (produced).

ALFRED ANDREWS. I am summoning-officer for the parish of Hackney, and constable for the Coroner. On Friday, 25th Jan., I went to the deceased's house, about half-past nine o'clock in the morning – Mrs. Gillett was there and the prisoner – Mrs. Gillett said to the prisoner, 'From what has passed between me and Mr. Andrews, he thinks there will be a Coroner's Jury' – the prisoner said, 'I don't think there is any necessity for a Coroner's Jury, as my poor dear husband died a natural death.' – I asked the prisoner whether she thought anything had been given to her husband, or whether she thought he had taken anything to destroy himself – she said, 'God knows, sir; he told me he had something to drink at Stamford-hill; but whether anything was put in his drink up there I can't tell.' – I saw her again that night, but the conversation purporting to have taken place that night is a mistake; it was on Monday, the 28th, an hour before the Inquest – she then stated that a piece of meat was cooking at the fire for her husband's lunch (alluding to the 24th); that he could not eat it, but had some gruel, while Ashby eat the meat; and that Ashby saw her make the gruel, I think she stated on Friday morning, the 25th – I asked her a great number of questions, and there was no answer – she said he had nothing to drink the first thing in the morning but the liquor of some Irish-stew made over night, and he shortly afterwards took a cup of tea; then he was very sick, but she thought nothing of his sickness, as he was so almost every morning – I think those were almost her precise words – I saw her on Monday, the day the Inquest was held, before the Inquest – I recollect Mr. Toulmin's assistant, and another medical gentleman coming to make the post mortem examination – I told her the gentlemen had come to make a post mortem examination of her husband's body – she said she had no objection from the first, but her husband had made her promise his body should never be opened, and was it not very natural that a wife should respect her husband's wish? The two gentlemen were ascending the stairs when the conversation took place – I said it was a very painful thing, the law must take its course, and we must find out whether her husband had died from natural or from foul causes – she started from her chair, walked across the room with her hands clasped, and said, 'Thank God I am innocent; if there is anything wrong I know nothing about it' – she said, in reference to her husband, 'Poor dear soul! I loved him too well to wrong him or to injure him,' or 'to injure him or wrong him,' I am not sure which – a day or two after this I saw the prisoner at Mrs. Gillett's – it was on the night of the 31st, the day I gave the prisoner the order for the burial of the body – when I gave it her Mrs. Gillett was standing near her, and she stated that the gruel her husband had left in the morning, she and her child Anne had eaten, and Mrs. Gillett could prove it, or 'Mrs. Gillett knows it,' turning to Mrs. Gillett for confirmation – Mrs. Gillett said, 'I know nothing of it; I have no recollection of it; or, 'I did not see that.'

Cross-examined. Q. Are you the Coroner's beadle? A. The Coroner's constable; I first communicated with the Coroner on this subject on 26th Jan. – I do not know whether my duty as Coroner's constable has reference to this matter – mine is a printed direction, filled up – I received that on the night of 26th – I communicated with him by the first post, the regular communication – I first commenced my conversations with the accused on the morning of the 25th – I had not been exactly acquainted with her; I knew something of her – as far as I was an officer she would know that my conversation was of an official character – I told her I was the Coroner's officer when I went into the house, and Mrs. Gillett knew it.

FREDERICK WILLIAM GROUND. My father is a chemist and druggist, in Church-street, Hackney, about half a mile from where the deceased lived – I assist him in his business in the shop – I have known the prisoner from her having frequented the shop – on Saturday afternoon, 19th Jan., she entered the shop, and asked me at first for two pennyworth of arsenic, which I refused to let her have – nobody but me was in the shop when she came – she said, 'Oh, your father knows me very well, he has often let me have it,' and gave me her name – I did not remember it; but having heard her name since, I recollect that Merritt was the name she mentioned – I did not know her by name at the shop, only by sight – I did not take her name down, as I knew her well – I was about to serve her with two pennyworth of arsenic in one packet, when she said, 'I want it in two separate pennyworths, one for myself, and one for my sister, who lives at a distance, and cannot procure it' – I asked her what she wanted it for – she said, 'To poison some mice or rats' – I then put her up two separate pennyworths, about half-an-ounce in each packet – I did not weigh it – I labelled each packet 'Poison,' a printed label with large letters, and on the reverse side I wrote 'Poison' twice, in case of accident; the packets were fastened with string – when she desired me to divide it, I was about reaching the bottle from the shelf, I do not think I had it down, I am quite sure a quantity of arsenic was not poured out – I put it in white papers, about this size (folding a piece of paper to the size of an ordinary powder) – it was whiter paper than this – the half-ounce would pretty nearly fill the paper; it weighs very heavy – I cautioned her as to the use of it, saying she was not to put it on bread and butter, as children were apt to take it up – she said, 'No, I cut a herring in two, and put it in the middle.'

We sell effervescing powders; they are the same colour as arsenic – white arsenic, divided into these portions, and folded in this way, would resemble effervescing powders externally – effervescing powders consist of two packets, one in blue paper, and the other in white, and one much larger than the other; the smaller is the white – she paid me, and left the shop – she had some pills at the same time – I observed nothing unusual in her manner – she was about the same as usual – she was not excited – she mentioned the death of her children, two I believe.

Cross-examined. Q. Do I understand you right, that you recollect that you put the label 'Poison' on the outside packet? A. Yes; I gave them to her in two separate papers about this size, not enclosed in a third – I have known her about twelve months – she had been in the habit of frequenting the shop.

JAMES COWARD. I am an inspector of the N division of police. On Saturday, 2nd Feb., in consequence of instructions, about half-past ten o'clock in the morning, I went to the prisoner's house, in company with young Mr. Ground – when I got there, I said, 'Mrs. Merritt, I have come here to ask you a few questions, which you can answer or not, as you think proper; but if you do answer them, I must make use of them elsewhere, for or against you.' – I first told her I should like to have some other females present to hear what I said – two other females came, besides one who was in the room with the prisoner; they were persons living in the neighbourhood – I am not aware of their names – when they came, I asked her whether she knew of any arsenic having been in her house lately – she said, 'No.' – I asked her whether her husband used any arsenic in his business, or for any other purpose – she said, 'No.' – I asked her whether she had purchased any arsenic lately – she said, 'No, certainly not' – I then called young Mr. Ground in – she saw him, and became very pale, and exceedingly agitated – I said, 'This young gentleman states that you purchased two pennyworth of arsenic of him about a fortnight since.' – she said, 'Well, I did, and I will tell you for what purpose' – she did not go on, for Mr. Ground left the house, and I went away directly, leaving her in the custody of a constable named Clark – when I returned, I took her to the station – on the way I asked her whether she had a sister living in the neighbourhood – she said, 'No, I have a sister living at Brixton, named Carr; her husband is a twopenny postman.' – I asked her whether she had purchased either of the packets of poison for her sister – she said, 'No, I bought it for myself, and intended to take it, but thought better of it afterwards' – I asked if she had not taken it, what had become of it – she said, 'I emptied one of the packets of powder into the other, and placed it in the cupboard, and burnt the paper containing the first packet' – she then added, 'My husband was very fond of soda and acid powders, and used often to take them, which Mr. Coleman knows.' – she remarked, 'Shall I tell you what a woman said my husband said to her a short time ago?' – I said she had better reserve what she had to say before the Magistrate – she said a woman living down the Lea Bridge-road, who her husband owed 10s. to, told her that her husband said he was often so troubled in his mind, that he had a good mind to throw himself into Clapton pond, or into the canal – I found a copy of the Rules of the Benefit Society in a drawer of a table at the prisoner's house, with Merritt's name on the title page – it was in consequence of what the prisoner said that I looked for it.

Cross-examined. Q. How long before 2nd Feb. was it you had seen Mr. Ground? A. Only the same morning – I did not know what he would state at the time I went to the house – I swear that – I had not talked to him – he had given me a description of a woman something like the prisoner, who had been to purchase arsenic a fortnight previously – on the morning of 2nd Feb., I desired he would go with me – I saw his father, and he told me his son had served the female; I had seen him the evening previous – the first time I went to Mr. Ground's house was the evening previous to my taking the prisoner; that was all the conversation

I had with the elder Mr. Ground – I told young Mr. Ground that it was my wish that previous to his entering the prisoner's house there should be other females present, that he might be able to identify her if he could do so – I told him on his entering the room, if he did identify her he was to lift his hat and bend his head towards her, as I wished to observe the expression of her countenance when she saw him – he said a female resembling the prisoner had purchased some arsenic a fortnight before; that was why I took him with me – I gave him an opportunity of seeing whether he could identify her or not, before questioning her.

Q. Did you not put question after question on the subject of her husband having arsenic in the house, over and over again, before you called in Mr. Ground? A. Certainly I did – I did not produce him at first, because I wished first to ask the prisoner whether she had purchased any arsenic, because from the description he gave me I thought it was her – I can give no other reason for putting the question before introducing Mr. Ground.

RICHARD CLARK (policeman, N 223). I went with Inspector Coward to the prisoner's house – I was left in charge of the prisoner while he went out – I said nothing to her after he was gone – she said, 'I suppose I shall be hanged, there are so many lies about it, but I bought the arsenic for my husband.' – I am quite sure those were her words – I produce sixty-four duplicates in a bag; I received them from Mary Sheen – I have examined them; they refer to articles of wearing-apparel, silver-spoons, and silver sugar-tongs.

Cross-examined. Q. Did you make a memorandum of that observation at the time? A. No – I did not hear her say she purchased it to take herself; I heard her say she had not purchased it – I was not in the room all the time of the conversation with Mr. Coward, I went out once – I did not accompany Mr. Coward to the station; I was left in the house.

MARY SHEEN. I delivered this bag of duplicates to the last witness; I found them under the dresser in the kitchen; I looked there for them – I was told by the prisoner they were there when she was being taken into custody – she told me I should find the tickets there, and she had pawned some of my things, and I was not to say nothing.

SARAH AVIS. I am a female searcher at the police-station at Hackney. I remember the prisoner being brought there on the 2nd Feb. – she asked me if I knew what she was there for; I said, 'No' – she said it was for poisoning her poor dear husband; that he had been poisoned, but she had not done it herself – she asked me if I had noticed the person in the station, meaning Mrs. Gillett; I said, 'No' – she said she had false sworn before the jury, at her husband's jury; it was against her wish, as truth goes furthest – she gave me six duplicates out of her pocket – she said she did not suppose she should be out again, and did not think she should want them; she wished me to burn them.

WILLIAM ALDERMAN. I am gaoler of the police-court, Worship-street. I had the prisoner in custody, after her second examination before the Magistrate on Friday, 8th Feb. – when I took her to her place of confinement, as we went to the cell, she said she wished to see her sister; I said she could do so in the presence of Inspector Coward – I was about to leave the cell, and she said, as she had no one to speak for her, she wished the Magistrate to know something of the case; she then stated that Mrs. Gillett, the witness, was the first instigator of her opening the boxes and pledging the property – she said she wished the Magistrate to know she had spoken the truth all through, except what she had stated to Inspector Coward, respecting the purchasing the poison – she stated she did purchase the poison; she placed it in a cupboard where her husband kept his acid powders, which he was in the habit of taking of a morning; that she emptied the powder out of the paper with the word 'Poison' on it, and destroyed that paper; she screwed the poison up in another piece of paper, and left it in the cupboard; and if he had taken the poison, he must have taken it in a mistake; that she afterwards destroyed the whole of the powders that were in the cupboard, put them in the fire; the said she bought it in a pet, and she intended to take it herself if her husband had gone on in the way he was going on.

Cross-examined. Q. How came you to go to the cell? A. It was my duty; I went to visit the prisoner – the conversation began with her – I went to look into the cell, to see if all the prisoners were right.

The prisoner's statement before the Magistrate was here read, as follows – 'I have nothing to say, but that I never intended him to take it – when I bought it I did intend it for myself if he came home as he had done for several nights past, for I could not live with him as I had done; he came home very comfortable, and I thought no more of it, till the Sunday following, when I burnt it, as it came into my mind that he might take it instead of the soda; as for my giving him anything, it never entered my head. What I said about hanging, was, if I should be hung that minute, I should be hung innocently of giving him anything to do him any harm.'

GUILTY. Aged 31. – Strongly recommended to mercy by the Jury, on account of her good character with Mr. Toulmin's family.

– DEATH.

Chapter 17

Aftermath

Saved by the *London Daily News*:

Editorial Monday March the 11th 1850

THE WOMAN UNDER SENTENCE OF DEATH IN NEWGATE

A case is now before the public that occurred at the sessions house, old
Bailey, on Friday last, which demands some interposition on the part of
friends of humanity. The woman is sentenced to be hanged, not on fact,
but on an opinion. Ann Merritt was charged with having poisoned her
husband by administering to him arsenic. The wretched woman admits
buying the poison, taking from it the label marked with the word 'poison'
and most thoughtlessly placing it in the only cupboard they possessed,
screwed up in a piece of paper, in which same cupboard, screwed up in
a similar piece of paper, were powders of soda and acids bought by the
ounce and not in doses, to form effervescent drafts, in the frequent use
of which her husband indulged. Her object in buying the poison, she
affirms, was to destroy herself, because her life was rendered wretched
by the drunken habits of her husband. He however, altered these habits
for a few days, and she repented of her purpose, and thought no more of
the poison. In less than a week the husband had again taken to drinking,
and on the morning of Thursday, 24 January last, goes to the carpet, takes
a Seidlitz powder as he thought, and soon after is seized with vomiting.
His wife prepared his luncheon for him about 11 o'clock, which he does
not eat, given the meat and potatoes to a fellow turncock, David Ashby,
and requested to have some gruel. A penny worth of oatmeal is fetched
by the child of a neighbour, being made into gruel in the sight of Ashby;
the deceased partakes of some of it, and his wife says she and her child
ate the rest. There was evidently no poison in the meat and potatoes,
and it is not too much to assume, therefore, there was some in the gruel.
During the day the man gets worse, and after going out about his duty,
comes home and goes to bed. Several medical men are sent for, and
none comes to see him till half-past 10 at night. Some chamomile and
opium pills are given him, and he dies about 12:30 the same night. On
a post-mortem examination of the body arsenic to the extent of 8 grains
is found in his stomach, in about a quart of liquid their remaining, and

resembling gruel. Dr Latheby, of the London hospital, gave it as his opinion that this 8 grains could not have been in his stomach more than 4 hours at furthest though he took no gruel after 11 o'clock. And upon this opinion the woman was convicted, the Lord chief baron admitting there was no evidence of her having administered the poison.

The woman's poverty prevented her from being properly defended. To the last moment it was hoped that her friends would have been able to procure counsel. But the depositions were obtained by the humanity of the sheriffs, and, almost without reading, placed in the hands of Mr Clarkson, who did all that could be done under such disadvantageous circumstances. It transpired, in court, as soon as the trial was over, that five friends of the prisoner were in the gallery (one the brother, another the sister, of the deceased) ready to speak to the characters of the accused. Many circumstances have also been since elicited, we understand, which render the unhappy woman's account of the transaction not unlikely to be true. The deceased was up and dressed as late as 8 o'clock on the night of his death, and several times during the same day took out of the screwed up papers the Seidlitz powders 'killed by' or the woman, under such circumstances about, to suffer the extreme penalty of the law, convicted, as she is, upon a chemical opinion? There is no saving clause to the opinion given by the chemist, such as supposing the common theory about the time substances remain in the stomach to be true, but we have positive dogmatism as to what time the poison was in the stomach: and on this dogma the woman dies!

Monday 18 March 1850, though the *London Daily News* received a plethora of letters as a result of its strong editorial, most of them were from concerned laymen, including an attack by an anonymous reader on Dr Latheby's record in general. It was replied to at great length by the doctor himself defending his record; his main comment on the trial itself being the inadequacy of defence counsel causing problems. The most important early letter of this date was from an eminent doctor who had been present in court:

To the editor of the *Daily News*

Sir, having been accidentally in court during the trial of the unhappy woman, Ann Merritt, charged with poisoning her husband and who has been found guilty but strongly recommended to mercy, I find it not unbecoming a member of the medical profession to advert to that portion of the evidence as to which the jury chiefly relied in arriving at their decision; and if any reasonable doubt can be thrown upon the evidence in question, the illustrious lady – known for mercy and goodness – to whom that recommendation will be submitted, will doubtless humanely give the case her royal and favourable consideration.

Dr Latheby who is an able toxicologist and whose truthfulness and experience of the position I do not for a moment question, swore, that the matter found in the deceased stomach, resembling gruel, but been taken only two or three hours before death, and founded his opinion on the theory that the average period for the digestion of liquid matter is from three to four hours, and in about five hours they pass entirely from the stomach into the small intestines. Guided by this opinion the jury could not admit the possibility of the husband taking the poison by his own act, either accidentally or designedly, and as he was unable to leave his bed from about 5 o'clock in the afternoon till almost midnight, a period of seven hours, when he died; and as no one but the wife had access to him, or was likely to administer the poison they were, by this evidence, fully justified in finding her guilty. Dr Latheby was pressed to state the usual and ordinary period that liquids required to pass on the stomach into the intestines, according to his experience in physiological laws on which digestions happen; that having been asked to give the exception to these laws he would doubtless have told the jury that some persons even in perfect health, from constitutional peculiarities, have remarkably slow digestion that account cannot take food at the shorter intervals than six, eight or ten hours and sometimes even longer. A Drunkard's stomach would certainly require a very long period for the digestion of this food and it was proved in evidence that the deceased had been drinking hard during the six weeks preceding his death. I am not aware whether the matter discovered in the unfortunate man's stomach was proven by chemical analysis to be gruel or even the remains of all food at all. Possibly the secretion of the stomach itself, and the softening of the mucous membrane by action of the poison on it, might have been mistaken for the supposed elementary matter found in the stomach after death. These considerations, added to the former reputation of the prisoner, the affectionate care she appeared to take of the deceased, in the absence of all malicious motives for depriving him of life without going into this question of the fallibility of all human means of detecting crime, however skilfully Dr Latheby's chemical experiments may have been conducted, I venture to hope, sufficient grounds for further investigation, so that the law and our common feelings of humanity may not be outraged by the commission of an error which afterwards would be condemned: for although some few women have been humiliating their sex by the perpetration of heinous offences, the natural attributions of women are kindness, virtue, and affection.

I have the honour to be, et cetera,
R.E. Davies M.R.C.S.

27th May 1850
THE LATE POISONING CASE AT HACKNEY
Anne Merritt, the unfortunate woman under sentence of execution for
poisoning her husband at Hackney, but respited, in order that further
enquiries might be made, has had the capital punishment commuted and
is ordered to undergo transportation for life.

Further research discloses she sailed on the *Emma Eugenia* on 25 October
1850 to Van Diemen's Land (Tasmania). Anne reached Tasmania on 7 March
1851, and married John Shipley on 19 July 1852.

Was she guilty?

Modern comment on this case cannot do better than an article of 27 March
1850, quoting *The Spectator*:

SENTENCE OF DEATH ON SUSPICION

Anne Merritt is under sentence of death because appearances are against
her. That is literally the case; in the mania for relying on circumstantial
evidence, a jury have gone to the extreme of condemning a woman on
suspicious appearances; a judge has sentenced her to death; and no
official sign has been given that the sentence will be commuted. Two
essential links in the chain of evidence are wanting. It is proved that
on 19 January Anne Merritt bought some poison – Arsenic: worn out,
she says, by her husband's debauchery, she resolved to destroy herself;
but for once he returned home sober, the regard revived, and she threw
the poison carelessly into a cupboard. Her husband was in the habit of
taking soda drafts, not effervescent, and the medical advice; and kept
the soda in that cupboard. On the 24th he was seized with sickness; he
asked his wife to making some gruel, which she did in the presence of her
husband and a friend. Merritt grew worse and sought medical aid, from
three medical men, who could not attend, but one sent some pills. At last
one, again summoned by message from Mrs Merritt, came; but the man
died soon afterwards. He was a member of a burial club, from which
Mrs Merritt received 7 pounds 10 shillings; on the other hand, had he
lived till 2 February she would have been entitled to £10; and the want of
his salary of ten shillings a week has forced her to send her children to the
work house. Arsenic was found in Merritt's stomach – 8 1/2 grains; by

whom administered – taken by himself in this state, or given by his wife? Dr Latheby deposed that it could only have been in his stomach four hours and he had been in bed from 5 to 12:30; so that in that case, it must have been given to him about 8 o'clock. But Dr Latheby's evidence is only a matter of opinion, much canvassed, and direct counter to the opinions of Orfila and Christison. This outline of the case we have abridged from the very clear analysis of the *Daily News*. The two links wanting in the evidence all – the motive, and the proof, even circumstantial that Anne's hand gave the poison. It is like the memorable case of Eliza Fenning, with this difference that Ann Merritt confessedly bought the poison. But the damaging point against is the profligacy of the husband: the jury seem to have thought it served him right, and that therefore his wife would not resist the temptation. But there really is nothing in the shape of proof, of course Sir George Grey will not suffer this judicial blunder to pass and redressed, in the meantime it is announced that Anne Merritt is to be hanged on Easter Monday!

Spectator

PART 8

Sarah Barber

Chapter 18

Early Life

The *Nottingham Gazette* 1 August 1851

LIFE AND BEHAVIOUR OF SARAH BARBER

We present to our readers this week with some particulars regarding the early life and character of the unhappy woman who now awaits in the condemned cell of the County Hall, the last dread sentence of the law being carried into execution. We do not give these particulars with the sole view of gratifying any morbid appetite for such details, which too often prevails. Our desire is to observe a far higher motive, that of setting before the public such a narrative, as may convey a salutary warning the inevitable consequences of crime, the fearful example as to the almost imperceptible steps of guilt, by which the height of delinquency is obtained, only expiated on the scaffold, a frightful spectacle of mourning to thousands. The tale is a brief but very melancholy one that cannot fail to strike the location of every reader, how important is the influence of early impressions. In early youth Sarah Barber was surrounded by circumstances of the most sad and unfortunate type, such as could only lead to inspire her with the most depraved tastes, lead to the formation of abandoned habits. To the circumstances may be traced in a great measure her subsequently miserable and guilty career. Too often may this result be referred to the pernicious example of parents, but in the present instance such is not the case. Very little is known respecting the parents of the murderess, as it is now many years, since their death. Mr. and Mrs. Simpson lived at the bottom of the hamlet of Nether Green, about half mile from Eastwood. The former died a short time before the birth of the unfortunate subject of our memoir, and from some unexplained cause, the child, after its birth, was put out to nurse to a woman of the name of Mackley. The mother married again, but died soon after, at which time Sarah Simpson was between the age of two and three. The child then remained for a short time under the care of her grandmother, who resided at Bomford-Row, which took its name from the husband of the latter, to whom the property belonged. The death of Mrs. Bomford, which took place shortly afterwards, the subject of this notice went to live with a cousin named Gregory, whose house was in the same row. A yearly sum of money accruing from the interest of small properly bequeathed by her grandfather, was to be appropriated in bringing her up. We are bound to say, however, that instead of proper care being taken to give Sarah a good education, she was entirely neglected and the most ordinary caution was not exercised to prevent her from associating with loose companions. It will scarcely be believed when we say that she was required do the most menial work, even at that tender age, and if we are rightly informed, she has been seen gathering manure in the streets and lanes. When not in the house she was allowed to run wild and join in the sports of all she met with. It is hardly to be wondered at, that her character gave unmistakable proof of the effects of this early training, and she soon gave evidence of that unrestrained looseness of conduct for which she afterwards became so unhappily distinguished. Having attained the age of nine or ten, her guardians, whom we may consider were Mrs. Gregory and another cousin named Springthorpe, were induced by the solicitations of some friends, to allow her to go to the church Sabbath School, at Eastwood, and shortly afterwards to the school in connection with the same. Every effort was now made to supply the inevitable results of former conduct, but as may be well supposed with scarcely any effect. Her self-will and temper during the time of her attendance, despite all the most patient kindness and labour which were lavished upon her by her teachers, was ungovernable. Such being the case, but little progress was made in her education, and we are informed that she cannot now write her own name in a manner fit to seen. She remained in the Sabbath School about four or five years, but we have not been able to ascertain the exact cause or time of her departure. When she was about the age of 13 or 14, she served for few weeks in the family of Mrs. Godber, of Sun Inn, Eastwood. We were somewhat surprised to learn from this lady that during this short period, the conduct of Sarah Barber was very steady. If such was the fact, which we would not dispute for moment, it forms the first bright spot in her unhappy career. She was an object of considerable notice in the neighbourhood from her commanding stature, being six feet two or three inches height. She entered very readily into the sports and pleasures of the neighbourhood, in the pursuit of which she showed but little of the modest reserve characteristic of her sex. When she was scarcely 15 years old, she attracted the attention of Joseph Barber, who at this time lived at Newthorpe, a distance of two miles from Nether Green. It is said, and with apparent good reason, that he was more lured by her pecuniary prospects rather than actuated by any honourable passion towards the unhappy object of his attentions. He was at this time about 27, and bore a very indifferent character. His conduct was very far from being creditable, and he was addicted to many vices, the principal of which seemed be the most unbounded sensuality. It cannot be a matter of surprise that the unfortunate criminal encouraged the attentions of a man of this description, when we reflect upon the loose and pernicious habits with which she was reared through the neglect and inattention of those who professed to act the part of guardians. As might be expected, it was not very long before improper intimacy look place between the guilty lovers, and common decency compels us to draw a veil over the depraved and abandoned pursuits of the man who has now come to an awful and untimely end. No doubt with a view to secure the property accruing her, Sarah Simpson, the early age of 17, was married to her depraved paramour, in Eastwood church, after which event, they came to reside at a small house in Brinsley. The results of such marriage, and the union of such a couple, produced no happiness. Besides the usual and frequent occurrence of matrimonial quarrels, the husband incensed his newly married wife with indulging his vicious propensities with the most indecent and unblushing effrontery. A very short time after the marriage, he brought a woman from the neighbourhood into the house where his wife was, causing the latter to leave the place for short time, and live with some friends at Codnor Park. She returned to her husband, but was a second time compelled to leave her home from the unnatural conduct of her spouse. Having resided above a year at Brinsley, the unhappy couple removed to Eastwood, in which place they continued to reside until the melancholy death of Mr. Barber. It was during their stay at this place that Mrs. Barber, unable to bear the conduct of her husband, left her home and went to France, it is said, in company with a man named Gillott. It is right to state that after the marriage, the conduct of the woman was anything but that of faithful and constant wife, and many vague rumours to this effect are afloat. After an absence of one year, Mr. Barber went to France and induced his wife once more to come home, after which time no further separation seems have occurred. There appears in the evidence what sort of life they led together, and we have it from eye witnesses that on more than one occasion, her husband put her to shame in a cruel manner, in the midst of company. Her language was the most coarse and unseemly imaginable, and in this respect she seemed to have been an apt scholar of her low and brutish husband. She also frequently joined with parties of men in the game of skittles, with all the zest possible. At the time of their marriage, Mr. Barber received from his wife's trustees the sum of £80, and about £210, when she reached the age of 21. He carried on the business of a horse dealer and higgler, which means was enabled to build four small houses, in one of which he lived at the time of his decease. During the early part of the present year she received £25 from her sister-in law on relinquishing claim to certain property devolving to her on the event of her sister marrying a second time.

Chapter 19

The Trial

From the *Nottinghamshire Guardian* Thursday 24 July 1851

THE EASTWOOD POISONING CASE.

SARAH BARBER, aged 22, dressmaker, and ROBERT INGRAM, aged 19, butcher, were charged with having, on the 24th of March last, at Eastwood, wilfully murdered Joseph Barber, the first-named prisoner's husband.

Mr. Macauley, QC, with Mr. Denison had been engaged for the prosecution, and on Wednesday Mr. Sergeant Miller and Mr. O'Brien were retained by Mr. Bowley, the prisoner's solicitor for the defence; but at 7 o'clock in the evening Mr. Sergeant Miller threw up his brief, which was then placed in the hands of Mr. Cockle.

When the witnesses were called upon to appear before the Grand Jury on Wednesday, Mr. Mather, assistant to Mr. Smith, surgeon, Eastwood, and was a material witness in the case, inasmuch as he opened the body of the deceased in the first instance, did not answer to his name, and his recognisance was ordered to be estreated. It afterwards transpired that he had absconded to New York. Mrs. Barber was attired in morning and kept a white handkerchief in her hand. She appeared somewhat subdued, and listened to the charge with considerable attention, and to which she pleaded 'NOT GUILTY' in slow and deliberate terms. Ingram listened collectedly to the indictment, having his hands joined together, and his left elbow raised upon the side of the dock, and pleaded NOT GUILTY in quickly uttered but low toned words. Several of the learned council, on seeing the female prisoner, inquired if she were standing on a stool or chair, her colossal figure towering much higher than the somewhat small person of Ingram.

Mr. Professor Taylor, the eminent analytical chemist of London, was seated on the Judge's bench, and appeared to be on familiar terms with his lordship. While the jurors were being sworn, the female prisoner, seeming all at once to be aware of the awful nature of her position, wept freely.

Mr. Macaulay in addressing the jury in support of the charge, made the following points:

- Ignore what you may have heard and concentrate on the evidence.
- He proceeded to outline the case as he intended to prove it.

- There was an objection by the defence on the use of England's evidence before the coroner's court, overruled by the judge. The statement was then read but, as the prosecutor observed, the whole statement was to be proved by other parties in evidence.

William Scott Smith being sworn was examined by Mr. Denison as follows: I am a surgeon, residing at Eastwood. My first visit to the deceased was on the 24th of February. My assistant attended him before then. He has left the country. I treated him for rheumatism in the lungs. I attended him for that up to Tuesday, the 18th of March. He got better of that complaint. He was then sufficiently well to warrant the discontinuance of my attendance for that. I attended him at his house. When I attended him he was always at home and in bed until the 16th or 17th. I believe the last day I saw him was the 18th, when I did not consider it necessary to administer any more medicine. He was up. The time I saw him before that he had been down stairs, and I found him sitting up in his bed room. He made no complaint of sickness either the last time or the last time but one I saw him. At the commencement of his attack, from the 24th of February to the 3rd of March, he was suffering from a feeling of sickness, and at times being sick, accompanied with diarrhoea. I attributed his sickness at that time to the medicine we had been giving him, which was emetic tartar and colchicum, and the diarrhoea was traceable in a great measure to colchicum. The sickness had ceased before I left off attending him; for a few days before I left him he complained 'of nausea, but not the last two times. The diarrhoea had entirely ceased up to my last visit. When I ceased to attend him he was in a convalescent state. The last time I saw him alive (on the Saturday I think) he was walking in the village. My professional visit was on the 18th; but the last time I saw him was on the Saturday. I was made aware of his death on the morning after his death, Friday, the 21st. I was surprised to hear of his death, judging from his condition the last time I saw him, and I could only account for it from the fact that after I had ceased to attend him my assistant Mr. Mather, prescribed for him.

By His Lordship – Mr. Mather has left the country, I believe.

By Mr. O'Brien – I did not see the mixture made by Mather, but I made a similar one the following day: it was a chalk mixture, to stop diarrhoea.

By Mr. Denison – I did not think his death at all likely. There is no circumstance beyond what was discovered at the post mortem examination, to explain the cause of his death. I was present at the post mortem examination. Mr. Mather made it, but I was present. That was on the 24th. Mr. Mather, myself, the two Messrs. Brown, surgeons, of Eastwood, and a relative of mine, in the army, were present. We examined the whole body, except opening the head. The general state of the organs was not such as to cause death. We found the right kidney diseased, and two or three ounces of fluid in the pericardium. The rest of the organs were not in such a state as would have accounted for decease, none of them indicating disease sufficient to account for death. The stomach was afterwards examined in my presence, by Mr. Thomas Wright, of Nottingham. That was on the Tuesday after the post mortem examination. There was inflammation of the upper portions of the stomach; and there was no substance in the stomach, but a quantity of fluid. I attributed the inflammation in the first instance to his imprudence in eating and drinking. It was such an inflammation in my opinion as would have been presented in the stomach of a person who died from imprudent eating and drinking. There was a little venous congestion on the coating of the stomach. There were slight appearances as if ulceration was commencing; which might have arisen from the inflammation he was suffering under. We preserved the fluid, stomach, and intestines.

By the Court – We did not preserve the liver.

By Mr. Denison – I did not observe the liver. Dr. Thomas Wright examined the fluid contents of the stomach in my presence. The contents of the intestines consisted of mucous, and the medicine he had taken. We examined the fluid on Tuesday, the 25th. We subjected it to Reinche's test. The result was very unsatisfactory.

By the Court – Previously to applying the copper we boiled the fluid. We could not satisfy ourselves of the cause of our failure, except that it was late in the evening, and dark. We also boiled a portion of the stomach itself.

By Mr. Denison – I did not make any other examination afterwards, nor saw any made. We used muriatic acid in the test. I left a portion of the intestines and fluid with Mr Wright, for him to go on with the experiments on the following day. That had had no tests applied to it.

By the Court – I took a portion of the stomach and intestines to Eastwood, which I locked up in the gig-house. I was suddenly called away, and on my return I found the stomach and intestines had been removed. There was the greater portion of the intestines, and about a third of the stomach. I discovered that they were gone on Thursday morning, the 27th. My gig-house had been broken open by my own servant, and I did not discover where it was gone to until yesterday. My servant is not here. I had to remain at the place I went to on the Wednesday, and sent my gig home, and my boy broke the gig-house open on purpose to put the vehicle in. I missed them immediately on my return, but could not ascertain where they had gone till yesterday.

By Mr. Denison – A part of the fluid I had put in my house. That was given to Mr. Swarm, junr., and sent up to Professor Taylor. I sent the whole of it to Dr. Taylor, and had nothing left.

By the Court – Before it was sent to Dr. Taylor I kept it locked up in my own house, under my own lock and key. I keep dogs, but had no reason to believe they had got it: they were not out that morning. The fluid was in a bottle.

By Mr. Denison – The examination of the fluid contents and the stomach, which was unsatisfactory in its results, was made at Mr. Wright's surgery. The post mortem examination was made at the deceased's house. A portion of the cardiac and a portion of the stomach and from two to three ounces of fluid were given to Mr. Gossett Browne, on the Monday afternoon, at the surgery. I did not examine that portion which was given to Mr. Browne. I did not detect any poisonous substance in the stomach or intestines.

By the Court – The portion of the stomach below that which I gave to Mr. Browne was inflamed.

By Mr. O'Brien – I was attending the deceased for rheumatic fever. During the time I attended I knew he was labouring under another disease, for which he had no medicine from me till after his recovery from the rheumatic attack. He might have the medicine for that disease on the 15th or 16th. Mr. Mather made it up. That disease (gonorrhoea) sometimes produces rheumatic affection in a severe form. Rheumatism acting upon the heart produces a severe disease called pericarditis, which is a dangerous thing. If a man died of an attack of rheumatism at the heart, I should expect to find a large effusion of fluid round the pericardium. I have examined Cases of that kind and have always found such effusions. I did not preserve the heart after the examination. I believe Mr. Mather cut it open, but could not say positively. Mr. Mather performed the operative part of the examination. I had frequently to call upon the deceased. His wife was sometimes present, and he told me she was kind and attentive to him from the commencement of my attendance upon her (3rd March). I saw him medico-professionally on the Tuesday, when he was improved. Before dinner on the Wednesday my assistant made up a bottle of medicine for the deceased which I never saw. I believe he did not take it to Barber himself. I don't know who took it: but the day after his wife fetched a bottle of medicine, of the same sort, as far as I know, that I had made up. It was the chalk mixture to remove the diarrhoea. Previous to that my assistant bad sent him some medicine for the gonorrhoea. It would be very likely to cause sickness. It was made of balsam of copaiba and sweet nitre, I believe. It generally produces nausea, and some stomachs will not retain it. The stomach of a man who had been attacked with disease would be more likely to reject it. Mr. Mather, Messrs. Brown, and I were the only medical men at the examination of the body on Monday. At that time we examined for the purpose of seeing whether the individual had had arsenic. Arsenic if administered in such portions as to cause death does not always produce evident appearances. At that time, my first examination, I was of the opinion that death was not caused by arsenic, and I then attributed his death to diarrhoea. I did not suppose the two or three ounces of fluid in the pericardium was the result of rheumatism of the heart.

By the Court – 1 do not know where Mr. Mather is.

By Mr. O'Brien – He left my establishment on the 23rd or 24th of March, or the beginning of April. The fluid in my possession was brought away in the stomach by Mr. Mather from the deceased's house. It was in Mr. Mather's possession when I left my house, and no fluid had then been extracted from the stomach or intestines. I left the deceased's house after the post mortem examination soon after 3 o'clock, and I saw the stomach again in my surgery three quarters of an hour afterwards. Mr. Mather was there with several patients. I found the stomach in a towel on my counter. After Mr. Mather had done with the patients, an hour after I left deceased's house Mr. Browne came in. I had tied the stomach and intestines in the towel in the deceased's house immediately after the post mortem, and they were carried away by Mather; and when I went to my surgery I found the stomach and intestines in the towel on the counter. The stomach had not been disturbed when I gave the fluid and a portion of the stomach to Mr. Browne at the deceased's house. When I saw Mr. Browne in my surgery, I gave him another portion of the fluid, keeping the other portion under lock and key till Tuesday, when I brought it to Nottingham. I took a portion of that back with me to Eastwood, and kept it under lock and key till it was sent to Dr. Taylor. On the Monday, about 3 o'clock, I sent for Mr. Brown, who came into my surgery. The stomach and intestines lay in the towel. I untied it and poured a portion of the fluid into a vessel he held in his hand, and also cut off a portion of the cardiac portion of the stomach which I also gave to Mr. Browne. The remainder I locked up in my surgery, where it remained until Tuesday, when I brought it to Nottingham to Mr. Wright. I put the hamper containing the contents in my gig up at the Flying Horse, and Mr. Wright sent up his man to carry it to his surgery. We poured the largest portion of the fluid of the stomach into a glass jar and a glass bottle. Upon a portion of the fluid I and Mr. Wright applied Reinche's test, but found no appearances of arsenic on the slips of copper. I left that portion upon which we had made the experiment with Mr. Wright, and took the remaining portion of stomach and liquid back with me to Eastwood. We put the liquid into a two or three ounce medicine bottle, which I took home and locked up. We got to Nottingham between two and three in the afternoon, and commenced the operation at 4 o'clock.

By the Court – The portion of stomach and intestines which I took back In the hamper I put in my gig house, and they wore taken.

By Mr. O'Brien – The deceased was about 35 or 37. He was not able to move his legs and arms for ten days after I first saw him. If he went out on the Tuesday it would very likely cause a relapse, and drive the rheumatism to other parts of his body.

By Mr. Denison – There was no numbness in the joints; he complained that the pain was very excruciating. From the first of March this gradually diminished, and the swelling disappeared, the pain ceased, and be was able to walk about.

By the Court – I attributed the effusion of the pericardium to the general inflammatory action all over the body, and not to the inflammation of the heart or pericardium.

By Mr. Denison – I am acquainted with cases of pericarditis which have produced sudden death. In those cases there would be great pain in the region of the heart, hurried circulation, and difficulty of breathing, of none of which the deceased complained. When I was called in on the 18th of March none of the symptoms of pericarditis were visible. He could not have walked about had there been. Vomiting is not a natural result of pericarditis; nor is purging, but thirst is, generally speaking. Chalk mixture would not be a proper mixture for pericarditis. Bleeding and blistering would be the proper treatment for that disease.

By his Lordship – The kidney was a little enlarged and hardened, but there was nothing to cause death in the appearance.

John Hill, being called, said – I am servant to Mr. Wright. I remember Mr. Smith coming to Nottingham in March. I went to the Flying Hone and fetched away a hamper, which a boy named Spray, whom I had met on the Poultry, he helped me to carry. I took it to Mr. Wright's kitchen in the state I found it.

John Spray corroborated this evidence, and further said he saw Mr. Wright open the hamper, and take out something in a towel.

Robert Gossett Browns, surgeon, Eastwood, said – I was present at the post mortem examination of the deceased's body. I observed that the left lung and also the apex of the right was studded with tuberculous deposits, and in the pericardium there was about two ounces of fluid. The muscular structure of the heart appeared pale and the liver was larger and somewhat softer than natural. The capillary vessels of the bowels externally appeared injected. The left kidney did not appear healthy. On laying open the oesophagus it was found more vascular in its upper and lower extremity than natural, and covered with mucus. I could not at that period see any appearances sufficient to explain the cause of death. At Mr. Smith's surgery I received nine grains of the fluid contents of the stomach, with a portion of the cardiac extremity of the stomach and with a portion of the oesophagus attached. I put them into a clean glass bottle, tied them over, sealed it, and locked it up. I walked from the house of the deceased with Mr. Mather to Mr. Smith's surgery, Mr. Mather carrying the stomach in a towel. During the post mortem examination a part of the liver was cut off, and I asked my brother, who is a medical man, to take it away. I afterwards made an analysis of that portion of the liver at my house. We went through several experiments, separately and conjointly. I reproduced metallic arsenic, and various preparations of arsenic, from the substance of the liver.

By the Court – I made these experiments on the Monday, the 24th March. I applied sulphate or hydrogen, Marsh's test, and Reinche's test. All were conclusive as to the appearance of arsenic, which in each test was obtained. We did not go on to produce metallic arsenic from those compounds of arsenic. I have no doubt from the result of those experiments that there was arsenic in the liver.

By Mr. Denison – The arsenic must have been absorbed into the system of the deceased during life. I observed that there were two dark patches on the stomach under the mucous membrane, which was very much infected, and somewhat softer than natural. I made an analysis of the fluid extremity of the stomach, which I tried by the same three tests, the result of which was proof of the presence of arsenic. I produced metallic arsenic by Reinche's test, the sesquisulphate of arsenic; and by Marsh's test, arsenate of hydrogen. These experiments proved that there was arsenic in the stomach as well as in the liver. There were two distinct tests both agreeing. I tried them several times; all with the same result. I should think there was about a grain of arsenic in the portions of the stomach and liver which I examined. A portion of that was in the fluid; that found in the liver was in the system. I had only about one-sixteenth part of the liver; and judging from an opinion expressed to me by Professor Taylor after I had told him the result of my experiment, I should say there was the twenty-fifth part of a grain of arsenic in the portion of the liver I examined. The appearances I observed on the body would be what I should have expected to find on the body of a person who had died from the effects of arsenic. That portion of the cardiac extremity that I did not examine I took to Professor Taylor.

By Mr. O'Brien. – I should think Mr. Smith was aware that I took away a portion of the liver. I went with Mr. Mather to the surgery, but seeing a patient there, from courtesy I went into the house, and stayed there perhaps ten minutes before Mr. Smith came. If by accident a twenty-fifth part of a grain had fallen upon the outer portion of the part of the liver I had I should have seen it, because I carefully examined it. If it were possible that the twenty-fifth part of a grain had been on the outer surface the result of the test would have been the same. I tried the muriatic acid before I applied the test. I subjected the liver to the three tests. There might have been one or two of the same vessels used in each experiment. I was examined twice – once before I went to London.

Thomas Wright, MD, (consulting physician to the General Hospital at Nottingham), was next called, but at the request of his lordship, Mr. Smith was again placed in the box, who, in reply to the court said – Mr. Mather made what I supposed was the chalk mixture on Wednesday afternoon, before I got home. I keep arsenic in my surgery, and Mather might have had access to it. There is a label upon the vessel of liquor arsenicolis. He had been in my service a year. The chalk mixture consists of chalk, aromatic confection, distilled water, and a small portion of opium, all of which constituents are kept in proper boxes or bottles, all of which are labelled. I had no other arsenic in my surgery at that time.

Thomas Wright said, on Tuesday the 25th of March last, witness came to my house, and I with him made some experiments which did not prove the presence of arsenic. The place in which the experiments were made is dark.

By the Court – The experiments were partly made by gas-light.

By Mr. Denison – On the following day I, with Mr. White, house surgeon of the Hospital, made some further experiments which were again unsatisfactory, not yielding evidence of arsenic. On the Wednesday and during the night we continued the experiments, and on Thursday morning we discovered slight traces which we believed to be arsenic. We made other experiments, and found arsenic in considerable quantity, which we estimated at ten grains. The portions of stomach we examined at the Hospital were the same as Mr. Smith had brought to me.

By the Court – From the appearance of the interior of the stomach, and the fact that some arsenic was found in the tissue of the stomach, I have no doubt arsenic was absorbed during life. We found several grains of arsenic in the stomach undissolved. I first used Reinche's test, but from a stain on the copper I was unable to prove that it was arsenic. That was the only test I applied. I attribute the failure of the first experiment probably to the existence of some fatty matter in the stomach.

By Mr. O'Brien – We found some portions of undissolved arsenic at the bottom of the vessel. This was tested and found to be arsenic. They were first noticed I believe by Mr. White. I believe it was on Friday, the 28th that the portions of arsenic were found within the tissues. I found that result by applying Reinche's test. Arsenic operates fatally by absorption into the system. The time intervening between the taking of the arsenic and its absorption varies.

Joseph White being sworn said – I am resident surgeon of the General Hospital. I and Dr. Wright made a first experiment on the 26th of March. At the conclusion of the second experiment, which was made hurriedly, I found indications of arsenic. There was not time on the first day to come to any decided conclusion. I then made a more careful analysis, commencing with the stomach. The portions which were there were put into distilled water and boiled for three hours, which had muriatic acid put into it, and a solution was obtained, divided into three portions. The first was examined by Reinche's process, and gave every indication of the presence of arsenic. The second portion was examined by Marsh's test, and gave every indication of the existence of arsenic. The third portion was tested with sulphate of hydrogen. In this there were about three grains of arsenic. The next portion that I examined was the upper portion of the intestinal canal, examined in the same way by Reinche's process, gave the same evidence of existence of arsenic, by Marsh's process, and by the sulphate of hydrogen, both of which proved the same result. The whole of that portion, about three inches of the intestinal canal would contain about a half-grain of arsenic. I next came to the examination of the fluid contents of the stomach, which had then stood for six days in my own cupboard under lock and key. For two days previously I had observed at the bottom of the bottle a heavy white powder. This was, carefully separated, boiled in ether, and, after being carefully dried, was found to be three grains and a one-tenth. I examined a portion of this powder, by being boiled in a watch glass in distilled water. It was indissoluble in a solution of potash. The solution which I obtained I tested with the ammonia–nitrate of silver, a yellow precipitate of the arsenide of copper was shown. A second portion was examined with the ammonia–sulphate of copper, which produced a green precipitate of the arsenite of sulphur. To a third portion a few drops of the hydro–sulphuric ammoniate was added. No visible effect was produced, by adding a few drops of muriatic acid. The witness detailed a number of tests, all proving the existence of arsenic of which he discovered altogether 8 grs. and 600ths.

Mr. Professor Taylor, MD examined by Mr. Macauley said – I am a professor of medical jurisprudence in Guy s Hospital, London. On the 1st of April Mr. Robert Gossett Browne brought me part of the contents of a stomach in a glass jar. There was a light coloured fluid, consisting for the greater part of mucus, of a reddish colour, from the presence of blood. There was no sediment in the bottle. I am acquainted with the appearances of stomachs after irritant poison; and this stomach presented those appearances, with the exception that it was diluted with water. That dilution might have been caused by the deceased drinking water just previously to his death. I learned from Mr. Browne that it had been diluted with water since death. I then and there made an examination of the fluid in Mr. Browne's presence, and detected about one-eighth of a grain of arsenic. The quantity of fluid was about six teaspoonfuls. I tested the muriatic acid, the water, and all the vessels, before making the experiment, and there was no arsenic in the materials or vessels. After boiling a short time the copper was coated with a grey metallic powder. I then applied heat and examined with a magnifying glass, and the deposit had all the appearances of white arsenic as it is commonly known. The proportion of arsenic which I obtained was about an eighth of a grain, the whole of which was extracted from the liquor. I then tried an experiment with the cardiac extremity of the stomach, which was three inches by one. It was 12 days after death, but it was well preserved. When arsenic is absorbed into the tissue it acts as a great preservative. There was a softening of the mucous membrane; and there were two spots where blood had been effused below the mucous membrane, which are appearances such as any irritant poison would produce. I examined the coating of the stomach with a magnifying glass, but could detect no appearance of arsenic. There were two or three yellow patches on the outside of the stomach resembling very much the appearances caused by arsenic. One appeared to have been partly occasioned by bile; but the other had a bright appearance as if caused by while arsenic, where it had been in contact with animal matter for a few days. There were two or three smaller marks of the same colour. I first experimented upon one square inch, the result of which was the detection of arsenic in a crystalline form. There was another jar which Mr Browne had brought, and which contained a portion of the intestines. The interior was very slightly inflamed. I tried it with the magnifying glass, and could detect no appearance of arsenic. It was 18 inches long; and I examined six inches by one process and six by another, having first boiled one of the six inches in distilled water to which I applied the test for arsenic, and no arsenic was produced. This is conclusive to show if there were arsenic it was absorbed in the tissues. I then applied further tests to the pieces of intestine, both tests proving the existence of arsenic, the proportions of arsenic being nearly the same although the processes were different – about an eighth of a grain to six inches. We generally allow about seven hours for the deposition of arsenic into the liver after being taken.

On the following day, the 2nd of April, Mr. Edward Swarm delivered to me a two ounce bottle containing an ounce of liquid said to be part of the contents of the deceased's stomach. I tested it for all the common articles of food, but was unable to discover any trace; the fluid consisted of water, mucus, blood, and some animal matter. There was a heavy sediment, which I dried on a glass, and examined it with a microscope, and found them to be crystals of arsenic, I found half-a-grain in an undissolved state. By other tests I found the fluid contained arsenic partly in a dissolved state and partly in an undissolved state; of the dissolved arsenic there was another half grain. I have known arsenic to remain two or three days in the stomach without being absorbed or thrown back.

There was no appearance to show that arsenic had been administered of large quantities at any time. The results I obtained were consistent with the opinion that the deceased had died from the effects of one or several doses. The quantity I found altogether was three grains and one-eighth, [The other medical gentlemen all together found eight grains.] I should infer from the appearances that arsenic had been administered in small doses. It is possible for a cessation of vomiting and purging five hours before death. From my observations I am of opinion that some arsenic must have been taken in powder.

By Mr. O'Brien. – Some poisons are considered accumulative, but this is not. The moment arsenic begins to absorb its action commences. It is a substance that a person can become accustomed to by frequent small doses Presuming a person had taken laudanum, the limits of time in which death would ensue varies, the average being twenty-four hours. The lowest that I know of is two hours. I have known one case in which six days intervened between the time of taking arsenic into the system and the death.

Francis Edward Swarm deposed that on the 31st of March be received a jar from Mr. Smith, and delivered it on the 2nd of April to Dr. Taylor in the same state as he received it.

Mr. Smith re-called and examined by Mr. O'Brien – I don't know that my assistant supplied the deceased with anything for an injection, but it would not have been an unusual thing to have done so. Solution of zinc or a preparation of lard would be used for that purpose, but I do not think such an injection was sent.

By Mr. Macaulay – The deceased never told me of having the gonorrhoea while I was attending upon him.

Elizabeth Barber being sworn said – Joseph Barber, the deceased, was my son. I am a widow, and live at Newthorpe, a little more than a mile from Eastwood. He was 35 years of age when he died. He used to deal with horses, sell hay, He had been married to his wife five years. She had no family. His wife sent me word by a little boy about half-past 11 on the day before he died that he was ill, and I got to him in about half-an- hour. He was in bed upstairs, undressed. His wife came up stairs and said he had had a very poor night of it. He said he had been very poorly that night, but was much better, and felt a deal better. He complained of his mouth being dry and parched, and that he was thirsty. He did not tell me he had been sick. His wife said nothing more than he had a poor night. She just came up stairs and said what I have just stated, and walked down again. I made him some gruel, and he drank about a pint, saying that it was very nice. He went on getting better, and told me that he felt a great deal better. I remained with him in the room all that night. He next had a little cold water, and some preserve, but had no other kind of food while

I was there. He drank a good deal of water that afternoon. I could only give him about three or four meat spoons full at a time, and I gave it him every quarter of an hour. He could have helped himself, for about one o'clock at night he went down stairs. About that time I made him some more gruel. He took nothing else. I was ill myself that night, and lay by his side. He got up several times during the night to bring me water and the smelling bottle. He only vomited once during that time, and that was at two o'clock in the morning, when he threw up two table spoons full of gruel. He was not purged while I was there. His wife was not in the bed room at all that night. She and I were not on very good terms, and I did not go so often as I otherwise should have done if she had been pleasant. When first his illness began, about five weeks before he died, she went away two nights because I was there. I did not know where she went. On the Thursday morning my son appeared to be, and said he was, better. I left him at 11 o'clock in the morning, when he talked of having a cup of tea and a new laid egg. I went home and heard no more of him till 3 o'clock the following morning, when Ingram (male prisoner) and the next door neighbour, Shaw, came to my house. On the day I was at my son's the prisoner Ingram gave him some medicine out of Mr. Smith's bottle. I know it was Mr. Smith's bottle, because my son told him to give him some out of it. It was half-a-pint glass bottle. I don't know what colour it was. He had two-table spoons full. I could not tell whether they emptied the bottle or not. I saw Mr. Bowker's bottles. My son told me to get them up from under the table. One dose bad been taken out of one and the other was full. They were the same sized bottles. One a kind of white and the other was slight red. He had had a dose out of the white mixture. My son told me to cork the bottle up again, and put them under his bed, for he would have no more of them, and I did so. This was before Ingram gave him the dose of Smith's medicine. My son and Mrs. Barber never quarrelled in my presence. I have heard them used abusive language to each other. She once left him, about two years ago, and was away many months. I have heard her say that she was in France. At that time my son went and fetched her back.

By Mr. O'Brien – They had been living at Eastwood about two years. I never heard that while she was absent she took service in a gentleman's family. They lived at Brinsley before they lived at Eastwood. He asked me about Bowker's medicine as soon as I got in on Wednesday. I found them under the dressing table, and by his orders I put them under the bed. He did not say why he would not take Bowker's medicine. It was about 4 o'clock when he took Mr. Smith's medicine. He did not send for Ingram. He came up stairs and brought a bit of coal. I don t know whether he asked Ingram for the medicine, or whether Ingram said it was time. In the morning my son said to his wife, 'Sally, where are the preserves.' I had not given him any during the night. Mr. Macaulay asked the witness it she knew with whom the female prisoner went to France. Mr. O'Brien objected to the question, but was overruled.

By Mr. Macaulay – I don't know that I ever heard her say that she went to France with a man named Gillott, or that such a fact was stated in her presence; but I know she did go with him. Dr. Taylor, recalled by Mr. O'Brien, said arsenic, if taken in small doses, did not taste; but if taken in large doses, half a teaspoonful, it would cause a rough, acid taste.

By the Court – Three grains of arsenic would destroy an adult; but that is the smallest quantity that could.

Thomas Hazledine, sworn, said: I live at Eastwood, and am in the habit of assisting my neighbours to make wills. The week before Joseph Barber died I went to his house. Mrs. Barber's brother, George Simpson, or Riley, fetched me on the Tuesday but one before he died. It was in the afternoon. Nobody was in the room with him at the time, but his wife came in. He spoke loud enough for her to hear. He told me he should leave his wife all with the exception of two rooms rent free and 6d. a week for life for his mother. He did not tell me what he was worth particularly. He mentioned his freehold property. I knew before that he had about three acres of land and about half a dozen houses. The land was worth about £8 a year to let. He said it would bring his wife in 10s. or 11s. a week.

By Mr. O'Brien – I know there is a mortgage to the amount of £46 upon the property.

John Wilson deposed – I am a farmer living at Heanor I knew the deceased, and also his wife and Ingram. I saw the deceased several times before his death. I was at his house the night he died, and also a fortnight before. I saw him on the Tuesday afternoon before he died, at Emmanuel Wilde's public house. I asked him to drink with me, and be refused. He said he felt better in health. He and I played at dominoes. He made bets of a 1d. upon the game. I was at Wilde's house on Wednesday morning. Ingram was there, and in his presence I asked Mrs. Wilde how the deceased was. She said she didn't know and she didn't care. Ingram did not say anything about Barber's health. A man named Gillott was there, and said he should like something to eat. Ingram said he would fetch him something from Joseph Barber's, and Gillott said he would not have anything from there, he did not mean to be poisoned. Ingram said 'Humph,' and made a puff at it. I could not tell whether it was an exclamation of approbation or contempt. Barber's house is 15 or 20 yards off the public house. Mrs. Wilde and the female prisoner are sisters. On Thursday night, about 11 o'clock, I went to Barber's house, hearing that he was worse. I met Ingram on the stairs carrying something down, and said 'Barber's worse; I think it will be a job with him.' I went into the bed room, where I found Mrs. Barber, Emmanuel Wilde, and Stubbs and Barton went in with me. The deceased said to Stubbs. 'My lad, I'm done.' He repeated the same to me when I spoke to him. Mrs. Barber was feeding him out of a pot or basin with a spoon. He kept saying, 'Give me a sup more,' it appeared as if he wanted to quench his thirst. He was very weak. I stayed about half-an-hour, when I went away. He seemed to get gradually worse. One day, about a fortnight before then, I was there and saw him in bed. His wife gave him some gruel, and he said it did not taste nice, it was nasty. She said it perhaps might be smoked. He wanted her to taste of it, but she would not, and set it down. Ingram was about the premises.

By Mr. O'Brien – I reached Joseph Barber's house the night he died about 11 o'clock. I did not stay till he died. He appeared perfectly sensible, He spoke to his wife. When he said he 'was done,' I told him not to harbour such an opinion. He said while I was in the room that he should die, and it was then I said 'Don't harbour such an opinion, so well you were the other day.' His wife had all the appearance of being kind and attentive to him while I was there. I heard Barber speak most affectionately of his wife's kindness and attention to him. I knew them both before they were married. I heard a report that he had some money by her.

By Mr. Macaulay – He said that she had waited on him uncommonly well, and that Squire Walker could not have 'been better attended to'.

Elisha Pollard deposed – I am a shoemaker at Eastwood. On Thursday night, the 20th of March, about ten o'clock, I went to the deceased's house. I went up stairs to his bed side. At first he did not know me, but his wife told him my name. Robert Ingram, William Plintoff, and Thomas Kelk were also there. He asked Thomas Kelk to pray. He said he thought if he should get better what a different man he would be; that he would go to chapel, and try to do what good he could. Mr. Flintoff began to pray, and the deceased got up, and got out of bed, but fell down by the side of the bed. We put him to bed again. He did not get up again. After that he said what a good wife his wife had been to him, and that Mr. Walker could not have been better attended to, and that he had left her about ten shillings a-week to live on. He called Ingram up to help him out of bed, and he died directly.

Eliza Shaw being sworn said – My husband, John Shaw, is a sawyer at Eastwood, and we live next door to where the Barbers lived. I was frequently in the habit of going to see them. During the time the deceased was ill his wife, Robert Ingram, and Robert Scrimshaw, of Shirland, waited upon him. Scrimshaw waited upon him in the first fortnight of his illness only, and left him about a month before he died. I don't know that anybody else but the prisoners, except his mother, waited upon him. Ingram's proper home is Langley Mill, about a quarter of a mile from Eastwood; but during Mr. Barber's illness he lodged in their house, and had his meals there. I saw the deceased out on the Sunday and Tuesday before he died. On Sunday I saw him and Ingram get into the gig to go to Bulwell. On the night he died I went to see him. I have seen Ingram give Barber medicine, and I have seen his wife give him tea. When I went in on Thursday night, about half-past nine o'clock, there were several people there. He asked me if I would stay with his wife all night. He did not complain of being full of pain, but he said he was thirsty, and asked for something to drink. I saw Mrs. Barber several times on Thursday morning, going in and out of the house. She told me in the afternoon that he was very ill, and that he had become ill on Wednesday morning. She said he had been sick on Wednesday, and also on Thursday. On Thursday afternoon she said she had sent for some arsenic by her brother Riley from Mr. Cullen's, a druggist, at Eastwood, on Wednesday night, and that she had lost it out of her dress pocket as she was returning home from the church lecture, together with five pennyworth of copper out of the change of six-pence she had sent for the arsenic. She said she had sent for the arsenic for the mice in the house. There were a great many mice both in her house and mine. Robert Ingram came the Friday before the deceased died to ask my husband to go with him to Cullen's to get a pennyworth of arsenic, because Cullen required a witness. My husband went with him. On the Sunday that Barber went to Bulwell I and my husband went into Barber's house, and my husband asked the female prisoner if she had laid any arsenic for the mice, and she said she had burnt it. On the Monday, the first day of the inquest, Mrs. Barber came into my house (before the inquest was held) and said, 'Mrs. Shaw, will you swear that you saw me burn the arsenic?' I said, 'I will not tell a story for any one.' My husband was present. She then went away. I saw Ingram shortly afterwards. He called me from my yard into Mrs. Barber's yard. I went to him, and he said, 'Mrs. Shaw, are you going to swear that you saw Mrs. Barber burn the arsenic' I said, 'I am not.' He said nothing more, and went away. On the Thursday after, I was in Mr. Godber's bar. Mrs. Barber was there, and she spoke to me alone. She said, 'Are you going to swear that you saw me burn it?' I said, 'I am not.' She said nothing more. I had not seen her burn it. When I saw the deceased out at the time I have stated it was very wet, and I said to him that it was a bad day for invalids. When Mrs. Barber was talking about the mice I saw some things that they had gnawed.

By Mr. O'Brien – During Mr. Barber's illness his wife was very kind and attentive to him. I heard Mr. Barber tell her to get something to kill the mice within about a week before he died. She did not say to me on the Monday, 'Don't you recollect I told you I burnt the arsenic?' but

'Will you swear that you saw me burn the arsenic?' She did not ask me to swear that she told me she burnt the arsenic, but to swear that I saw her burn the arsenic that she had told me she burnt.

By Mr. Cockle – Barber and Ingram were on very intimate terms. When the deceased was taken ill he had Scrimshaw to attend upon him, but he dismissed him and sent for Ingram.

John Shaw being sworn said – I am husband of Eliza Shaw. Am a sawyer, and lived next door to the deceased's house at Eastwood. On the 14th of March (Friday) Ingram asked me if I would go with him as a witness to Cullen's shop for some arsenic to kill mice with. I saw Mr. Cullen give him a pennyworth of arsenic (about half an ounce.) I went back with him, and left him at Barber's door. On the Sunday following, when Barber went to Bulwell, I went into the house and asked Mrs. Barber if she had found any mice that had been killed by the arsenic, and she said she had burnt it, adding that if her husband was to die people would say he was poisoned, so she would not have it about the house. On that day I heard her say to my wife, 'Mrs. Shaw, will you swear that you saw me burn the arsenic?' and my wife replied, 'I will not tell a story for anybody.' I heard her say no more then, but the same day she said to me. 'My husband has been in the habit of going to the stable to take medicine; I don't know what it is; it will be hard for me to suffer, as I am innocent.' That was on her return home after the first inquest.

By Mr. O'Brien – I know that Barber had a stable, and I have twice seen him drink something out of a bottle. I saw him take it once about the time of his illness.

Robert Stances Bowker, of Bulwell, surgeon, said – I knew the deceased, whom I recollect coming to Bulwell, five or six miles from Eastwood, in a gig with another man I did not take much notice of. I did not know the prisoner Ingram at that time. It was between 11 and 12 o'clock. I saw them against Mr. Buckle's, druggist's shop. I asked Barber how he was, and he said he wanted to consult me. I said 'if you will go to my house I will come to you. 'I afterwards saw him in my parlour, and I prescribed some copaiba, potash, in sweet nitre, to be taken internally, and an injection, composed of sulphate of zinc. I went with him to Leavers public-house, and there I saw a man with him. He told me he had rheumatic fever. I asked him if he had ever taken copaiba, and he said he had taken buckets full. Supposing he had taken the injection instead of the copaiba it would not produce death.

By Mr. Cockle – I don't know how the other man was dressed; but I believe he had a rough coat on.

By the Court – I am sure I did not put arsenic into either of those bottles. I keep arsenic in my surgery in a powder state.

Dr. Taylor, in reply to the Court, said it would require a very large quantity of zinc, 2 grams and a half, to produce serious effects. A scrapie (the amount in the injection) would cause sickness, but not death.

George Gosling being called, said – I am a frame-work-knitter, and live at Bulwell. I have known deceased for six or eight years. I did not know the male prisoner. On Sunday the 14th of March I saw the deceased in a gig or light cart, driving to the door of Buckle's shop. The man at the bar was driving. I believe he is the man. At about half-past 11 o'clock in the morning. The horse's head was up the town towards Leavers's public-house. I saw the other man, whom I believe to be the prisoner, get out of the gig and go into the shop. When he came out he got in again, and they drove a yard or two and stopped to wait for Mr. Bowker. Whilst they were waiting at the bottom of the yard next to Buckle's shop, Mr. Wilmot, the coach proprietor, drove up in a four wheeled carriage, and shook hands with Bowker, and spoke to Barber. I heard Mr. Bowker tell Barber that he could not leave at that time, and that he must go and put up, and he would go to him as soon as he could. I believe the prisoner is the man. I saw him again three weeks after, at the last inquest.

By Mr. Cockle – The prisoner was dressed in a rough short coat when I saw him at Bulwell. The shutters of Mr. Buckle's shop were closed. I saw him knock at the door, and it was opened from within. I did not see Mr. Buckle. When I was taken before the jury I picked the prisoner out without his being shown to me.

By the Court – To the best of my knowledge I believe the prisoner is the man.

Walter Charles Buckle, druggist, Bulwell, said – On the 16th of March a person came to my shop and asked for a pennyworth of arsenic. I believe it was the prisoner Ingram. I wrote 'Arsenic, poison,' on it. He gave me 6d., and I returned him 5d. in copper. He said he wanted it to poison rats and mice, in a barn, I think. I said, 'It is a curious thing to come for on a Sunday,' and he said 'We can't get any in our place.' I asked him where that was, and he said 'Eastwood.' It was between 11 and 12 o'clock. The shutters and door were closed. A part of the door is ribbed glass, so that a person can't see through it distinctly. He came in by himself. In a few minutes after I had served him and he had left the shop I heard a cart or gig drive from the door towards Leaver's. I have very little doubt the prisoner is the man, but owing to the shutters being closed I did not see his face distinctly. I saw him at the inquest, and pointed him out as being like the man.

George Leavers deposed that his father kept a public house at Bulwell. He remembered the deceased going to his father's house on Sunday, the 16th of March, in a light cart, with the prisoner Ingram.

By Mr. Cockle – While Barber was at Mr. Bowker's, Ingram could not have gone to Buckle's shop and back.

Benjamin Cullen, grocer, Eastwood, being sworn said – I also sell drugs. On Friday, the 14th of March, the prisoner Ingram came to my shop, and asked for a pennyworth of arsenic for destroying rats and mice. I gave him the arsenic, and wrote upon it, 'Arsenic, poison.' A man was with him. I never sell arsenic without there is a witness. On the Wednesday following the female prisoner's brother, Riley, came to my shop, and asked for a pennyworth of arsenic, with which I served him. He had a man named Simpson with him. On the morning of the same day, a woman named Betty Lees had called for a pennyworth of arsenic, and I had refused to let her have it.

By Mr. O'Brien – I have an indistinct recollection that some considerable time ago the deceased applied to me for arsenic, but I don't remember that I served him with any.

Mr. Christopher Swank, coroner for the county, said: I held the inquest on the body of the deceased, commencing on Monday the 24th of March. There were five adjournments. On the first day, Monday, the prisoner Ingram gave evidence upon oath. Elisha Pollard was examined first, and Ingram next. What he stated was written down by me in answer to questions of mine. Questions were also put to him by members of the Jury, and his answers I reduced to writing the same as the others. I took down all he said; and he signed it in my presence as his deposition – The deposition which will be found in the opening address by Mr. Macaulay, was read by the clerk of the Assize, and put in as evidence.

Mr. Swank's examination resumed: Ingram was apprehended under my warrant. On the day on which the witness, Gosling, picked out the prisoner Ingram, the two prisoners were not sitting or standing together, but were several yards apart. Ingram sat against the Jury, and he might have been mistaken for one. After the whole of the witnesses had been examined, I asked Ingram if he had anything to say, and he said, 'I have nothing to say further than I have said.'

By Mr. Cockle: I believe Mr. Bowley, his solicitor, advised him to say nothing. Mr. Cullen, recalled by Mr. O'Brien, said he knew Ingram when he fetched the arsenic, and had known him some time before.

At this stage of the proceedings (half-past 7 o'clock), the Court adjourned until half-past 8 o'clock next morning, the Jury being ordered to be taken to a place where they would not be able to see any one, but where comfortable arrangements would be provided for them.

Dr. Taylor, recalled by Mr. O'Brien, said arsenic, if taken in small doses, did not taste; but if taken in large doses, half a teaspoonful, it would cause a rough, acid taste.

By the Court – Three grains of arsenic would destroy an adult; but that is the smallest quantity that could.

(Friday). Mr. Baron Parke took his seat on the bench at a quarter to nine o'clock, on Friday morning. The prisoners were immediately placed at the bar with little alteration being visible in their appearance. The petit jury having answered to their names.

Eliza Goodwill, Eastwood, single woman, said: I live with my brother Henry Carr, who keeps a grocer's shop. I have known the prisoner Mrs. Barber a long time. On Wednesday, the day before her husband died, she came to my brother's shop, and asked for half a pound of crushed sugar, she then asked me if we keep arsenic and I said I thought we did keep it, and I looked but could not find it. I don't know what time of day it was. She said she wanted the arsenic to kill mice. I asked her how her husband was, and she said 'very poorly'.

By Mr. O'Brien: She had been in the habit of buying articles at my brother's shop now and then. There is service on Wednesday at Eastwood church, when Mr Plumtree is at home. It begins at seven o'clock.

Elizabeth Lees, being sworn, said – I live at Eastwood and am a widow. I have known Mrs. Barber all my life she lives about a quarter of a mile from my house. On the day before her husband's death, about 11 o'clock, she came into my house, and asked me if 'Nanny,' my late husband's sister, was in, she wanted her to go of an errand for her. I told her she was not in, and she then asked me to go to Mr. Cullen's, to buy a pennyworth of arsenic. I asked her what she wanted it for, and she said she had got mice in the house which had eaten a carpet and many more things besides. I asked her if Mr. Cullen sold it, and she said 'Yes, for Mrs, Jackson had bought some there, and it had killed all her mice for her.' I went to Mr. Cullen's house which is about 20 yards from mine, and if she came direct from her house she would have had to pass it. I then went to Mr. Cullen's shop, but did not get the arsenic. I went back to Mrs. Barber and told her Mr. Cullen would not let one person have it I gave her the penny, and she went away immediately.

William Roe, builder, Eastwood, deposed – I had known the deceased and his wife many years, and saw them frequently. Two years next November I was building some houses for him between Eastwood and Langley Mill. He latterly lived in one of these houses, but at the time they were building he lived in another house close by, and I used to go in and get my breakfast there. There was a little variance between them at times. On one occasion in the year 1849 while in a passion, I heard her say 'She would poison him if it was longer first'. I heard her say so two or three times. What caused her to say so I can't tell. He had offended her in some way, and she broke out in a passion.

By Mr. O'Brien: I continued to get my breakfast there up to the time the buildings were finished in Spring, 1850. I have seen them on friendly terms after those bursts of passion. I never heard him say he beat her home with a stick once. I seldom went after I had finished the houses.

Thomas Barnes, grocer, Eastwood, said – I knew the deceased, Barber, well. I lived about a quarter of a mile from his house. They lived on not very good terms. I was once present when angry words passed between them. That was about eighteen months since I was in their house. I believe Mr. Barber had been out all night drinking. They were quarrelling about that and I heard her say she would poison him. I believe he had not said anything violent to her. She was angry. The exact words were that 'She would poison him, he had been along with his __ all night.' I heard nothing more that took place between them.

By Mr. O'Brien: I saw them frequently after that. About a month before his illness I saw them together. I was examined before the coroner on one of the last days. I had heard that Mrs. Barber had been taken up.

John Shaw, of Eastwood, police-officer, being sworn, said – I have been at Eastwood nearly two years – On the 31st of last January I went to his house to search for a stolen gun. Both Barber and his wife were in the house. I told them I had come to search his house because he was suspected of having a stolen gun in his house. His wife said: 'You see what disgrace you have got yourself into by keeping such bad company, but blast you I'll poison you and put a stop to it, if it's longer first.'

By Mr. Cockle – I apprehended Ingram on Tuesday, the 4th or 5th of April, at Langley Mill, on the turnpike road near the bridge. He came to me, and I took him into custody.

By Mr. Macaulay – I saw him going in the direction of his own house, and I stepped towards him. He then came to me and said, 'I suppose you want me, Shaw.' I said 'Yes, I want you on a charge of poisoning Joseph Barber.' He said 'he was as innocent as the babe unborn.' He also said 'he thought he would go away until the biggest part of the throng was over.' He was about 200 yards from his house when I apprehended him.

Edward Adolphus Browne, surgeon, said – I am brother of Mr. Robert Gossett Browne. I was present at the post mortem examination. Mr. Mather gave me a portion of the deceased man's liver, in the room at the deceased's house, to carry to my brother's house for my brother and myself to analyse. I put it in my pocket handkerchief. I and my brother analysed it together and separately. It was the same portion of liver delivered to me by Mr Mather and in the same condition.

By the Court – I saw it cut from the body. The rest of the body was left in the room. My brother walked with me.

Robert Gossett Browne recalled by the Court, said – When the stomach and intestines were taken by Mather to Smith's house, I walked with him to the surgery. I left the surgery at Smith's for about ten minutes, until Mr. Smith returned. My brother walked with me as far as Mr. Smith's surgery, where we parted. There was someone in the surgery with Mather when I left the remains with him, and the same person was with him when I went into the surgery again. In the portion of the stomach I took to Dr. Taylor there was some distilled water, which I had put there. I received a portion of the duodenum from Mather on the Wednesday night I and my brother tried experiments upon it, and reproduced arsenic. When I found that the other medical men's analysis were contrary to our own, I requested to see some more portions of the remains. I saw them in the stable. Mather showed them to me on the Wednesday night; and it was the portion of the duodenum which I then took, and the portion I took to Dr. Taylor was a portion of that which I got from the gig house. I had about 18 inches of the duodenum, and having taken off an inch for my own experiments. I put it in a bottle and sealed it up.

By Mr O'Brien – 1 also sent to Dr. Taylor a portion of the cardiac extremity of the stomach with a part of the oesophagus attached, which I had received from Mr. Smith's surgery. I did not take all the remains from Mr. Smith's surgery. I think Mr. Smith has heard me say I had had a portion out of the gig house.

John Wilmot, of Lenton, coach proprietor, said – I remember on the Sunday before Barber died, driving through Bulwell, and pulling up to speak to Mr. Bowker and Barber the deceased, There was another man with him. I did not notice him particularly but I think he had a fustian coat on, but I really could not say.

Christopher Swann being called deposed that Thomas Mather, surgeon, was bound over to appear at this assize to give evidence against Sarah Barber and Robert Ingram, on a charge of murder.

John Thomas Brewster deposed as follows – I am in business with my father, Brewster and Son, conducting this prosecution. I did not know where Mather was till ten days ago. I enquired of Oldknow, the parish constable of Eastwood, when I was taking the examinations of the witnesses, and in consequence of what he told me I wrote a letter to Mather addressed to Crow Oaks, Stand, near Manchester. Either Mr. Swarm, jun., or the constable, gave me that address. On the 22nd I received the following letter from the brother of Mather. 'July 21, 1851 gentleman – in my brother's absence, I opened the letter addressed to him, respecting the case of Joseph Barber, and in reply I have to inform you that Mr Thomas sailed for New York, on Monday, 7 July. Signed James Mather, Addressed to 'Messrs. Brewster, and Son – and dated.' Crow Oaks, Stand, Manchester.

This closed the case for the prosecution. After a short pause during which a breathless silence pervaded the court, Mr O'Brien proceeded to address the jury on behalf of the female prisoner.

- He implored, at considerable length, the jury to forget about anything they had read or heard about the trial outside the evidence in court. He knew how difficult that was, but it was their duty to do it.
- It appeared that the woman at the bar had been married to the deceased for about five years, and that a separation had taken place about two years ago. The evidence gave ample reason to understand why the female prisoner should at times been inclined to separate from her partner. At the period of his sickness, however, it was admitted on all hands that the deceased being in that state in which the slightest neglect is looked upon with irritation and petulance, expressed his grateful sense of the kindness, attention, and affection which the woman had for him. The mere existence of poison in the deceased man's body proved no crime whatever, because it might have been taken innocently, it might have found its way into his stomach by his own act, or it might have been mixed inadvertently in his medicines.
- It was quite clear that that portion of the human body which found its way to Dr. Taylor's laboratory in London was strongly impregnated with arsenic. But how was it watched from the inquest-room to the time it reached Dr. Taylor? It was necessary that it should be proved to the jury to have been in the same state as when removed from the body of the deceased. It was shown to have been in the possession of Mr. Mather, and Mr. Mather had not been produced to say whether it was in the same state when he gave it into the possession of Mr. Smith as when be received it. Mr. Mather, although bound under recognisance to appear to give evidence at the trial had from some cause or other removed himself from the jurisdiction of the court.
- He would proceed to write this to show them that there was nothing in the facts of the case inconsistent with the idea that the deceased might have administered the poison himself, or that it might have been given to him by accident in some of the medicine that had been thrown out. It had also transpired that at the time of his death, Barber was suffering from another and more loathsome disease than that of rheumatism, for which Mr. Bowker, Mr. Smith, and Mr. Mather prescribed. Some care had been taken to show that the medicines prescribed by the two former contained no poisonous ingredient; but it still remained unproved that Mr. Mather's medicine did not, for of the bottle of medicine sent by him on the day but one previous to Barber's death they had no account whatever. Then there was the

bottle of stuff which they had evidence to show the deceased used to keep in his stable, and of which no account was given.

- With respect to the purchases of arsenic it had been proved that there was no false attempt at concealment, no recourse to places where the suspected persons were not known, and no false pretences made when the purchases were effected. It had been proved beyond doubt that mice existed in considerable numbers in the house, and that Mrs. Barber had even been told by her husband to get something for them.

- It was then suggested by the prosecution that for the sake of that 10s. or 12s. a week (left her by her husband) she entered into a conspiracy to destroy his life. This was the motive suggested in order to bring the facts into shape.

- With regard to the threats which it had been stated the woman had at times uttered against her husband, he looked upon them merely as the result of passion, and called forth by extreme provocation, observing that the best evidence that this was the fact was to be found in the subsequent conduct of the deceased towards her.

- To take the worst view of the case it was a matter of great doubt, and it would be their duty to give the benefit of that doubt to the prisoner. In conclusion he urged upon the jury to consider the extremely awful responsibility of their position. In the case of the prisoner, if their deliberations should unwittingly be formed upon false conclusions, and she should be condemned to death, there would be no future mode of reparation, for the scaffold gave not up its victim.

Mr. Cockle next addressed the jury on behalf of Ingram; requesting them, in the first place, to consider the charges against the prisoners as separate and distinct and to be especially careful not to apply the evidence which had been adduced against the woman, to the man, unless the facts warranted such a step.

- In cases of this kind, too, it was necessary to prove some motive for perpetrating so dark a deed; but what motive had been proved against the young man Ingram? None.

- On the contrary, it had been proved that he was a friend of the deceased, by whose express wish it was that he went to live in the house for the purpose of attending upon him during his illness. There had been no evidence to show that he had had anything at all to do in the preparation or administering food to the sick man, his duties being merely to give medicine and wait upon him.

- Then with respect to his purchasing arsenic at Cullen's shop, he contended that Ingram's conduct had been like that of an innocent man. He knew that there were mice in the house, and where did he go for the poison? – To a shop where he was well known, and taking with him as a witness his next door neighbour.

- If the medical men were unable to detect symptoms of anything wrong, not only while the deceased was living, but even up to and for a time after several examinations had been made of the body, surely it ought not to be looked upon as suspicious that the lad had not seen anything wrong going on in the house. If the fact of his buying arsenic at Cullen's shop was to be considered as a matter of grave suspicion against him, then the present charge would apply fairly against all the parties who had bought, or who had attempted to buy, arsenic for the female prisoner, and in that case the old woman, Mrs. Lees, the man Riley, and the witness Shaw, ought to have been placed at the bar.

- Then as to the deposition he had made before the coroner and which had been put in as evidence against him, he contended that it rather went to establish his innocence than his guilt, inasmuch as every particular had been borne out by the evidence for the prosecution.

- It had been proved that he had asked Mrs. Shaw whether she was going to swear that she saw Mrs. Barber burn the arsenic. That could not be looked upon as a suspicious circumstance, fixing any guilty knowledge upon him; because it might have been that, having had such an opportunity of witnessing the woman's conduct towards her husband, and believing that, though perfectly innocent, she was in some danger, he might from motives, certainly not of a criminal nature, have been induced to ask the question. In conclusion he adjured them, unless they were of opinion that this evidence was of the most convincing kind, to return against the prisoner Ingram a verdict of not guilty.

The Learned Judge in summing up the evidence, said:

- This very serious case had been protracted a long time, but not to say unnecessarily; and now that it was drawn to a conclusion it became their duty to pronounce an opinion upon that most important question, whether it appeared to them that the prisoners, or either of them, were guilty of the heinous crime laid to their charge, in this case they were charged with the wilful murder of the female prisoner's husband. No doubt the most satisfactory proof of any crime was by the direct testimony of an eye witness who had witnessed the commission of the act, and who was himself beyond all suspicion a man of known integrity of character; but it was impossible that secret crimes could be proved by such evidence, and they must therefore be dealt with by what was called circumstantial evidence, which however required a most careful consideration. The course he advised them to pursue was to weigh the facts of the case clearly, and to their entire satisfaction, and then to see whether they could draw any other inference from those facts than that the prisoners, or one of them, were guilty of the offence.

- It was imputed in the indictment that the deceased died from the effects of arsenic contained in gruel. This was immaterial, for if it could be proved that both prisoners had administered any poison, in any other shape, they would be liable to a conviction, the real charge against them being that of wilful murder by poison. But if a poison was administered in this case, unquestionably it was arsenic, not probably administered in the shape of powder, but in a little tea or gruel.
- His Lordship then virtually reiterated the prosecution's version of the facts of the case.
- It had been thrown out as a suggestion by the learned counsel for the woman's defence that every proper measure had not been taken at the coroner's inquest to ascertain the nature of the medicines the deceased had in his possession; and it was certainly to be lamented that the police officers and constables did not, when circumstances of suspicion occurred, and cause every bottle found on the premises to be placed in the hands of justice, in order that there might have been a more full investigation of the case. However, that was neglected.
- It was suggested by the defence that the different portions of the stomach that had been subjected to examination had not been sufficiently proved to be in the same state when examined as at the time of death. For that they were in the possession of Mather in Mr. Smith's surgery for ten minutes while Mr. Robert Gossett Browne was in an adjoining room awaiting the arrival of Mr. Smith, and it was thrown out as being possible that Mather might have introduced arsenic into the contents at that time...
- Then came the more serious and more difficult inquiry whether they were of opinion that the prisoners at the bar or either of them were guilty of introducing the arsenic into the body of the deceased. Before arriving at such a decision they must satisfy themselves beyond all reasonable doubt that death was not attributed to design on the part of the deceased, to accident, or that it was caused by any other persons than the prisoners or either of them. There was no reasonable ground for showing that he took away his own life. He seemed to have been fond of life, and it was unlikely that he should have used that means of destroying it which was generally attended with much pain, although in this case he appeared not to have suffered extremely.
- Having excluded the probability of his having destroyed himself, then came the question of accident, with respect to which they would have to say, looking at the whole of the evidence, whether they thought

it was likely he had taken the poison which was introduced into the house, in mistake for salt or by any other accident...

- Then they would look at the evidence to see whether his death was, in their opinion, the result of design. The charge against the woman was that she entertained a design of taking away the life of her husband. Where a case depended upon circumstantial evidence they were to take into their consideration the motive in conjunction with the facts of the case. It appeared that the female prisoner and her husband during their lifetime did not live together upon peaceable terms. Of course the jury would reject any thing which was the result of a mere ebullition of temper, which took place some times between persons who loved each other sincerely. But they would judge whether the expressions used by her at various times showed that she disliked her husband, and that she was a person of furious temper, and likely to commit such an act of violence against her husband. No person could, in mere passion, use such expressions as were attributed by witnesses to the prisoner at the bar. Once about two years ago; again about eighteen months since; and a third time so late as January last, she swore she would poison her husband if it were longer first: on the first occasion she said, 'she would poison him,' on the second, that 'she would poison him if it were longer first;' and on the third, when a search was being made at her husband's house for a gun supposed to have been stolen, she said, 'You see what disgrace you have got yourself into by keeping such bad company, but blast you I will poison you if it be longer first.' Whether she intended to do what she said was another matter; but at all events it showed that she was a person of violent temper. This was the evidence so far as it showed her dislike to her husband.

- The next evidence proved the making of the will and the bequeathing to her the bulk of his property; and it was suggested by the prosecution that this, to a person like she was, having no affection for her husband, was the cause of one of the motives that induced her to commit the crime. On the 11th of March the will was made, and on the 14th she procured arsenic according to the testimony of Mrs. Shaw, and this was a point deserving the particular attention of the jury, the female prisoner said she burnt that arsenic on the Sunday because her husband was ill; and because if he should die people would say he had been poisoned. On a subsequent occasion she asked that witness to swear that she saw her burn the arsenic. Then came the important point for their consideration. After having told Mrs. Shaw that she had burnt the arsenic, and expressed her anxiety not to have any in the house while her husband was ill, why was it that on Wednesday following, when he was worse, she should get more arsenic? It was certainly a fact in her favour that she did not procure the arsenic secretly, or under a pretence which was afterwards proved to be utterly false, because it was proved beyond doubt that there were mice in the house. Then a suggestion had been made in her defence which required some attention, to the effect that she could not have had those feelings of hostility and dislike to her husband in his last illness, because she treated him with attention and kindness. The judge constantly made points denigrating the defence. There was no doubt that at that time she did treat him with much apparent kindness. It might be considered that she adopted this mode of behaviour in order to secure his good intentions towards her in the first instance in making his will on the 11th of March, in her favour, and afterwards to prevent him from altering it. Then it was suggested as being unlikely that she could nave meditated her husband's death, when at the same time she sent for his mother to go and see him. Still it was not inconsistent with the idea that she intended to take away his life, because she might resolve not to do it until after his mother had left him. That the poisoning commenced after his mother left him was quite consistent with the testimony of Dr. Taylor.

With regard to Ingram the case against him was considerably different.

- It was supposed that he had been guilty of assisting the female prisoner in committing the murder from some motive in his mind. There was a total absence of proof that there was a criminal intercourse between the prisoners before or after the decease, and it was upon evidence only that they should act.
- What they would particularly have to inquire into with respect to him would be the account he gave when examined before the coroners' in which he was found to give a very favourable colouring to all the acts of the female prisoner, and to swear that he believed the deceased died a natural death. In that statement he admitted having purchased poison once at Eastwood, but denied that he had ever obtained any at any other time. In answer to this, very strong evidence was offered by the prosecution to show that the prisoner at the bar himself purchased on the Sunday he went with the deceased to Bulwell, a pennyworth of arsenic at the shop of Mr. Buckoll, representing that he could not get it at his native place. It had been suggested by his counsel (Mr. Cockle) that he might have thought, without being *particeps criminis*, that he should be giving some advantage to the female prisoner by swearing that he never got any other arsenic than that which he presumed had been sufficiently accounted for, one packet she having destroyed, and the other lost on the Wednesday evening as she was returning from

church. So that with regard to Ingram the case was not by any means so strong as it was against the female prisoner, inasmuch as there was a total absence of all motive.

His lordship having finished his summing up, which occupied two hours and ten minutes, the jury withdrew at five minutes past five o'clock, to consider their verdict. They were absent two hours and a quarter. On their return the court was hushed in breathless silence. The woman appeared calm and collected, almost indifferent, while Ingram appeared fearfully anxious. In reply to the usual formal question by the clerk of Assize the foreman returned the following Verdict: Wilful Murder Against Sarah Barber; Robert Ingram Not Guilty.

The moment the verdict of acquittal was pronounced against Ingram, he dropped on to his knees in deep emotion, and remained in that attitude until sentence of death had been passed upon Sarah Barber. The female prisoner received the announcement with remarkable composure, and she listened attentively and seemingly unmoved to the solemn form of condemnation which the learned Judge, having placed the black cap on his head, with considerable emotion pronounced the usual homily and sentenced her to death upon your soul. The condemned woman, with considerable composure, turned towards the jury and said firmly, 'Gentlemen of the jury, if you have found me guilty in this world, you cannot prove me guilty in the next. Gentlemen, I am not guilty; I am as innocent as a child just born.'

Chapter 20

Sarah Barber: The Case Re-Examined

London Evening Standard Saturday 9 August 1851

THE CONVICT SARAH BARBER

(From the *Nottingham Journal*) ...She is said to have hoped there would be a great many persons in the hall to hear the proceedings, and to have expressed her pleasure at finding that such was the case. On returning to the gaol after condemnation she was for some time considerably agitated, but this in a few hours subsided, and the matron, who stayed in the same room with her during the night, was surprised at her sleeping so well. Several members of her family visited her on the Monday following, and the firmness she exhibited during the whole of the interview was certainly most astonishing. On Wednesday, the 30th ult., she asked to see the governor, and on Mr. Hildyard proceeding to visit her she informed him that she had a statement to make, which she wished he would take down. Finding, in answer to some questions he put to her, that she desired to make something like a confession, he asked her whether she had any objection to make it to a magistrate. She replied that she had not, and Mr. Hildyard then went into the hall, where the magistrates were then sitting in Petty Sessions. He related what had occurred, and Captain Legard, one of the visiting justices, returned with him into the gaol, and there received the woman's statement, which was immediately written down. We are unable this week to give the exact words of this statement, as the magistrates have arrived at the determination not to allow it to be published until the fate of the prisoner is finally settled. It is, however, to the effect that on the Sunday the deceased and Ingram went to Bulwell to consult Mr. Bowker, the surgeon, Ingram did purchase some arsenic at Buckoll's shop, as it was supposed he had done, and that on the way home he took the opportunity of dropping the arsenic into one of the bottles of medicine procured of Mr. Bowker. On their reaching home nothing (declared the prisoner) was said to her by Ingram about this, and when she gave her husband some of the medicine she was utterly unconscious that she had administered poison to him. He died in consequence, but she strongly protested she knew nothing about the cause of it until two days after his death, when Ingram confessed to her what he had done. She further alleged that after the first day's inquest had been held, she said to Ingram, 'Robert, you had better go out of the way for a short time,' and that he replied he had no money. She then gave him 5s., and he left the village and went to Sneinton. During the time her statement was being made, the high sheriff and Thomas Nixon, Esq., another magistrate, entered the gaol; but hearing what was proceeding in the condemned cell, they waited in Mr. Hildyard's parlour until Captain Legard and the governor returned, (it was then read over to them, but neither they nor the Rev. Mr. Plumptre, who afterwards heard it, appeared to be satisfied with it). It was agreed that it should be left in the governor's hands. On the following Friday Mr. Hildyard and one of the turnkeys were sitting in the room with her, when the former told her that her statement was not believed, and asked her whether she had anything further to say, and whether she had told the whole truth. She replied that she was certain she had told the truth, and, further, named certain facts as a proof that her statements were true. Among these she said that they would find the two bottles in which Dr. Bowker's medicine had been kept, and which it will doubtless be remembered could not be found on the search being made in the house, among the rubbish of the ash-pit attached to her deceased husband's house. She also said that the statement she had previously made as to her losing the packet purchased by her brother, in addition to the 5d. change which he gave her, could have been in some degree corroborated by Mr. Mather, who had unfortunately left the country. After she had received the packet and the change she went to Mr. Smith's surgery to purchase some powders, which her husband would have to take in linseed tea. She procured the powders, and then commenced talking to Mather, the assistant, about the linseed. While so doing she suddenly put her hand into her pocket, and then discovered that both the packet and the money had disappeared. She told Mather of her loss, though she did not name what the packet contained, and he kindly lent her fourpence to pay for the linseed at the shop she was going to, in order to save her the trouble of proceeding all the way to her own house for it. After Mr. Hildyard had heard all she had to say, he proceeded to Mr. Swarm, the coroner, related what the prisoner had stated, and asked him whether he would accompany himself and the chaplain, the Rev. W. Butler, whom Mr. Hildyard had previously seen about the matter, to Captain Legard, at Lenton, in order to obtain that gentleman's opinion respecting it. Mr. Swarm at once kindly consented, and a cab having been procured the three gentlemen proceeded in it to Lenton Hall. They immediately saw Captain Legard, and informed him of what the prisoner had further stated; after which it was agreed that Capt. Legard should instantly go forward to Eastwood, in his magisterial capacity, the other gentlemen accompanying him. On arriving at

Eastwood, they first called at Mr. Plumptre's house, but that gentleman being absent, they went forward to Mr. Godber's, the Sun Inn, where they were afterwards joined by Mr. Plumptre, and also by Mr. Smith, the surgeon. A long consultation took place, after which the statements of several persons were taken, respecting observations which they had heard made by Mrs. Shaw, who was one of the witnesses examined at the trial. This woman, it will be remembered, was called to prove that the prisoner Barber had asked her to swear before the coroner that she had seen her (Barber) throw one of the packets of arsenic upon the fire, when in fact she (as she herself swore) had not seen her do so. The persons, however, who made their statements before Captain Legard, said that they had on various occasions heard this woman (Shaw) really say that she had seen the prisoner burn the packet; and thus, if this were true, considerable doubt was thrown upon the veracity of her evidence. The chaplain and Mr. Hildyard afterwards drove down to Langley Mill, in search of Ingram. They found him standing at the door of his father-in-law's (Mr. Brierley's) house, and asked him if he had any objection to accompany them to the inn? He said he had none, and consequently he returned with them to Eastwood. A number of questions were there put to him with a view of testing the accuracy of part, at least, of the woman's statement, and among others it was asked him in what manner he had travelled to Sneinton from Eastwood at the time of the inquest! He replied, that it was by railway. They then asked him where he obtained the money to pay his fare, and he rejoined that it was his own which he had earned. Mr. Hildyard told him that he did not think that could be the case, as he had himself told him that he had been out of work at his trade for some time, and had no money. He then said that his sister had given it him. Captain Legard asked him whether he was sure this was the truth, and he, in reply, called upon Heaven to witness the truth of what he had said, and further expressed a wish that he might never enter into the kingdom of Heaven if what he said was proved to be false. By Captain Legard's directions, inquiries were made of the man's sister as to the accuracy of his statement relative to the alleged loan, and she at once denied that there was any truth in the matter. This was therefore, told to Ingram, and he then, notwithstanding the awful imprecation he had so shortly before used, acknowledged that he had told a lie about the matter, and begged their pardon! In reference to several other matters of a similar description, Ingram was also guilty of like falsehoods, and, consequently, the conclusion the gentlemen present came to in reference to the credibility of any statement he might make, may well be imagined. We ought previously to have mentioned that before any questions were put to the man, he was informed that whatever he might say it could not, after his acquittal, imperil his safety in the least. He was then asked whether he had any objection to tell the whole truth, and he replied he had not. He accordingly made certain statements which we have not yet obtained but we understand they were not of much importance and coupled as they were with the audacious falsehoods' he told respecting other matters, not much dependence can be placed upon them. Before the magistrate and the other gentlemen returned to Nottingham directions were given to have the ash-pit alluded to by the prisoner Barber emptied and properly examined. This was accordingly shortly afterwards done, and the two bottles were discovered, as it had been intimated they would be. Both without loss of time were conveyed to the General Hospital at Nottingham, and on an examination being made, Mr. White, the house surgeon, immediately detected a portion of arsenic in a sort of sediment at the bottom of one of them. Further experiments were subsequently used, and the result was, that altogether nearly two drachms of undeniable arsenic were found. On Saturday, Captain Legard wrote out a long statement of the result of his inquiries, the examination of Ingram, and was desirous of sending it by a trusty hand to Baron Parke, the judge who tried the case, and who was then at Warwick. Mr. Hildyard was first suggested as a proper person for the office, hut he being unable to leave Nottingham that day, Mr. Patchitt, the clerk to the magistrates, volunteered to go and set off the same morning. While these proceedings were taking place nothing was said to the prisoner as to what they were doing, and Friday was appointed for her as the day to take a last farewell of her relatives, many of whom had visited her several times since the trial. On the Friday, however most of them were unable to attend, and therefore only her aunts Gregory and Hunt, and an uncle named Gregory, saw her on that day. On the one following, her sister, Mrs. Wild, and that person's husband, George Riley and Mrs. Riley, an 'aunt named Springthorpe, and two or three children, visited her for the purpose, as they supposed, of seeing her for the last time alive. The interview with her adult relatives did not seem to have the slightest effect upon her feelings. They were all weeping most bitterly, but she remained perfectly calm and composed, and said several times to them, 'Why do you cry! I don't cry.' At last, However, one of the children, who had previously it seemed been a sort of favourite with her, approached her, and getting upon her knees, addressed various observations to her. Its infantile prattle seemed to have the effect of awakening her hitherto slumbering feelings, for after listening to it for a few minutes, she commenced weeping in a most distressing manner, and it was some time before she again recovered her composure. Her drunken brother, George Riley, who was in the public-house opposite the prison during the former part of her interview with the relatives named, came in just before it had concluded. He was approaching to kiss her, but the smell of liquor and tobacco which he brought with him, and to which she during her confinement in the purer air of the gaol had been unaccustomed, seemed to overpower her with disgust. When Riley was about to leave the place, she said to him, 'George, go home and lead a new life, for yours has hitherto been a shocking bad one; my life has been a bad one too, but yours has been far worse.' On Sunday (which she supposed would be the last Sunday of her existence), she attended Divine service twice in the chapel attached to the gaol. In the morning prayers only were said, but in the afternoon, what may be termed the condemned sermon was preached by the chaplain, the Rev. W. Butler. The text was the 18th chapter of St. Luke, from the 9th to the 13th verse. It was, we are told, a really excellent and appropriate sermon, and was listened to with great attention not only by the wretched woman herself, but also by the other prisoners. The executioner for the district, Thomas Jeffcott, arrived on Monday, when the erection of the scaffold was commenced and preparations for the formation of the barricades in various parts of the street were made. These, however, it soon appeared, were not, on that occasion at least, to be required, for by the mail train which reached Nottingham at three o'clock in the following morning arrived a messenger from the Home Office, bearing an order for the respite of the execution of the prisoner for 14 days. In order to account for this generally not expected document, we must retrace our steps slightly. Mr. Patchitt, it will be remembered, left Nottingham on Saturday, taking with him Captain Legard's statement. He found Baron Parke at Warwick, and laid before him the document with which he had been entrusted, and this his lordship read carefully over. He also re-perused those portions of his notes of the trial which relate to the matters referred to in the woman's statement, as well as in the subsequent proceedings before Captain Legard. The result he came to was that it was a case deserving of a more careful consideration than it would be possible to bestow upon it previous to the following Wednesday, the day on which the execution was fixed to take place, and consequently he forwarded a recommendation to Sir George Grey to grant a respite. For fear, however, that any mistake should occur, his lordship, we are told, gave Mr. Patchitt an order to respite the execution, to be used, however, only in the event of nothing being heard from the Home Secretary in time. This, however, as has already appeared, it was not found necessary to use. We may here observe that on Monday Mr. William Hannay, a magistrate for the town, accompanied by other gentlemen as a deputation, waited on Mr. Waddington, the Under Secretary of State, at the Home Office, with a petition, signed, we are informed, by upwards of 11,000 inhabitants of the district, asking for a reprieve of the unfortunate woman. Whether this had any influence on the mind of the Home

Secretary, it is of course impossible for us to say, though it appears most probable that the principal, if not the sole reason for the respite being granted was the recommendation of the Judge. Mr. Bell, the messenger, arrived in the town, as before stated, at about three o'clock on Tuesday morning, and immediately hastened to the County Gaol, where he called up the governor and confided to him the important document of which he was in charge. Mr. Hildyard immediately drove over to Gonalstone, where he arrived at about a quarter past six o'clock and had an interview with the High Sheriff. The governor breakfasted with Mr. Franklin and they then returned to Nottingham, arriving at the gaol about twenty minutes past nine. The sheriff immediately went into the condemned cell, accompanied by the governor and chaplain, and informed the prisoner that her Majesty had been pleased to respite her execution for 14 days in order that she might have more time to make her preparations for entering upon eternity than she had at present. She, in reply, made several courtesies, and said, 'Thank you, thank you.' The sheriff intimated that it was not him she had to thank, but that it was the governor. Although she was thus quite composed during the time Mr. Franklin was present, yet immediately after his departure she was deeply affected and slightly convulsed, and continued to express her thankfulness for some time. The arrival of the respite was soon known generally throughout the town, and in the course of a few hours the portions of the scaffold and barricades already erected were removed, and the various preparations for the execution, were put a stop to. On the Wednesday morning, however, at an early hour, great numbers of country persons who had not heard of the respite assembled on the High Pavement to see the execution, and although on their becoming acquainted with the fact many of them appeared to be very well pleased, yet still considerable numbers, some of whom no doubt had been deceived on the former occasion, seemed to be grievously disappointed, and gave vent to their displeasure in expressions not particularly polite.

Chapter 21

Afterwards

As already mentioned in the introduction, I am most indebted to Mike Sheridan for the meticulous research in Australian records in discovering what happened to Sarah Barber after the reprieve.

> The Australian Convict Transportation Registers – Other Fleets & Ships, 1791–1868
> Name: Sarah Barber
> Vessel: Anna Maria
> Convicted Date: 23 Jul 1851
> Voyage Date: 4 Oct 1851
> Colony: Tasmania (Van Diemen's Land)
> Place of Conviction: Nottingham, Nottinghamshire, England

The boat arrived in Hobart in late January. Female convicts worked as servants in free settlers' houses, or were sent to a female factory (women's work house prison). Sarah was sent to Cascades then to Brickfields, with its less strict regime. In fact female convicts were ardently sought after and there were a number of short periods of hire. Eventually on 6 August she was discharged to Mrs Frank Pogdon. There she met John Hunter, a discharged convict himself. John Hunter regained this certificate of freedom on 9 February 1852.

Any man wanting to marry would simply attend the line-up at the factory and drop a handkerchief at the feet of the woman of his choice. If she picked it up, marriage quickly followed. The romance between John and Sarah was also brief and they were quickly married at St John's Presbyterian Church, Hobart on 23 August. On the marriage certificate their ages were both given at about 21. It wasn't true for John. In fact he was 34 years old when he met Sarah. He was also only 5 foot 9¼ inches tall. He was a shoemaker by trade and could earn a living by making and repairing shoes. Their first child was born in December 1853. Samuel, their second child was born in August 1856. Sarah was recommended for a conditional pardon effective on 10 November 1857. In March 1857 Thomas, her third child was born. A conditional pardon was approved on 6 July 1858. In 1859 Alfred, their fourth boy was born.

Sarah and her husband were now free settlers themselves, and could earn money without limits. Her life was full and she had obviously finally found things that had always eluded her: her own family, a sense of belonging and an inner happiness. Unfortunately it was not to last long. On 20 May 1860 Sarah went into labour and died, while her baby was delivered stillborn. At an inquest the following day the coroner's jury made a decision her death was from the effects of delivering a dead male child and nothing else. She was still only 31 years old.

Source Information

Ancestry.com. Australian Convict Transportation Registers – Other Fleets & Ships, 1791–1868 [database on-line]. Provo, UT, USA: Ancestry.com Operations Inc, 2007.

Original data: Home Office: Convict Transportation Registers; (The National Archives Microfilm Publication HO11); The National Archives of the UK (TNA), Kew, Surrey, England.

PART 9

Elizabeth (Lizzie) Pearson

Chapter 22

Precursor: Mary Ann Cotton

Born Mary Ann Robson and one of the UK's most prolific serial killers, she killed husbands, and possibly even her own children. She was hanged in Durham prison on 29 March 1873, aged 40. She stood to gain from insurance policies, and killed using arsenic in cups of tea.

Born in the small English village of Low Moorsley in October 1832, Mary Ann Robson did not have a happy childhood. Her parents were both younger than 20 when they married; her father barely managed to keep his family fed by working as a miner. When Mary was eight the family moved; Mary and her brother Robert went to a new school, where shy Mary found it difficult to make friends. Not long after the move her father fell down a mine shaft to an early death. Life in Victorian England was never easy, but especially so for a widow and her young children. The shadow of the workhouse and separation from her mother must have left dark shadows on Mary, and indeed it is reported that she suffered bad nightmares. The workhouse and probably homelessness was avoided when Mary's mother remarried. Mary did not like her new step father, but she liked the things his good salary could buy. Finally, at the age of 16, she could not stand the hard discipline of her step father, so she moved out to become a serving girl at a nearby house.

After three years service, and many a scandal in the local village about the many male visitors Mary took, she left to train as a dressmaker. It was not long before she married, already being pregnant. Her first husband was William Mowbray, a miner. During the first few years of their marriage, they travelled all around the country in search of work, William taking work as a miner and sometimes on the railroad. During the first five years together Mary had five children, four of them dying as infants. Even though infant mortality was high in Victorian England, this was unusually high, but was probably viewed as just 'bad luck'.

She moved around the country marrying a number of times (sometimes bigamously) insuring spouses and step children, finishing up with Mr Cotton.

Mary was eventually caught when a post mortem examination on one of her children revealed arsenic poisoning as the cause of death.

Convicted of only the murder of her step son, she was suspected of killing at least six people, and it is believed that she actually took the lives of more than 20 victims over a 20 year period,

Cotton was pregnant with her seventh child at the time of arrest and trial and the execution had to be delayed until after she had given birth. However, because of her pregnancy, there was a petition for her reprieve. This was denied and she was hanged in the prison yard.

Chapter 23

Background and Early Years[1]

Lizzie Pearson was born in Blackwell, Darlington on 27 December 1845. She was the second child of gardener William Sedgwick, and his wife Elizabeth. While still a baby she was handed over to her mother's sister Jane, the childless wife of a farm labourer called John Robinson who lived in Ravensworth. The Robinsons raised Lizzie, and she grew up looking upon them as her real parents.

John died in 1857. In 1860 Jane met and married James Watson, a widower living in Church Road, Gainford, and she and Lizzie moved into his home. James, then 59, was an agricultural labourer who had lived in Gainford for many years raising a family of four children with his first wife Hannah until her death in 1858 and the family seemed to get on well together.

According to reporters at her later trial she was both ugly and ill tempered. According to one she was about 5ft 2 in tall, stout, dark-haired with a sallow complexion and a singularly reserved and dogged expression who 'seldom bent except to express herself in a sharp shrewish manner'. Another described her as 'a reticent morbid minded sort of creature, gifted with little that was likely to find favour with those around'. Some claim that she bore a considerable resemblance to Mary Ann Cotton. One must be cautious about reporters' descriptions and characterisations gleaned from court appearances. Contrast the actual photograph of Mary Ann Cotton with drawings of her used in national newspapers of the time.

At the age of 21, Lizzie was courted by 24-year-old railway plate layer John Pearson and married him on 27 July of that year. The couple moved into a house in Church Road, Gainford which had been rented by his parents for many years and was just two doors down from Lizzie's aunt and uncle.

The first child, Alice Jane, was born in January 1870 but lived for only a week. A second, Ada Jane, born in August 1871, survived, as did her third, Dora Jane born in February 1874. Ada died the same year.

By this time her uncle James was 73, and having lung problems. He still had to work to pay rent on his cottage. He had a job as a groom for a local wine and spirit merchant, Mr Wheatley, and he took in a lodger of the same age, George Smith. In the 1861 census George was recorded as living next door to the Pearsons in Church Road. He was a well-known village character, making a living as a mechanic and razor grinder.

James Watson died, and at first the circumstances of his death were considered innocent enough. After all, the old man had been seriously ill, and the local people looked upon it as a sad event but nothing more than that.

However, when the inquest opened on Friday, 19 March in the Lord Nelson, Dr Humphrey admitted that he was not totally satisfied about the cause of death.

He confirmed he'd seen James at 1 p.m. on the day he died, and thought he'd got over the worst of a bout of pneumonia and was well on the road to recovery. Yet within a few hours James was dead, which greatly surprised him. Near neighbour Ann Hall's description of how he died, in severe pain, clenching both his teeth and hands, suggested something peculiar had taken place.

He concluded that the death had taken place under strongly suspicious circumstances and his doubts were increased when, during the post mortem, he found something in the body which he could not readily identify. The deputy coroner, Mr Dean, asked if this indicated poison, and Dr Humphrey replied there was nothing to confirm it. However, now the question of a possible death by poisoning had been raised, the jury decided to seek professional advice, and the inquest was adjourned until further evidence could be obtained. Based upon medical evidence, given again at the three levels: magistrate's court, grand jury and at the trial (where the full details are given), the coroner's jury returned a verdict of wilful murder against Elizabeth Pearson.

Chapter 24

The Trial

Compiled from the best detail obtainable in the local papers, *Northern Echo* and *Sunderland Gazette*:

THE GAINFORD MURDER

Before Mr Justice Archbold

Elizabeth Pearson, a married woman of respectable appearance, 25 years of age, was placed at the bar and charged with the wilful murder of her uncle, James Watson, 73 years of age by administering prison to him at Gainford, on the 15th of March 1875. Mr. Skidmore and Mr. Milvain prosecuted. There was no counsel engaged for the defence of prisoner, but at the request the judge, Mr Ridley agreed to conduct the case on her behalf.

Mr. Skidmore in opening the case for the prosecution, gave a brief statement of the facts of the case, and pointed out the motive for the crime in the desire shown by the prisoner to possess herself of the old man Watson's furniture.

The following witnesses were then called and examined by Mr Milvain:

Jane Pearson, said: I am the mother of the prisoner's husband. I know the prisoner well. I knew James Watson, the deceased. He lived in the same house as the prisoner. My son and a little girl, and a lodger named George Smith, lived in the house also. I live near my son. Some time ago, I was going to the shop of Mr Corner, grocer, and the prisoner asked me to get three pennyworth of mice powder. Because the mice were eating her featherbed. I got it and brought it to her. She was alone in the back kitchen when I gave it her, and she put it on the shelf above her head. Some time after, she asked me to fetch her another three pennyworth from the same shop. I bought it to her when she was sitting at the table side getting her tea. There was a lodger in at the same time, sitting on the sofa. I was close up to the prisoner, and gave her the powder, and she put it into her breast when I was going for the powder, she said I had not to tell anyone, not even her husband, because he would scold her so about it. He did not like mice powder that is why I sat close up to her. I am sure no other person saw me give it her, because I was close to her. She took it in hand, and popped it into her breast. I never went to see

James Watson, who was in the house. Lizzie, the prisoner, attended on him at that time; there was no one else to do so.

Watson's son has the furniture now, at Barnard Castle. Before he got it, the prisoner took it up to her own house. The prisoner had her own house.

The prisoner had been brought up by her aunt, Mrs. Watson, since she was fifteen months old, until she got married, and when Mrs. Watson died, about a year ago, shut up her own house (although she retained possession of it) and went to keep house for her uncle.

Cross-examination: There were two houses; one she shut up her own when she went to attend on the deceased. After Watson's death, she and her husband went back to their own house. Nobody has been in the prisoner's house for a good while – all the time she attended on her uncle. She told me there were a great many mice in this house. I never was in the house. When I gave the powder to the prisoner, James Watson was ill upstairs. He had been ill for some time. The deceased was a countryman, and was a needy man. The prisoner and the deceased were on very good terms, the old man, I believe, was very fond of Lizzie; and he said he was never better waited upon in his life and he was with the prisoner. I don't think they were on bad terms about his two sons or his daughter.

Re-examined: I don't know anything about the deceased means, further than he worked for his living.

By the judge: He first worked at breaking stones, and then he was a groom. He stopped work sometime before his death.

John Corner, grocer, Gainford, deposed that: I succeeded William Anderson in my business. I took his stock. In that stock there was some Battles vermin powder. I supplied Jane Pearson with two packets of Battles powder, one on the 2nd of March and the other about a month before that. On the first occasion Jane Pearson said she wanted the powder to kill mice, on the second occasion I asked her if she was going to commit suicide, as he thought she was coming too frequently for it. She replied, 'No, the last packet has killed about a dozen mice.' 'Poison' was printed upon the paper envelope.

Cross-examined: The vermin powder is much used for destroying vermin. It is well known in the trade.

By His Lordship: The first packet was not entered on the poison entry book. I made an entry on the second. His Lordship advised the witness to be very careful in future. It was a very dangerous thing for him to sell if he did not observe all precautions.

Witness: I shall sell no more.

Robert Watson said: I am the son of the deceased, and live at Barnard Castle. I last saw my father alive on 13 March. I had some conversation with deceased. When the prisoner was present, I wanted my father to give up his house and go to lodgings, or come to stop with me. My father said he would like to spend his time in Gainford. I said 'If that is your wish to stop there, and allow you to do so for a week; but you must sell off your furniture. We can't pay this rent.' He paid £7 a year rent for that house. The furniture was his. I arrange to come on the Saturday following. When I was speaking about removing my father to Barnard Castle, the prisoner said, in his presence, but the old man would never come downstairs again. I said 'Lizzie, how is that?' 'Well,' she said, 'the doctors said so.' I went downstairs and the prisoner came to me and said my father changed his mind, would come to live with me at Barnard Castle. My father died on the Monday following and I went to his house that night. When I was going in my father's house, I met the prisoner's husband's sister carrying some clothes horses. On Tuesday morning he saw the prisoner in her own house, and asked her about the furniture, and for his father's money to bury him. The prisoner replied, 'You said you would bury your father you can go and bury him now.' He asked her then how she meant the body to be buried, but she only laughed at him. Witness afterwards saw prisoner's husband, who asked him if he would be content with what his father had signed over to the prisoner with regard to the furniture, and witness replied that he would. The prisoner, however, said that rather than he should have them she would make firewood of them, and said (addressing her husband), 'What's mine is mine, what's thine is thine and what I have I will stick to.' I saw some of my father's furniture in her house. I've got the furniture now, but none of the luminal bedding. Sometime after the husband sent me, and I got the furniture. The husband could not find any of the linen or the bedding. My father had been a healthy man all his life, but four years ago he broke down. He recovered since. I never knew of him taking a fit.

In cross examination: Deceased was 74 years of age, his second wife's death preceded his own by about a year. I did not support my father at all. My father got part of his furniture by his second wife. I have not been down often to see my father upwards of 20 years. When before the magistrates I did not say how I found the house nor did I mention the interviews on the Tuesday. I did not care about the furniture, but I went to see about the money. The prisoner did not say she had a right to the furniture because it had been her aunt's. I went to a solicitors to know who had the right to the furniture. I wanted to get something to bury my father with. I buried my father. I have not paid the rent yet, the last place he was at, groom to Mr Wheatley he got 15 shillings a week. Before this he worked at Mr Nation's, in minding the beasts. The prisoner had been married for eight or nine years.

Mary Brown said: I am the wife of Christopher Brown, and live at Gainford. I live next door but one to James Watson. I remember James

Watson being ill. I used to see him three times during the day. On a Saturday in the early part of March, he was taken upstairs. The following Tuesday, that before he died, I saw him. Next Saturday morning I saw him at 10 o'clock. The prisoner was upstairs with me. I asked him how he was, and he said he was better. I saw him the morning before he died, about 9 o'clock. The furniture was in the house in the morning. I saw the featherbed taken away before my window.

Cross-examined: Monday morning, deceased said he would come downstairs. I sent a telegram to his son when I heard his father was dead.

Re-examined: I never saw Smith attending upon the deceased.

Ann Hall said: I am the wife of Robert Hall, and live at Gainford. I know the prisoner, and I also knew James Watson, the deceased. I last saw the deceased alive on Monday, the 15th March. I was in the bedroom near 5 o'clock in the afternoon the lodger, Goldsmith, pulled me in. The prisoner was in the whole time. Smith was downstairs. The prisoner was standing by the deceased, holding both his wrists in the hands. He seemed to be suffering. The prisoner said she thought he was going to have a trembling fit. The deceased said to me 'Ann, don't leave me.' I knew him for long before but never knew of him having fits before after advising water, I heard the deceased give a groan, and saying he could not tremble it out. I immediately went downstairs to send of my little girl for Dr Humphrey, and got the bottle filled with hot water. The prisoner called me to be sharp, and come away I went immediately upstairs, took the hot water bottle in my hand. The deceased was then lying with his head thrown back, his teeth firmly set, and his eyes fixed. I could just observe a slight heaving of the chest, the prisoner was in the room then, but not holding his hands, which were clenched over his chest. She said 'Call George.' Smith came upstairs, and looked at the deceased. He said nothing at all. The deceased did not tremble. We were neighbours for eight years.

Cross-examined: When George Smith called me he said he believed the old man was dying. I was out on the road very short time. I did not wait till the doctor came. It would not be much after 5 when he died. I have not been in the house for a month previous. He said nothing more than I have mentioned. First time I noticed nothing particular the matter with his face. I did not see his feet. I did not notice anything the matter with his breathing.

Dr. Humphrey, physician and surgeon, practising at Gainford, said: I was called in to attend the deceased on March 6 and found him suffering from chronic inflammation of the right lung, and I saw him every day till his death. I saw him last alive four hours before his death, on March 15, when he was a great deal better. On the last time I saw him prisoner said that he wanted a little opening medicine. I said I would make him a mild pill, and she said 'Could not you give him a powder, I could get it into him far better.' I said 'Very well, it makes no difference to me, and I thought he could swallow a pill better. Send out to me, and I will make him a powder'. I made up a powder composed of 2 grains of calomel and one grain of jalap and I left it in the entrance hail of my house, where I always left medicines which were to be called for. I did not make any medicine that day containing strychnine or Prussian blue. I went into the country, and, returning about a 5:15 o'clock, I received a message to go to Watson's at once as the old man was much worse. On my way to the house I met a second messenger who said that Watson was dead. There was nothing in his symptoms, the last time I saw him, to cause me to expect his death so soon. I heard from the prisoner that the deceased took fits. Prisoner told me on my first visitation – 6 March – of the deceased took fits every 20 minutes. She said his hands were clenched, his back was bent, his mouth was shut, his lips turned blue and he was stiff all over. I asked the deceased if he knew anything about the fits. He said he did not remember anything about them. I made two post-mortem examinations the first was on 18 March. The lungs were in a state of chronic inflammation. They were not very bad. Only the right lung was affected but not sufficiently to cause death. The brain, heart, liver and all the internal parts that I examined that day were healthy. On the 19th I made another examination. I open the stomach, which contained a large tablespoonful of some fluid matter. On the coats of the stomach there was a slight excoriation, and a little redness around the mucous membrane of the stomach. I placed the stomach and all it contained in the transverse colon and a portion of the liver in a carefully cleansed glass jar, which I gave to Superintendent Thomson. After my first three days attendance on the deceased he began to improve. I never said that Watson would never come downstairs. I felt almost sure he would come down again, because he improved so much under my treatment. I certainly consider that his death was caused by strychnine.

Cross examination: I gave observations on account of the fits before the coroner and I think I did so before the magistrates. I don't know how to account for them not being down in the depositions. I did not believe prisoner's statement about the fits, and did not treat him for these fits. I never saw Smith upstairs. I am quite positive I never expressed any apprehension to the prisoner about the deceased. I have no assistant whatsoever, always make my own medicines. Mrs Humphrey only assists me in wrapping the bottles and paper, and inputting in the courts. The redness and excoriation on the coat of the stomach might be caused by any heart or irritated substance.

Corner, recalled, said: He supplied a glass jar to superintendent Thomson. It was quite clean and had not been near any vermin powder.

James Robinson said: On 15 March the prisoner asked him to do some errands. He said she told me to go to Dr Humphrey. I saw Mrs Humphrey there she gave me a little folded up paper. I brought it straight down to Mrs Pearson (the prisoner) and gave it to her. This was about 4 o'clock. She was in Mr Watson's house when I gave it to her. 'James Watson' was written upon it.

Thomas Scattergood said: I am a surgeon at Leeds, and lecturer on medical jurisprudence. I received a jar from Superintendent Thomson on 23 March. The jar was securely sealed with the seal. I understand it to be Dr Humphrey's seal. The jar contained the human stomach, which had been cut open, the contents of which had escaped into the jar. Attached to the stomach was nearly 12 inches of: colon, large bowel, piece of liver, weighing 8 ½ ounces. The liver and bowels were healthy. I examined the stomach. There was a small patch of reddening on the external surface. I made an analysis of the stomach, the liver, bowel, the escaped contents of the stomach which I obtained by washing the viscera and the jar with pure spring water. I found strychnine in all of them. The stomach contained about a 20th of a grain. The liver contained a much smaller quantity, the bowel a small quantity, and the contents washed from the jar a small quantity. In the latter I found small particles of Prussian blue, and also some unbroken granules of starch. On 13 April I received by post, from Superintendent Thomson, a letter (produced) containing two three-penny packets of Battles vermin powder, the two envelopes of which were marked, in large letters, 'Poison'. I am well acquainted with Battles powders. I made an analysis of one. Its component parts are wheat flour, strychnine, and Prussian blue. One packet weighed 13 1/10 grains containing 8 or 9 /10 per cent of strychnine; there would be about 1.4 grain of strychnine. The contents of one three-penny packet will be sufficient to cause the death of a man. I have several cases in which death has been caused by one packet of this powder, five or six of which were adults. Less than the whole of one packet would be fatal to a failing old man. Strychnine, when taken, would result in a series of tetany attacks, in which the body is rigidly extended, the hands clenched, feet often arched the head thrown back, the back very often arched, so that the body rests upon the head and heels with jaws fixed, and the eyes stare. I am describing an extreme severe paroxysm. After the paroxysm, which is extremely painful, the person is often bathed with sweat. The paroxysm returns in quick succession until the patient ... Before the first attack there is a shivering trembling. From the evidence I have heard, and the analysis I made, I have come to the conclusion that the deceased died from strychnine. I have no doubt whatsoever.

Cross-examined: What I found in the stomach was not sufficient to be fatal; I applied several tests, every one of which answered. In the other part of the contents there was less than 100th part of a grain; in the liver there was more. There was not sufficient to cause the death of the patient in what I received. The smallest fatal dose to an adult that I heard recorded is half a grain. There are no symptoms after death is solely characteristic of strychnine; but the appearances during life are characteristic. Taking all the strychnine that I found in the jar, bowels, stomach, there was not sufficient to cause death.

Re-examined: Strychnine is very rapidly absorbed into the system. Its presence in the liver showed that it had been absorbed, although contacting the jar might have caused that.

By his Lordship: Within a few minutes after the strychnine is taken into the stomach it is absorbed. Absence or presence in the stomach would be no guide to the quantity consumed. In one case of death by poisoning, half an hour after the taking of the dose for this the quantity taken was known to disappear.

Isaac Thomson said: I am superintendent of police, and live at Barnard Castle. I was present when Dr Humphrey made a post-mortem examination, on 18 March. On the following day he examined the stomach. I got a jar from John Horner. It was quite clean. On the 19th I saw the stomach and its contents put into the jar. I saw them sealed up. On the 23rd, I handed over the jar to Dr Scattergood. On 12 April, I purchased two three-penny packets of Battles vermin powder from John Corner, and forward them to Dr Scattergood, by post, on the following day. On 15 April, I took the prisoner into custody; I charged her on suspicion of causing the death of James Watson. She replied 'I am innocent.' I said 'I'm going to search the house; have you any of Battles vermin killer?' She replied 'I never had such a thing in my life.' I searched the house, but found nothing.

Cross-examined: I did not find any of Dr Humphrey's powder in her own house. On the 18th, I looked through James Watson's house, and found nothing in it. There were further beds in the prisoner's house, but there was no powder about. I saw George Smith at the inquest on the 19th but never seen him since. I have tried to find him, and sent all over for him, but he has not been found yet. I never charged the prisoner with robbing the house.

Dr Humphrey recalled said: Having heard Dr Scattergood's evidence, account of his analysis, and what was found in the organs, and also with my own knowledge, in attending him, of his condition; opinion is that the cause of his death was poisoning by strychnine.

Dr Scattergood, recalled: It is usual to find some congestion of the brain and part of the spinal cord in cases of strychnine poisoning.

Mr Milvain in an address at considerable length and after reviewing the evidence, argued, firstly that the deceased had died from strychnine poisoning; and secondly, that the prisoner had administered the poison. There had been some talk of Smith. There had been no witness to say they saw Smith waiting upon the deceased: and although Smith was not to be found, that was no reason to assign this dastardly cruel and heartless murder to a man – a razor grinder, who could have no possible motive, who could have no possible object, who could have no possible opportunity of administering, while he was under the watchful care of his niece. But what could be the motive of the prisoner in committing such a deed? There was a great deal of jealousy about furniture. Before the deceased would sell his furniture, before the son could have become possessed of it and all things belonging to the deceased there was a motive for her to possess herself of them first; she accomplished that motive in the cruel hard, cold manner in which she affected the death of her uncle, which characterised every action after she accomplished that. He asked the jury to do the duty – painful though it might be – return a verdict according to the evidence they have heard.

Mr Ridley, on behalf of the prisoner urged that there was not clear proof that the deceased, James Waters, died from strychnine poison: that if he had, there was not any proof that the prisoner had administered the poison; and Mr Smith's flight caused it be more likely that he, either by accident or otherwise, poisoned the old man. The learned counsel founded his case upon the discrepancies of evidence, and upon the fact that some important evidence given that day, but never been so much as mentioned before the magistrates and asking, if there was any doubt, that the prisoner should have the benefit of it.

The Judge next summed up, and the jury retired. They returned into court after about an hour's deliberation, and the foreman announced they found the prisoner GUILTY.

On being asked if she had anything to say why sentence of death should not be passed on her, the prisoner said 'Yes' but made no further comment.

The Judge then put on the black cap and gave the usual homily ... crimes of this kind especially are undertaken and endeavoured to be carried in secret, but it so happens in the order of Providence that whilst the perpetrators think the crime is secret, it is the one all others which said to write its own history in the traces it leaves – the clear traces which science enables us now to decipher and to read without any doubt or uncertainty...

As the cathedral bell tolled 8 on the morning of 2 August 1875, Lizzie Pearson walked resolutely to the scaffold of the city's jail, her hands pinioned to her sides, her face expressionless. Executioner William Marwood placed a cap over her head and the noose around her neck. Then he pulled the lever to open the trap beneath her feet. He had invented an instantaneous form of death, the long drop and so she died.

Was Lizzie Pearsons Guilty?

There are problems with the reporting of this case that appear to be absent in all the other cases I have discussed. Even local papers, usually so reliable and meticulous in their reporting, tell us little about the defence argument, and the Judge's summing up to the jury is absent in all.

There is no doubt that Lizzie bought two lots of vermin powder, and whilst she may well have used the first lot for killing mice, as her mother-in-law testified, the second lot was not only unaccounted for but she lied to the police about it.

On the other hand the hole in the prosecution bucket is the disappearance of George Smith, the lodger who lived with Lizzie's uncle.

Recall what the prosecutor, in a pre-emptive strike, had to say about his flight from the trial: 'There had been some talk of Smith. There had been no witness to say they saw Smith waiting upon the deceased: and although Smith was not to be found, that was no reason to assign the committal of this dastardly cruel and heartless murder to a man…'

So, firstly, the deceased was a man and everyone knew this was a woman's crime. Secondly, there was a perfectly innocent reason for the flight, and the jury were asked to assume that: most unlikely. As he assumed in his address to the jury Lizzie was in such constant attendance on the deceased there was no opportunity for the lodger to get at him. Again, most unlikely.

A good defence lawyer properly briefed would have been able to answer or question the problems with this case.

Was Lizzie guilty? Probably – but beyond reasonable doubt?

PART 10

Mary Lefley

Chapter 25

Trial of Mary Lefley

Abridged from *Boston Guardian*

THE WRANGLE MURDER CASE

Wednesday morning Mary Lefley (49), of Wrangle, was charged before Mr. Justice North with the wilful murder of her husband William Lefley, (60), cottager, Wrangle, on February 6th, 1884. The court was crowded with spectators there being an unusually large number of ladies present. The prisoner was assisted into the dock by a warder of the prison. She wore a heavy crepe fall and a velvet jacket.

Mr. Etherington Smith and Mr. Cassidy, instructed by Mr. Page, of Lincoln, appeared for the prosecution, and Mr. Lawrance, QC, MP, instructed by Mr. B. B. Dyer, of Boston, for the defence.

The prisoner pleaded not guilty to the charge in a distinct tone, and was then allowed to be seated. Mr. Etherington Smith, in opening the case for the prosecution, summarised the evidence he intended to produce for the prosecution.

The following witnesses were called:

SAMUEL SPENCE, examined by Mr. Cassidy, said: I am a carrier and live at Wrangle. I know the prisoner and her husband. They lived alone in nice little cottage. My journey is from Wrangle to Boston, and on Wednesday Feb. 6th, I had amongst my passengers William Lefley and his wife, the prisoner. William Lefley rode with me about half-a-mile and then got out. Prisoner went with me to Boston. Lefley was in his usual state of health. I have known him several years. He has lived on his own property as cottager at Wrangle. He had about 10 or 11 acres of land, all near his cottage. I brought the prisoner back in my van the evening. The distance was about eleven miles. I reckon to start in the morning about half-past eight from my home. Lefley talked with me a little while in the cart,

Cross-examined by Mr. Lawrance: Mrs. Lefley was in the habit of going with me on Market days; she went sometimes once a fortnight or perhaps once in three or four weeks. They have lived for more than five or six years in the cottage. She used to take butter to the market when she went with me, and I took it when she did not go.

By Mr. Smith: She took some butter with her that day. or at any rate she had her basket with her.

MARY ANN MAIDENS, examined by Mr. Smith, said: I am a widow residing in Wrangle. On Wednesday, Feb. 6th, I went for John Bowson, the man for whom I was working near Mr. Lefley's house, to borrow a hook of Mr. Lefley. I saw deceased in his own yard. He had been borrowing a measuring staff, which he had in his hand. He lent the hook and bit of rub stone to sharpen it with. I asked him what o' clock it was. He said, 'I will go and look.' He went in the house and said it was half-past ten as near he could tell. I don't know whether he had to unlock the door or not. He appeared then to be quite well – as well as I am just at the present. The door of the cottage does not face the road and I could not see it where I was, when he went for the time he went out of sight, and I could not see him enter the house.

Cross-examined Mr. Lawrance: Deceased went to fetch the hook first and did not go into the house then, but I suppose he went in to look at the time.

AUGUSTUS FREDERICK NESBITT, examined by Mr. Smith, said: I am a carpenter residing in Wrangle parish. I have been well acquainted with the deceased as neighbour this last 12 years and saw him often. I was passing his house after dinner (between one and two o'clock) on the Wednesday. He was digging a hedge bottom in the field near his house. I had some conversation with him. It would be about two o'clock as near I can say. He appeared quite well.

By Mr. Lawrance: The nearest house to Lefley's would about 40 or 50 yards off on the same side of the road. On the left the nearest is nearly a quarter-of-a-mile away.

ELIZABETH HILL, examined by Mr. E. Smith, said: I am a maid servant residing with Dr. Bubb. I did not know William Lefley. He came to the doctor's on Wednesday, February 6th, between two and three o'clock. He came to the kitchen door. He asked me if the doctor was at home, and I replied no. He asked if Miss Bubb was at home, and said yes. He then said he wanted to see her in a minute. He did not say why, except that he was ill. He appeared to be very faint and ill, and vomited near the surgery door. He was carrying a small basket with him. He seemed faint and fell down in the yard. He brought the pudding with him in the basket. I and Miss Bubb looked at the pudding, which was in a basin with a cloth over it. Afterwards I went to him in the straw place. I wrapped him up with rugs as he complained of being cold, and I think was very cold. Dr. Faskally saw him afterwards, and Mr. Chapman took him home. I saw him go away a short time afterwards. He vomited several times, in the straw place and near the surgery door too. Deceased several times got up and came into the yard, and walked to the surgery door when the doctor came. Deceased was in the straw place between two and three hours before he got up and walked to the surgery door.

He fell down several times on the way, and seemed to be in pain all the time. I did not see him anywhere else from the straw place.

By His Lordship: He asked me to hasten the doctor and said he had been poisoned. He also said he was dying as fast as he could. I first heard him say that after he had been an hour. He came out of the straw place and said so. He said so several times after that, and afterwards said something else. The basin was here produced and identified.

HANNAH MARIA BUBB, examined by Mr. Cassidy, said: I am a sister of Dr. Bubb, of Wrangle. She confirmed the events and conversations given in evidence by Elizabeth Hill.

GEORGE BLEEK FASKALLY, medical practitioner who had been acting *locum tenens* for Dr. Bubb, examined by Mr. Smith, said: Being out that afternoon I came home between half past four and a quarter to five. When I got back deceased was in the closet. I went to him there and he came out into the yard. He seemed very weak and more or less staggering at the time. He spoke of his illness and said he was dying. He said he had been eating some pudding, he went with me to the surgery and pointed out the basin (produced) which contained a portion of pudding. I treated him for collapse, which was his condition. His symptoms were to a certain extent consistent with his having taken metallic poison. There was an absence of two symptoms generally very prominent in metallic poisoning, which were not well marked in this case. These were thirst and pain. After treating deceased for some time I sent him home in a cart by man named Chapman, about 5.20 p.m. I took charge of the basin and locked it up. Next day I examined it and found traces of metallic poisoning therein. I then handed it over to Supt. Crawford in the same condition as when I first found it. I followed deceased to his house and found him in bed. I stayed about two hours until eight o'clock with him. Mrs. Lefley had just come back when I arrived, and there were in the house Mrs. Longden and Mr. Wright. When I went up to the deceased his condition of collapse was unchanged. He had vomited again, I had ordered that hot bottles be applied to him, and all my directions were carried out with regard to his treatment. Before I left the house I said that in my opinion there was no chance of Lefley's recovery, that I could do nothing for him. When I first saw him I was not quite confident be had been poisoned, and hoped be might recover. I did all I could for him. Had the state of collapse not been caused through poison he might have recovered. The reason I did not use the stomach pump was because the man was too far gone. It was also of no use applying antidotes at that period. A quarter-of-an hour after entering the deceased's house I came to the conclusion he would not recover. I saw the prisoner, when I went downstairs, go away. She asked me what I thought his condition was, and if it were true he had been poisoned. I replied as regarded his condition there was no chance of his life, but as regarded the poison I had not made up my mind whether he had been poisoned. I further said he had accused the prisoner, to me, of having poisoned him, to which she replied, 'If he has been poisoned, I am innocent.' She also said, 'People don't know that he went out the other night and wanted to hang himself. If he has been poisoned I don't know where he would have got it.' I had not seen her upstairs at all while I was in the house. I think she said he had told her to go downstairs. She also said she hoped I would be able to do something for him to get him better, or words to that effect, expressing anxiety. I had some vomit, discharged deceased, given to me. I put it in a bottle and locked it up with the pudding. I tested the vomit and found traces of metallic poisoning. This was also handed over to Supt. Crawford.

JOHN ROBERT CHAPMAN, examined by Mr. Cassidy, said: I am a bricklayer, of Friskney. On February 6th I went to Dr. Babb's surgery, and saw Lefley there. I took him home in my cart and left him there. Mrs. Longden took charge of him. It was about half-past five. I helped him upstairs and left him there. There was no one at home when we got there. Lefley took the key from a place and unlocked the door. I now think Mrs. Longden got the key from the place. She came up soon after I got there.

ANNIE MARIA LONGDEN, examined by Mr. Smith, said: I am the wife of Francis Longden, cottager, of Wrangle. My house is near to Lefley's. There is no house between these two. On Wednesday, Feb. 6th, a little after five o'clock. Chapman called for me to go to Lefley's. I knew Lefley well. When I got to the house I saw Chapman and Lefley standing there. We got the key out of Lefley's pocket and unlocked the door. The deceased looked very bad, and I and Chapman helped him up to bed. After Chapman had gone away Wright came in. He came up into the bedroom and helped me. After that Mrs. Lefley came in home and entered the kitchen. I was upstairs, and Mrs. Lefley came up also. She said to her husband 'What all this about, what's the matter?' He said 'You know all about it my dear; go down and don't let me see you any more.' She said nothing, but walked downstairs and did not come up again while Mr. Lefley was alive. Mr. Lefley died about nine o'clock. Mrs. Lefley came in a little after six. After she had gone down the doctor came and stayed till eight o'clock. After the doctor came deceased vomited but did not seem in so much pain. He did not appear able to talk much. I went downstairs to prisoner after she had gone down. She offered me half a glass of beer. After this she got some tea for both of us, saying at the time 'Let us have some tea, for I have had nothing all the day; I feel queer.' I went several times downstairs, on one of which occasions she said her husband told her she need not make any pudding, there being plenty of food cooked in the house, but she told him he always had one so she would make one that day. She first said she put the sugar and rice together and left it for Mr. Lefley to put the milk to. I stayed at the house all night and Mrs. Lefley was there all the time. I had seen Lefley on the afternoon previous, when he seemed well.

Cross-examined by Mr. Lawrance: I live at the nearest house to Lefley's and have lived there four years. From what I know Lefley and his wife have lived on good terms.

RICHARD WRIGHT, examined by Mr. Cassidy, said: I was a neighbour of Mr. Lefley. I am parish clerk for Wrangle. I knew Lefley. I went to his house about half past five on Wednesday, February 6th. I went accidentally and was not called for. I saw Lefley and Mrs. Longdon. The former was in bed. I had some conversation with him and remained there until nine. I was there when Mrs. Lefley came home. She also came up into the bedroom, and said to her husband, 'Now what's the matter?' He replied 'You know what's the matter. Go down, I don't want to see you any more.' She did not reply, and went downstairs, not returning again before Mr. Lefley died. I remained with him all the time with the exception of ten minutes. I went downstairs after Mrs. Lefley had gone down to fetch him a cup of tea. I had some talk with the prisoner but could not say who spoke first. She said 'I suppose he says he has been poisoned. We haven't any poison in the house to my knowledge. We have not had for years.' She also said, 'I felt very impressed while going in the van to Boston, thought I must have got out and come back.' Lefley then called me and I went upstairs, when he was sick. I preserved that vomit and gave it to Dr. Faskally, who was not there at the time. Mrs. Longdon brought some tea up after this.

ELIZA CURL, wife of PC Curl, of Wrangle said: On the evening of Feb. 6th, I went to Lefley's house, about 8 o'clock. I asked her how Mr. Lefley was. She replied that he was no better. I said it was a strange thing if he was poisoned, how did she think he had got it. She said that he said it was in his pudding. I asked her had she made the pudding. She said yes, and put it in the oven ready for him. I asked her had she made it in a dish. She said no, in a little basin, producing one similar. I asked her if she had been upstairs and she said yes, and be said 'Go down, my dear and don't let me see you any more, you know what all this is about.' I said it was strange he should say you had poisoned the pudding and not have you upstairs. She said it's his badness. He has been an old brute ever since Christmas. I will go up again I will tell him a thing or two. I said she was better away. I stayed about ten minutes and then went away.

Cross-examined by Mr. Lawrance: Mrs. Longden was present part of the time when this conversation took place. The reason I went was because I lived near and heard Mr. Lefley was ill. My husband was at home but did not know where I was going. I did ask her if there was any poison in the house, and she said they had none in the house since they had lived there. I was not called before the magistrates when Mrs. Lefley was committed. I was there but not called. My evidence was taken after the adjourned Inquest and before the magisterial enquiry.

PC CURL, examined by Mr. Smith, said: On Feb. 6th about 12 o'clock at night, I went to Lefley s house. Sergt. Elvin was there. I saw Mrs. Lefley there and heard Sergt. Elvin ask some questions. Sergt. Elvin asked whether deceased had been ill, and prisoner replied no. Sergt. Elvin asked deceased's name and age and Mrs. Lefley looked in Bible and said his age was 60. A few minutes afterwards she said, 'It seems strange to me; he was well this morning. I made him a rice pudding in a basin, put it in the oven for him to cook for himself, as I always do when I go to Boston. If he has got any poison he must have taken it himself for I know nothing about it. I've not had any poison in the house for years.' I and Elvin then went away. Two days afterwards on Feb. 8th I was present when Dr. Pilcher and Dr. Faskally made an examination. Dr. Pilcher handed me a jar, which was sealed up with blue wax, and I handed it to Supt. Crawford just as I received it.

Mr. Lawrance: I had seen my wife before I went and knew she had been to the house.

SERGT. ELVIN, examined by Mr. Cassidy, confirmed the evidence given by PC Curl. He continued: On Thursday Feb. 7th, I went to the house and searched it downstairs. I found a small quantity of white powder in the cupboard in the front room. And handed it to Supt. Crawford the same day.

Examined by Mr. Lawrance: I have not heard that the powder had been analysed and turned out not to be poison. Nobody told me it was not arsenic. I only know it is not by the doctor's evidence given in the papers. I went to the house that night because I was fetched by Curl. I lived about three miles off. and came about 10 o'clock. I did not know then that Lefley was dead. From what I had heard I thought it right to go there, and when I arrived I was told he was dead, saw Mrs. Longdon and Mrs. Lefley. When I got to the house I and Curl went into the front room with Mrs. Lefley. Mrs Longdon told me Mr. Lefley was dead. I had not seen Mrs. Curl on my way to the house. It was in this room with Curl present that I ask her.

JAMES WILSON COOPER, miller and baker. Wrangle, said: On Thursday, Feb. 7th, the day after Mr. Lefley died, I saw Mrs. Lefley and had some conversation with her. She said while on the road to Boston she felt very queer and asked herself a question: What am going to Boston today for. I have nothing to go for today but to the shop. Every time the cart stopped I had good mind to get out and go home. We talked together about his will and his being buried. I was present when Lefley died, the day previous, I got there about 7 o'clock and some little time after I had been upstairs I went down to haste them with some brandy the doctor had ordered. She said, 'This is a strange job.' I said I was afraid it would be a very serious job, and went upstairs again to Lefley. I spoke to her again after and she said she had had a deal of trouble with him since Christmas. She said she had felt very uneasy. I said something about him being ill and she said Dr. Atkinson could always set him right. I asked if we had not better have Dr. Atkinson and said I would go upstairs and see him again before I sent. I did so and looked at him. I told them that Dr. Atkinson and no one would be of any use to him. I went upstairs and looked at him again, and then went down and told Mrs. Lefley he was fast dying; would she come see him. She said 'How is he' but did not go. I went upstairs again and looked at him and asked her again to go and see him. She made no reply.

In what state did she appear be? She looked rather wild and turned into the kitchen. She did not go upstairs again. I stayed an hour after the man was dead.

By Mr. Lawrance: I was examined before the magistrates, did not then give evidence of more than what the prisoner said in the van. I was not asked about anything else but have spoken of it, although it was not taken down. I have talked to the neighbours about what took place.

THOMAS POCKLINOTON SAUL, farmer, Wrangle Hall, examined by Mr. Cassidy, said: Mrs. Lefley came me about her husband death and I told her I had been away from home and had not heard of it. She said 'I've come to ask your advice as to whether I should employ a solicitor to attend on my behalf at the inquest.' I said, 'Did you poison him.' She said, 'No.' I said 'Then I don't think you will require a solicitor.' She made some allusion to telegraphing to her solicitor at Louth to come down. She also said she had not lived on very good terms lately with her husband. She said a few nights previous her husband had gone out into the yard about midnight. She thought he had gone to hang himself. I said, 'Did you go out after him?' She said, 'No.' She also said she went to Boston market by the carrier the morning previous and before going she had made the pudding as usual and put it in the oven.

MARY ANN SNOWDEN, examined by Mr. Smith, said: My husband is named John Snowden, and we live at Wrangle. I remember being at the house on Friday, the 8th February, and having some talk with Mrs. Lefley about her husband. She said on the Wednesday she had made the pudding as usual and put the rice and sugar in first, telling her husband she had done this and that he might put the milk in himself. But he said, don't bother yourself to-day, as there's cold meat in the house. She replied 'I always do make you a pudding,' and thereupon put the milk to and put it in the oven, I asked her if she thought there was anything littered among the rice or sugar. She said to me it was the jar she always made it out of, and she had put two more pounds in when she came home from Boston. Mr. Lefley was cousin to my husband.

WILLIAM LISTER, examined by Mr. Cassidy, said: I am a labourer, living at Wrangle. Deceased was my uncle. About five months ago I went to lodge with him in his house at Wrangle. I continued to do so about five months, going first in September. I don't remember the day of the month I left there, but it was the Saturday before the Wednesday he died. During the time I lodged there they had a few words together. I heard uncle one night threaten do violence to himself. He came to me the night before I left, and said he had attempted to hang himself. They had a quarrel that night about a cask of ale being sent in during that day. My uncle did not like it being ordered, that being done by the prisoner. I went to bed, and it was between twelve and one o'clock, when he came to me and made the above statement. He got into bed, and when I awoke was gone. He told me he had been back to his own bed. Mrs. Lefley that morning said her husband had been round the back place to hang himself. Lefley was not there at the time. He told me himself had been to do so

MAIDENS SMITH, examined by Mr. Smith, said: I am a potato dealer residing in Friskney. I remember Lefley dying on the 16th February. I was at his house on the previous Saturday. Mrs. Lefley was accusing him of letting a neighbour have some potatoes, and she said he had better let the neighbour have some coals to cook them with. She asked him if he were going to sell the remainder of the potatoes. He said he thought not at present. She told him he never would sell his things like anyone else, and she wished he was dead and out of the way. This took place in the house, and continued for about five or ten minutes. She spoke very angry.

Cross-examined by Mr. Lawrance: I suppose Mrs. Lefley meant he had sold the potatoes too cheaply or had given them away. There was no other cause for the quarrel mentioned. I had had no quarrel with Mrs. Lefley about the potatoes, but she had accused me of being too long before settling for them. She looked more sharply after me than her husband. I did pay for them, and do not owe anything now, and there was nothing more between me and Mrs. Lefley.

ROWLAND WALKER, examined by Mr. Cassidy, said: I am an evangelist, and know the prisoner. I saw her on Feb. 5th (Tuesday). I went to her house on that day, and saw her. I said I had received a letter from my wife at Partney to ask me if I would go to Eastville station the next day and meet Lizzie Holmes by the noon train. Lizzie Holmes is a niece of prisoner's. I was to take her to Mrs. Lefley's at Wrangle. I told her I was going to the station. She said 'The walk is too far; Mrs. Holmes is mad to want you to do it.' I said, 'Don't think about that, It is nothing.' The distance from the place to the station is about seven miles. Before I left the house I wrote a letter saying I would meet the child at the station next day and take her to Mrs. Lefley's. At the Wesleyan Chapel that night I again saw Mrs. Lefley, when she said she had asked Mrs. Holmes to send Lizzie through to Boston, which is nine miles off Wrangle. I believe the train is due at Eastville about half-past eleven. I went there expecting to meet my wife, and got back about one o'clock.

SUPT. CRAWFORD, examined by Mr. Smith, said: On Feb. 8th I took the prisoner In custody on a charge of murdering her husband on Feb. 6th. by administering arsenic to him in a rice pudding. At the moment she made no reply, but shortly after said 'Where did the arsenic come from?' I said I can answer no questions, but whatever you say I shall take down and use in evidence against you. I received from PC Curl on Feb. 8th a jar, tied with string and sealed with sealing wax. On the following day I handed it to Dr. Stevenson, of Guy's Hospital, London. I also received from Dr. Faskally, on the 7th Feb. a basin which I delivered to Dr. Stevenson at the same time. On the 8th Feb. I received a bottle from the same gentleman, which was also given to Dr. Stevenson. On the 7th and 8th Feb. I went to Lefley's house and searched, bringing from thence some rice and a quantity of moist sugar. These were all handed to Dr. Stevenson. Sergt. Elvin gave me a paper containing some white powder, which was similarly disposed of.

DR. FASKALLY recalled, examined by Mr. Smith, said: On February 8th I and Dr. Pilcher, by order of the Coroner, made a post mortem examination of the body of William Lefley. Generally the condition of the body was healthy, except the stomach and part of the small intestines, which were acutely congested. I did not open the stomach, which we put in a jar, sealed up and handed to the police. The appearance of the body was consistent with the supposition that death resulted from arsenical poison, and there were no apparent signs of death by any other cause.

WILLIAM JOHN PILCHER, of Boston, said: I am Fellow of the Royal College of Surgeons. He confirmed that in his opinion having made a post mortem that some mineral poison had been the cause of the action. The viscera were not opened but placed in a sealed jar, and given to PC Curl. On the previous evening (7th) I received a basin from Supt. Crawford, containing some dark mixture like rice pudding. I took a quantity of the pudding, from the bottom, the sides, and the middle. From the result of chemical and microscopic examination of the same, I found that the pudding contained common white arsenic.

HIS LORDSHIP: How soon can a man ascertain that he has taken arsenic – Almost immediately when the dose is large and the stomach empty.

DR. T. STEVENSON, of Guy's Hospital, London, said: On February 9th, 1884, I received personally from the hands of Edwin Crawford, superintendent of police, Boston, the following articles in a box which he opened in my presence:

An earthenware jar, a quart spirit bottle, a screw of paper containing whitish powder, another earthenware jar containing a quantity of rice, a similar jar, also containing rice, and in paper some sugar and a basin containing some cooked pudding. All these items were produced to the court.

I have examined and analysed the articles delivered to me.

The large jar contained several of the viscera of an adult human being, to wit: the brain, which was healthy; ... the heart, which was healthy; one lung, it was gorged with blood, but was healthy; two kidneys ... they were healthy; the spleen ... was healthy; the pancreas, was healthy; the liver, was healthy; the stomach, which was tied at both ends, was unopened. It contained a thickish fluid; the stomach itself was red and highly inflamed from the administration of an irritant poison; a large mass of small and large bowel, greatly Inflamed so far as regards the small bowel – this had the appearance commonly observed after the administration of an irritant poison. The jar also contained bloody fluid. I found arsenic, in the stomach itself, in the bowel, and the liver. The results enable me to say that arsenic was present. The spirit bottle contained ... vomit ... It contained arsenic ... The sugar, and both the samples of rice, were free from arsenic. The white powder had been administered during life and already absorbed in the system. In the paper this was free from arsenic. The basin with pudding was a pint basin in which a rice pudding had been baked. This I produce, also some of the pudding ... They were highly arsenical, and contained visible particles of white uncoloured arsenic. There was a further quantity of arsenic forming a creamy layer at the bottom of the basin, having sunk through the pudding. The arsenic had been cooked in the pudding; the creamy layer at the bottom of the dish could not have arisen from arsenic added after the cooking of the pudding. The quantity of arsenic found ... are in my opinion, inconsistent with the administration of any quantity of arsenic short of a dose that might be fatal.

Cross-examined by Mr. Lawrance: If the whole pudding had contained the same proportion of arsenic as the portion I examined there would be sufficient to kill nearly 150 persons. I do not think, however, that the portion eaten did contain as much as that left.

MR. EVERINGTON SMITH said that was all the evidence he proposed to call, and he proceeded to address the jury.

MR. LAWRANCE then addressed the Jury on behalf of the prisoner.

In concluding, pleaded that no motive for the alleged crime had been shown at all, and no fact had been produced as evidence to warrant the Jury in coming to the conclusion that the poison had been administered by the prisoner. They had only the fact that she made the pudding, about which there was no doubt. There might be grave suspicions against the woman, and she was not in a position to rebut anything that had been said against her, but suspicions were not sufficient to bring in a verdict of Wilful Murder upon her. If that were brought there would never be an opportunity of reversing it, and he was of opinion that they would not see their way to a conviction in consequence of the evidence being so incomplete.

His Lordship then summed up, and reviewed the evidence in detail. Referring to the conduct of the prisoner on the night when the deceased died, he asked the jury if they considered that her conduct was consistent with her innocence in the matter. If she were innocent, and supposing they did think he was unjustly accusing her of poisoning him, was it the part of a woman to stay away from him altogether, would she not go to the bedside and make his last moments as comfortable as possible? If she knew that he was accusing her unjustly would she not have done her best to repudiate the charge made against her? Did they suppose that her staying away from the bedside that night was consistent with her innocence? After an absence of thirty-five minutes, the jury returned into Court with a verdict of Guilty. In reply to the usual inquiry from the Clerk of Arraigns to why she should not be sentenced to death, the prisoner ejaculated, 'I am not guilty, sir.' His Lordship then assumed the black cap, and said 'Mary Lefley, the jury who have tried your case have come to the conclusion that you are guilty of the crime for which you are arraigned, that crime being the horrible one of the wilful murder of your own husband by arsenic poison. Full consideration has been given your case, and that is the conclusion to which the jury have come. I will say nothing farther than that I advise you – nay, I earnestly entreat you – to use the few days which in all probability will remain of your life in seeking from a higher source that mercy and forgiveness which has never been denied a penitent offender.' Mr. Justice North then pronounced sentence of death in the usual form. The prisoner, on being removed from the dock, said: 'I am not guilty, and never poisoned anybody in my life.'

Chapter 26

Documents from Home Office file[1]

Letter from solicitor

To the Secretary of State

Sir

Mary Lefley... Was on 7 May convicted and sentenced to death at the Assizes held before Mr Justice North on a charge of having murdered her husband William Lefley by poisoning him with arsenic.

I was the solicitor engaged in the defence of the condemned woman and I beg to urge upon you that in the consequence of the incomplete nature of the evidence upon which she was convicted it would be very hazardous to allow the actual penalty of the law to be carried out. I am emboldened to make this statement partly in consequence of the nature of the learned judge's charge to the grand jury that they might throw out the bill and the woman could be charged again provided more evidence warranted it. His Lordship made that suggestion on consideration of the same evidence upon which the woman was convicted and I venture to submit that the meaning of this was although the learned judge considered that there was a cause of suspicion that the evidence was not strong enough for conviction.

I beg therefore and respectfully submit that notwithstanding the consequent verdict of the jury it would be painfully insecure and haphazard dealing with the death penalty in this instance to be allowed to be carried out.

It appeared from the evidence... That they lived happily together and never had more than an occasional domestic difference of an ordinary nature. No sort of motive is ever been suggested such a crime [he then reviewed the evidence in detail]... The prisoner would be away all day so she prepared his dinner... Part of which was a rice pudding... Placed on the table by her... Ready for him to place in the oven when he was ready for it having cooked the rice pudding he sat down very soon after eating some of the pudding he was seized with pain and vomiting which led him to believe he was poisoned. He immediately put the pudding in a basket and went to the doctor's stating he'd been poisoned. He rapidly grew worse and after being conveyed home by the same evening. His wife the prisoner arrived from Boston and after expressing surprise that the occurrence went to where he lay and asked him what was the matter upon which he said to her 'You know my dear. Go away and do not let me see your face again.'

The pudding was proved by analysis to have been highly charged with arsenic and the post-mortem examination showed he died from arsenic poisoning.

These are the main facts on which the conviction was obtained... There was nothing of a greatly material character bearing against the prisoner. Not the slightest trace of arsenic in her possession and no theory advanced as to how she procured it. While she was away the pudding stood upon the table; it is possible that a subtle enemy of his might have quietly slipped into the house to poison the pudding – no evidence was produced at trial which would do away with this theory and the implied accusation with his dying words was a natural consequence of the meal being prepared by his wife...

Under all the circumstances of the case I beg respectfully the prisoner's guilt was not sufficiently clearly made out and to ask that you will advise Her Majesty to grant a respite of capital punishment in this case.

I have the honour to be
B B Dyer Two Church Lane Boston

File note

Mary Lefley – Date execution Monday, May 26.

Mr B.B. Dyer the solicitor who defended the prisoner states from the incomplete nature of the evidence the extreme sentence of the law should not be carried out. (P) details the facts of the case that the prisoner's guilt was not sufficiently proved and requests that Her Majesty be moved to grant a respite.

He suggests that while the pudding had been prepared by the wife before it was consumed someone may have slipped quietly into the house and introduce the poison. He urges the absence of motive and evidence of obtaining the poison.

(Endorsed nil by Secretary of State)

Letter from Judge

(Home Office stamp 25th May!)

Mr Justice North acknowledges the Home Office letter conveying the decision in this case. He presumes the Secretary of State considered the fact that there was no proof of purchase or possession of poison by the prisoner and that the evidence of actual motive was slight and he states he would not have been very much surprised if the jury considered the evidence insufficient to sustain a conviction in a capital case, though he himself considered the verdict of guilt warranted by the facts proved.

Sincerely et cetera
(mark on next sheet 'Destroyed 6-12')

Home Office note

Points advanced in the judge's notes & have already been fully brought under the consideration of the Secretary of State. The judge himself remarked on the absence of evidence as to the possession of poison. The absence of motive on the part of the prisoner and the possibility of a stranger having committed the deed was urged in the appeal of the prisoner's solicitor and attention was called to this in the minutes of that paper and the argument formed part of the defence submitted to the jury.

The judge considered the verdict warranted on the facts, though he would not be surprised if the jury had said case not proven.

The woman's conduct after she came home and found her husband in the dying state when he immediately accused her of knowing all about it was most heartless and not that of an innocent wife charged with a horrible crime of poisoning her husband, see the evidence of Mr Langdon in trial notes

The last documents on the file are a press cutting from the *London Evening Standard* 7 May 1892 and a file note:

DEATH-BED CONFESSIONS

Our Hull Correspondent telegraphs that a succession of death-bed confessions has resulted in the elucidation of a mystery which surrounded one of the most cruel murders in the annals of Lincolnshire. Mrs. Lefley poisoned her husband with arsenic in the village of Wrangle, near the South Lincolnshire coast, but until now it has never been discovered where she obtained the poison. Mary Lefley was the last woman to be hanged at Lincoln Gaol. She protested her innocence to the last, and for this reason some people doubted her guilt. That doubt can no longer be entertained. The man who bought the arsenic has confessed his complicity on his death-bed. He was one of Mrs. Lefley's lovers; yet even when he died some time ago the truth did not become known. He bound the woman to whom he told his share in the crime to secrecy. She kept her word until she was approaching death, when she revealed the secret to a woman who was attending her. It was on the 6th of February, 1884, that Mrs. Lefley went to Boston market, leaving her husband engaged in trimming the hedge of the little farmstead which they owned at Wrangle, she was forty-nine years of age, and her husband was much older. They had been married over twenty years, but had no children. William Lefley was an intensely religious man, and on the night before he was poisoned he gave out a Hymn in the village chapel. While he did this Mrs. Lefley winked and nodded to another man, who is said to be the man who confessed on his death-bed. Next day Mrs. Lefley went to Boston, after placing a rice-pudding in the oven for her husband. It was really an arsenic pudding, mixed with rice: for Dr. Stevenson, of Guy's Hospital, asserted that William Lefley had partaken of enough arsenic to poison forty people. Mrs. Lefley returned in the evening just before her husband died. After the post-mortem examination she was arrested. A nephew was arrested on suspicion of complicity: but he was discharged. Frank Reeson lately occupied another of the small homesteads at Wrangle. A woman, named Mrs. Daniel Humble, tended him in his sickness, and he begged of her to stay with him throughout his last night. He told her he dare not die with something on his mind. He then said, 'It was I who bought the arsenic for Mary Lefley; I gave it her, knowing for what purpose it had to be used. Mary Lefley wanted to get her husband out of the way. I helped her, we were false to him.' Mrs. Humble died recently, but before her death she told Mary Ann Jarvis the secret, it was not until a few days ago, after having quarrelled with her relatives, that this girl revealed the secret to a friend, and left the village in haste, and has not since been found.

This cutting was followed by the last file note in the folder.

H.O. had not at the time any clue as to whether the arsenic came from.

The judge and S.S had no doubt whatsoever, after careful examination of the facts, as to the prisoner's guilt.

The present statement appears to clear out the only doubtful point in the case.'

Comment: I am unhappy about the deathbed confession. The reliance is on a series of deathbed confessions ending with a woman-to-woman conversation where the original woman has left the district and can no longer be found. There was no evidence given of lovers in the trial, the police certainly never found one and it would have given the prosecution a far better motive than the one they used. The content is so dubious given the 'Chinese whispers' and 'urban myth' overtones that the complacency of the final Home Office note cannot be shared.

Was Mary Lefley guilty?

Boston Guardian Saturday 16 February 1884

SINGULAR COINCIDENCE

Mrs. Lefley, is like the notorious Mrs. Biggadike a native of Stickney, and singular to state many circumstances in the two cases are exactly parallel. Mrs. Biggadike went out on the day she arranged to poison her husband, and upon her return she, like Mrs. Lefley walked straight up to her husband's bedroom. She said 'What's the matter my dear?' He said 'You know very well what's the matter. Go down and don't let me see your face again.' She went down, was apprehended by police and afterwards tried and executed for the murder of which she was undoubtedly guilty.

With a paragraph in the paper like this interposed in the report of earlier proceedings Mary Lefley never had a chance.

There are many unanswered questions about this case:

1. Lefley saw seven people, excluding his wife, between his arrival at the surgery and his death. He told the Dr first, Kelly, Miss Barb and Elizabeth Hill that the pudding was poisoned and of course he sent Mary away from his bedside. Otherwise, he said nothing to any of the seven which they mentioned in their evidence. A curious reticence.
2. The pudding contained enough arsenic to kill a hundred men. Could Mary possibly have been so naive as to believe this massive dose would be undiscovered?
3. Is it also possible that her husband could have cooked and eaten part of such a saturated pudding without noticing the grittiness in taste and appearance?
4. Then there was the suicide evidence. Surely a weird coincidence that whilst the husband was contemplating suicide his wife was planning murder. She knew about the suicide attempt too. Why didn't she wait?
5. Why did Mary not concoct a plausible story about self-administered poison? Again, no plausible evidence of motive or unhappy marriage or access to poison was given at the trial.
6. I firmly believe that by the standards of the time she should have been acquitted.

PART 11

Florence Maybrick

Chapter 27

Precursor: Catherine Flannagan and Margaret Higgins 1883

Looking for an easy way to make money, Catherine Flannagan, 55, and her sister Margaret Higgins, 41, decided midway through their lives to go for the big insurance payout. One of the victims upon whom the sinister sisters alighted was Margaret's husband Thomas, 36. Throughout 1883 they laced his food with arsenic until, in September, he died. But the police got suspicious and started investigating. They discovered there had been another mysterious death in the household, that of an 18-year-old lodger, Mary Jennings. Her body was exhumed and it too contained arsenic. The sisters were also suspected of poisoning Mrs. Higgins's 10-year-old stepdaughter Mary and one of Mrs. Flannagan's sons, John, 22. Each time there was a death they collected on the insurance money. After a three-day trial in February 1884, they were both convicted of murder and hanged on Monday, 3 March that year at Liverpool's Kirkdale Prison. Police inquiries that continued after the double execution suggested that the sisters might have poisoned several other family members, friends and lodgers, for the small insurance pay-outs. At the time of her arrest, Catherine claimed to her solicitor that the murders the sisters committed were not isolated, and provided a list of six or seven other deaths that she claimed to be murders related to burial society fraud, as well as a list of five other women who had either perpetrated those murders or provided insurance to those who did. This raised the possibility that Flannagan and Higgins were only part of a larger conspiracy of murder-for-profit – a network of 'black widows' – but no convictions were ever obtained for any of the alleged conspiracy members other than the two sisters.

The sisters had developed and perfected, from victim to victim, an almost perfect method of murder – distilling the poison by dissolving flypaper in water.

As a recent *Liverpool Echo* article remarked 'They used this method nine years before the infamous "Flypaper Poisoner", Florence Maybrick, was convicted in Liverpool of the murder of her cotton trader husband, James Maybrick using the same technique.'

The case provoked an outcry at the time and prompted the Home Secretary to review the law which allowed people's lives to be insured without their knowledge.

* * *

Preliminary Reflections on the case of Florence Maybrick

The trial and conviction of Florence Maybrick in 1889 is the last case in chronological order that obviously belongs to this study of miscarriages of justice against females accused of poisoning their husbands.

The problem for anyone trying to compress a trial that took three times as long as any other trial examined in this book is that the wild meanderings of a badly conducted prosecution carefully countered by the greatest advocate of his age (Sir Charles Russell, who went on to become Lord Chief Justice of England) had no effect on a trial judge suffering from advanced mental illness instructing a British runaway jury.

It should be noted that there were also undertones of xenophobia since Florence was an American by birth.

This notorious case has had 350 books devoted in whole or part to the trial alone and it must be one of the most studied cases in British criminal history. The most important book on the case that I have come across is a contemporaneous treatise published in 1891 and over 600 pages long, with a title to match: *The Maybrick case. A treatise… On the facts of the case, and in the proceedings in connection with the charge, trial, conviction, and present imprisonment of Florence Elizabeth Maybrick* written by Alexander William McDougall[1].

A barrister by profession practising in Lincoln's Inn he lived in London from about 1870 and died in the city in November 1917 aged 80. As I found with many of my own cases, notorious cases attract fanatical supporters willing to go to great lengths to achieve justice for the unfortunate victim. Mr McDougall was clearly one of these. He not only spared no trouble or expense in mastering the properties and characteristics of the various forms of arsenic found in the great prosecutorial trawl of bottles and other objects found in the Maybrick premises, he interviewed a large number of witnesses scattered throughout the country, witnesses that should've been unearthed by the investigation to find the truths of the red herrings. His insights are adopted here in italics.

The central facts of the case were simple and surrounded, as already remarked, by a crowd of irrelevant, sometimes sinister, evidence with innocent explanations. The real interest of the case is what happened after the unfortunate Florence Maybrick was condemned to death, and the further research into the evidence available to the prosecution and not produced at trial.

A Mad Judge

Florence Maybrick's trial was presided over by Sir James Fitzjames Stephen, 1st Baronet, KCSI (3 March 1829 – 11 March 1894). Although only 60 at the time of her trial he was clearly suffering from what we would now recognise as an advanced stage of Alzheimer's.

The Reviews Reviewed, contemporaneously, (as noted in *Crime Archive: Mrs Maybrick* by Victoria Blake,[2]) a publication of the National Archives, described the behaviour of Judge Stephen in his summing up of the case as follows:

> He came into the court and charged horse foot and artillery upon the wretched and forlorn woman in the dock. The judge began by getting confused over the quantity of arsenic found in James Maybrick's intestines … He then rambled obscurely on those quantities. Before long he addressed various letters and telegrams that have been found … Claiming that they showed Florence was a liar. They had not, however, been produced as evidence! After lunch … Judge Stephen made further errors of fact, saying that one of the bottles held in evidence had contain 94 per cent arsenic, when the percentage cited in court was actually 2.94 per cent then he launched into a tirade which ended: 'It's easy enough to conceive how a horrible one, in so terrible that position, might be assailed by some terrible temptation.' The judge seemed to be asking for the jury to reach a verdict of guilt based on motive rather than the facts. His summing up took 12 ½ hours. The jury was out for only 38 minutes.

As the Directory of National Biography noted:

> Stephen's final years were undermined (by) … steady mental decline. Despite accusations of unfairness and bias regarding the murder trials of Israel Lipski in 1887 and Florence Maybrick in 1889, Stephen continued performing his judicial duties. However, by early 1891 his declining capacity to exercise judicial functions had become a matter of public discussion and press comment, and following medical advice Stephen resigned in April of that year.

He died in a 'nursing home' (a reputed private asylum) in 1894.

He was heard by his fellow judge on circuit with him and who had the bedroom next door in the judge's lodgings, pacing his own bedroom on the night before he concluded his summing up muttering 'she is guilty, she's obviously guilty'.

Chapter 28

Summary of the trial

Day 1

Mr Addison, for the Crown, began by laying out its case and called the first witness Michael Maybrick. After Sir Charles Russell's cross examination the court knew Florence had written to Michael, worried about a white powder her husband was taking (Michael said he destroyed the letter); that James had a mistress; and that nothing had been administered to James from the bottle of Valentines meat juice which had been found to contain arsenic. Also noted was the fact that Florence had been prevented from reclaiming the cashbox at the bottom of her wardrobe in Battlecrease house.

Dr Hopper gave evidence about the Maybricks' argument and reconciliation. Hopper confirmed that James was a hypochondriac with a habit of doubling the dose of any medicine his doctor prescribed him: 'I said to him it was a dangerous habit … He would sometimes do himself great injury.' James had handed him a number of prescriptions that he been taking in America; they included strychnine, and confirmed Florence's concern about the husband's habit with white powder.

Mrs Briggs in cross examination: She had suggested that Florence write a letter to Brierley asking for financial assistance and had then taken it straight back; that she had also thought James very sick on the day Florence wrote that he was 'sickened death' and that she knew that James had a habit of dosing himself; none of the poison found had been hidden in any way. When she left the witness box spectators disapproved. This woman, pretending to be a friend, had behaved like an agent provocateur.

The Edward Maybrick cross examination established that from the Wednesday before James's death it would have been very difficult for Florence to administer any poison because of the ever present nurses. When asked whether his brother took any sort of arsenic Edward replied he did not. Later in the trial, when he was recalled, it became clear that he lied about that.

The chemist who sold Florence the fly papers gave evidence next. Sir Charles established that the second set of fly papers were bought at the same time as Florence was having a face lotion of benzoin and elderflower made up and that arsenic was used as part of a cosmetic.

At the end of day one the local papers were coming round to Florence's side.

Day 2

The first witness was Alice Yapp: It was observed she was very subdued. In cross examination it was established she was only a nanny. She was constantly asked why she had opened the letter she had been given to post, which as Victoria Blake commented had made her appear deceitful and disloyal, undermining the character of one of the prosecution's key witnesses.

Then the Battlecrease house servants (Bessie Brierley, Mary Cadwallader and Mrs Humphries the Cook) trooped through to give evidence.

Dr Humphrey admitted that if Michael had not come to him with his suspicions he would have given the cause of death as 'acute congestion of the stomach' and would have certified the death was caused by 'gastritis or gastroenteritis'. He had tested James's urine and faeces two days before death and found no arsenic.

The press had come round in support of Mrs Maybrick as Victoria Blake noted, and at the end of the second day the correspondent of the *New York World* stated that 'A great rebound of popular opinion in this is in Maybrick's favour and makes a disagreement of the jury, if not an absolute acquittal, looks quite probable.'

Day 3

Dr Carter testified he was sure that James Maybrick's death was caused by an outside irritant, by arsenic poisoning, but agreed that his suspicions had not been aroused until a conversation with Michael Maybrick. He also agreed that gastritis could be caused by the ingestion of impure blue.

Dr Baron, who attended the post-mortem as Florence's representative stated that death was due to 'acute inflammation of the stomach probably caused by some irritant poison' but he could not say how the symptoms of death by poisoning differed from those of death by arsenic poisoning

Dr Edward Davies, analytical chemist, next gave evidence. He presented an enormous list of items taken from Battlecrease house in James's office (see Home Office files); there were a number of items that had not been produced before the trial, including Florence's dressing gown and a handkerchief which bore traces of arsenic but could well have been accounted for by her contact with the original fly papers.

He testified that the arsenic in the packet marked 'Arsenic. Poison for Cats' was not mixed with sort of indigo, as required when arsenic was sold to the public. It had instead been mixed with charcoal. No explanation was offered by anyone as to this.

Day 4

The three private nurses were first called.

Alfred Schweisso, a waiter at Flatman's hotel confirmed Florence and Brierley had been together.

Dr Thomas Stevenson was lecturer in forensic medicine chemistry at Guy's Hospital London and official Home Office representative in such trials. He had received all the viscera in 11 jars but had only found traces of arsenic in the liver (under a 10th of a grain) and the intestines (under a 50th of a grain). He admitted the quantities were tiny, and that a fatal dose was two grains. He was dogmatic that James's death had been caused by arsenic poisoning but admitted under cross-examination 'There is no distinctive diagnostic symptom of arsenic poisoning. The diagnostic thing is finding the arsenic.'

Sir Charles Russell opened for the defence after lunch. The defence was that there was reasonable doubt as to whether James Maybrick had died of arsenic poisoning, and even then Maybrick was a drug addict known to dose himself.

Mr Nicholas Bateson, Capt Robert Thomson and Thomas Stansell, gave evidence as to James taking drugs including arsenic in America.

Edwin Garnett Heaten, a local chemist, recently retired, recognised James's picture in the local paper as being a regular customer who bought a tonic and insisted that arsenic drops be added. Over time the arsenic drops increased from four to seven and James had dropped in for his tonic two to five times a day.

In cross examination it was established that there was no evidence in his books and argued that recognising someone's picture in a paper was insufficient proof. In fact it transpired that, on the list presented by the prosecution of goods and in the Home Office records, was an entry of a bottle found bearing the address of the chemist who was incorrectly recorded as Easton by the police.

There were other witnesses as to hypochondria and drug taking and in particular John Thomson, wholesale druggist, who had employed one of Maybrick's cousins and suspected him of supplying Maybrick with drugs.

The formal evidence for the defence closed with its doctors.

Dr Charles Tidy, who had the same qualifications as Dr Stevenson, and had been involved with 40 post-mortems concerning arsenic poisoning was adamant 'That (the death) it is due to gastroenteritis of some kind or another but the symptoms of the post-mortem distinctly point away from arsenic.' This ended the formal evidence for the defence.

Day 5

The day began with a statement made by Mrs Maybrick, allowed by the judge, in evidence.

'Before my marriage and since I have been in the habit of using a face wash prescribed for me by Dr Greggs of Brooklyn. It consisted of arsenic ... and other ingredients. I mislaid the prescription last April.' She went on to say she had learnt how to make up this prescription as a young girl.

She next explained about the bottle of meat juice.

'On Thursday night, 9 May, after nurse Gove had given my husband beef tea, I went and sat beside him ... Under his pressure she consented to put 'his powder'. She went on to relate that he upset the bottle and added a considerable amount of water. She put the bottle of juice (possibly containing arsenic) out of sight in his room and Michael removed the bottle.

She concluded 'I have only to add for the love of our children a perfect reconciliation had taken place between us and on the day before his death, I have made a full and free confession to him, and received his entire forgiveness for the fearful wrong I have done.'

Sir Charles asked the judge if he could bring corroborative evidence but was not allowed to do this.

Sir Charles, in his closing statement portrayed James Maybrick as a hypochondriac in the habit of dosing himself with all sorts of drugs.

He dealt with the flypaper evidence placing emphasis on buying it from two chemists who knew her by name and the openness of the soaking of flypaper.

Addison portrayed Florence as a liar, using the evidence of the letters to link the hotel and the purchase of two sets of fly papers so closely together. He asked why, if Florence had been so worried about what her husband had been taking, she put it in his meat juice.

Victoria Blake chronicles that a reporter from the *New York World* tracked down Dr Greggs in Brooklyn and when asked about Florence Maybrick he said 'All I know about Mrs Maybrick is that she called upon me to prescribe something for her complexion, which I did.' He also confirmed that there had been arsenic in the prescription.

The rest of the trial was occupied by the judge's summing up (already dealt with).

The case for the Crown

1. Ignore the man's habit of dosing himself.
2. Take the Brierley incident, 16 March, as the 'first date in the case'.

3. 1/10 of a grain of arsenic was found in the man's body.
4. Arsenic was found in the house after death.
5. Mrs Maybrick was seen soaking flypaper, which has arsenic content, before the death and the prosecution theory was that arsenic in solution was the cause of death.
6. Mrs Maybrick committed adultery with Brierley in March.
7. Adultery is the motive for the murder.
8. Therefore Mrs Maybrick is the person who put 1/10 of a grain of arsenic into the body which was found there and arsenic was the 'cause of death'.

The defence had a field day with this mishmash of false reasoning unsupported by the evidence, that in reality based itself on the supposition that since Mrs Maybrick was clearly guilty of an affair with Brierley she was capable of anything and must be guilty.

The key finding was that less than a 1/10 of a grain of arsenic was found in the body and the experts agreed that it took three grains to cause death. The actual cause of death it was agreed by all was gastroenteritis.

The medical evidence brought by the Crown which said that it was arsenic which might have caused the gastroenteritis were:

Dr Carter, Dr Humphrey and Dr Stevenson. Dr Carter and Dr Humphrey had no previous experience of death by arsenic to draw upon. They gave an unqualified opinion.

MacDougall[1] puts together all the medicines that were poured into Mr Maybrick by Dr Humphrey that might have caused the gastroenteritis by being an irritant poison:

> April 28 Diluted prussic acid, April 29 Papaine, iridin, May 3 Morphia suppository, May 4 Ipecascuanha, May 5 More prussic acid, May 6 Fowlers solution of arsenic, May 7 Jaborandi tincture, antipyrine, May 10 Sulphonal, cocaine and phosphoric acid.

The good doctor admitted in the witness box that some of these were patented medicines manufactured abroad and he was not aware of the contents.

A conspiracy?

Most of those writing about this case have remarked on a Cabal of prosecution witnesses who exhibited some malice towards Mrs Maybrick.

The five are:

Alice Yapp, children's nurse and threatened with dismissal by Mrs Maybrick

Michael Maybrick, brother of the deceased, gaining under a will of the deceased that he was aware of.

Edwin Maybrick, another brother.

Bessie Brierley, friend of Alice Yapp and housemaid for seven months.

Mrs Briggs, friend to the Maybricks for eight years. Exposed as agent provocateur of dubious correspondence.

This is the group who searched the house for objects immediately after Mr Maybrick's death. They went straight to places open and accessible to everybody, and only to those places, and put their hands, without any difficulty, on large quantities of arsenic in all sorts of forms: arsenic, mixed with charcoal, 'poison for cats', bottles of arsenic in a state of solution, and arsenic in crystals, enough altogether to poison fifty people. The remarkable circumstances in connection with these things is as McDougall observes 'Nobody had ever seen any of it in the house before, and nobody at the trial could say where it had all come from':

- 'Arsenic, poison for cats' - the parcel contained arsenic mixed with black charcoal, commonly used and bought for vermin control. The word arsenic printed on one side and the phrase 'poison for cats' in pencil handwriting on the other. No attempt by prosecution to get a handwriting expert on the sample. Discovered by Yapp and Brierley. It later transpired that their nickname for Florence was the old cat.
- Yapp's evidence that she saw Florence Maybrick transferring liquids from one bottle to another. In the presence of the professional nurse employed, both bottles had been tested negative for arsenic.
- The purloined letter and evidence of adultery, opened on the excuse that it had been dropped in a puddle by the Maybrick's youngest child and got wet. Yapp was unable to explain why the original envelope was dry and showed no watermarks.
- Two bottles of meat extract, one testing negative for arsenic, see Mrs Maybrick's statement (the white powder was clearly a red herring but she believed it was poisonous), the other containing arsenic but without a chain of evidence to prove it was ever near Mrs Maybrick. What was made clear by following the evidence of Mrs Hughes was that she had been made aware by Michael Maybrick that there was arsenic in one bottle of meat extract before the analyst had informed anyone of its presence. On the evidence, Michael Maybrick becomes a suspect for the death of his brother in so far as that death was unnatural.

- Much play made by prosecution and judge on the three days unaccounted for in Florence's trip to London for her assignation with Brierley. Suggestions made that she had other lovers, without evidence. In fact she was staying with a relative and seeking the services of a solicitor.

Public opinion during the course of the trial

Public opinion, totally guided by the local press, was uniformly hostile to Florence Maybrick from the coroner's court to the opening of the trial. The factors mainly prevailing were the adultery, the Liverpool experience of serial killers Catherine Flanagan and Margaret Higgins seven years before and the common factor of arsenic in the flypaper.

Chapter 29

Aftermath: The Home Office[1]

The verdict was wildly unpopular. The headlines in the *Pall Mall Gazette* of 8 August chronicled what happened:

GREAT OUTBURST OF POPULAR INDIGNATION IN LIVERPOOL JUSTICE STEPHEN DEPARTS AMID A STORM OF GROANS MRS MAYBRICK CHEERED BY THE CROWD

On 7 August, the same day as the verdict, Sir Charles Russell wrote a letter to the Home Secretary Henry Matthews:

I am sorry to say it will be necessary for you fully to consider this case. Against her there was a strong case undoubtedly of the means being within reach to poison her husband and of the existence of a motive but there was no direct evidence of administration by her. But further; but a small quantity of arsenic was discovered in the body after the death and none in the stomach, bile, heart, spleen.

The symptoms – all were agreed – with those of gastroenteritis; but while the witness for the prosecution attributed it to arsenical poisoning a very strong body of evidence was given for the defence that it was not so.

The woman had been unfaithful to her husband and I am afraid this fact and a subsequent improper letter to her paramour unsettled Justice Steven's ordinarily fair judgement.

In a long experience I have never heard any summing up which gave a jury less chance of differing from his clearly conveyed adverse view. Indeed he seemed to have told the jury to consider the case as a whole and not dispute its consideration; and thus he appears to suggest it to them that even if the cause of death was doubtful they might look at the other facts – whereas he ought (I think it clear) to have said they were to look at all the evidence and facts bearing on the cause of death and if in the result there was doubt – to acquit even though the prisoner might've sought to poison her husband.

Very strong feeling is very widely expressed and I hope you will get the best reports of the evidence you can. I will send you the local papers.

The Russell memorandum

On 14 August Russell followed this up with a seven-page memorandum to the Home Office
It began:

> There were two questions
> (1) Was it proved beyond reasonable doubt that the deceased died from arsenic or poisoning? And if so,
> (2) That the prisoner criminally administered that poison?

This was followed by a detailed examination of arsenical poisoning, symptoms and post mortem appearance. It concluded:

> It is no exaggeration to say that every point made by the prosecution was put by the learned judge and with greater insistence as well as other points which the prosecution had not made ... In short period he had honestly but mistakenly taken the view that the woman was clearly guilty ... That view he persistently and permanently impressed upon the jury in the summing up of two days and in a manner which would justify the trial being described as a trial by judge rather than jury...
>   On the whole it is submitted that looking to all the facts... The verdict cannot be regarded as satisfactory and the irrevocable penalty ought not to be inflicted.

The memorandum was accompanied by a covering letter 'The case demands independent examination by you.'

The Home Office conference

The Home Office file discloses that on 16 August a high-powered conference was convened at the Home Office to discuss the case.

Present: Home Secretary Henry Matthews, Lord Halsbury (the Lord Chancellor), Judge Stephen, Doctors Stevenson and Tidy, Mr Lushington (Home Office?) and Dr Poore (the Prince of Wales's doctor).

The Home Secretary opened with the purpose of the meeting. To reconcile the difference between his two Home Office consultant doctors, Stevenson and Tidy. Both of them stuck to their guns and at the end of the conference Judge Stephen summed it up: 'You get a contradiction between two experts which you cannot reconcile.'

On 22 August, four days before the execution, the Home Secretary decided on his course of action. The press report issued from the Home Office stated:

> We are given to understand that the Home Secretary, after fullest consideration and after taking the best legal and medical advice that could be obtained, has advised Her Majesty to respire capital punishment of Florence Elizabeth Maybrick and to commute the punishment to penal servitude for life: insomuch as, although the evidence leads to the conclusion that the prisoner administered and attempted to administer arsenic to her husband, with intent to murder him, it does not wholly exclude a reasonable doubt whether his death was in fact caused by the administration of arsenic. This decision is understood not to imply the slightest reflection on the able and experienced practitioners who gave evidence, or on the tribunal before which the prisoner was tried. We understand that the course adopted has the concurrence of the learned judge.

It was a typical pragmatic compromise at Florence Maybrick's expense. Judicial face had been preserved, and the normal life sentence translated into 20 years in prison.

Chapter 30

The Fight for Freedom

The enormous volume of Home Office files bears witness to the unending transatlantic campaign to free Florence Maybrick. From America, a petition to the Queen was signed by the wives of the President, the Secretary of State, the Secretary of the Treasury and the Secretary of Agriculture and sent on 7 August 1891.

On 1 June 1892 the Home Office received a similar petition signed, amongst others, by the Vice President of the United States, the Speaker of the House of Representatives and the head of the Catholic Church in the USA.

It was received with contempt by the Home Office, an official making the following written comment 'A truly astonishing document; for if ever there was a criminal not entitled to mercy it is Mrs Maybrick. How persons occupying stations of such high responsibility could sign this document on a slight and imperfect knowledge of the facts I cannot imagine.'

On this side of the Atlantic Sir Charles Russell led the campaign to free Francis. On every change of government he pleaded her cause, continuing when he became Lord Chief Justice of England in 1894 until he died in 1900.

All the agitation was in vain. Even if one of the many successive ministers constantly bombarded by letters and petitions had been inclined to recommend a pardon they would have been blocked by the implacable enmity to Florence's cause from Queen Victoria.

Queen Victoria is not Amused

We are indebted to Victoria Blake for uncovering a communication from the Queen to Matthews at the time of the commutation of Mrs Maybrick's sentence: 'The only regret she feels about the decision is that so wicked a woman should escape by a legal quibble! The law is not a moral profession she must say. But her sentence must never be further commuted.'

It was not until Queen Victoria's death in 1901 that the Home Office reconsidered its options:

Memorandum 10 July 1901
It would be possible to fix 15 years as the period at which she might be brought up for licence, I think it would be well, if this decision is come to,

to inform the American ambassador at the interview on Friday that it has been so decided and to communicate the decision to the prisoner. This will give her three more years to serve. I think it should be understood that although in the ordinary course she will be licensed when she has served 15 years that the decision is not irrevocable but will depend on her conduct, and that the difficulty of acting on it will be increased if agitation against the justice of a conviction is renewed.

Florence was finally released on 20 January 1904. The rest of her life was spent in a long period of declining health and the constant need for money, satisfied initially by her autobiography and lecture tours degenerating to relying on charity from others. In October 1941 she suffered a mild stroke and died two days later at the age of 79.

Was Florence Guilty?

The most conclusive piece of evidence to my mind is the original of Florence's American facewash prescription including arsenic which was discovered by her mother when it fell out of Florence's Bible some two years after the trial. It proved her use of arsenic as a cosmetic, and demolished the entire basis of the prosecution's flypaper evidence. A certified copy of the prescription exhibited to a lawyer's affidavit sits in the archives to this day.

The more I read and studied this case of an American woman's experiences at the hands of a British court of justice the more I was reminded of a case I was involved in, a British young woman at the hands of an American court of justice at the turn of this century. Louise Woodward was charged with the murder of a young baby while she was an *au pair* to an American family. She too had the services of a defence team led by one of the greatest American defence lawyers of our age. Both juries were uneducated (the Maybrick jury consisted of three plumbers, a wood turner, a provision dealer, two farmers, a grocer, an ironmonger, a milliner, a house painter and a baker) and faced complex medical evidence. The jury preferred the evidence of a local medical practitioner who was asked by the local attorney to perform the autopsy, against more eminent medical evidence produced by the defence team which included scientific evidence making the alleged crime as charged by the prosecutors an impossibility. Nevertheless the young woman was convicted by a runaway jury. The great difference was the trial judge, who disagreed the verdict, had powers to set her free and exercised them.

Chapter 31

Was Florence Maybrick married to
Jack the Ripper[1]?

James Maybrick - Jack the Ripper suspect

In 1992 Michael Barrett, a former Liverpool scrap metal merchant, produced a journal which, he claimed, had been given to him by a friend, Tony Devereux, in a pub the previous year.

Although the author of the diary doesn't actually identify himself by name, it is quite obvious from various personal references, and from other information contained within the journal, that the diarist is meant to be that of the Liverpool cotton merchant James Maybrick.

In the diary, the author makes the claim that he had seen his wife – whom calls 'the bitch,' or 'the whore' in the pages of the diary – with her unnamed lover in the Whitechapel district of Liverpool. The subsequent rage that he experienced following this sighting sent him on a murderous rampage in the Whitechapel district of London in the course of which he mutilated and killed five prostitutes.

The journal contains a somewhat long-winded description of the murders before ending with the assertion: 'I give my name that all know of me, so history do tell, what love can do to a gentle man born. Yours truly, Jack the Ripper.'

Until the emergence of the diary there had never been any suggestion that James Maybrick may have been Jack the Ripper and the only real evidence against him as a suspect is his own supposed confession in the pages of his diary. So his viability as a Jack the Ripper suspect comes down to whether or not he wrote the diary and, if he did, does what he wrote about his crimes correspond with the known facts.

It has to be said that the provenance of the diary has proved a hugely dividing issue amongst Ripperologists. The first reaction from experts on examining the diary was encouraging. Several of them agreed that, if nothing else, it was most certainly of the correct period to have been written by James Maybrick. A set-back to establishing the authenticity of the diary came when Michael Barrett informed the *Liverpool Post* that he had in fact forged the diary. However, he then withdrew his confession and, in addition, his wife, from whom he was by then separated, stated that the diary had in fact been in her family's possession since the Second World War.

There is, however, another intriguing piece of memorabilia that links Maybrick to the Jack the Ripper crimes. In 1993 Albert Johnson purchased an antique gold watch on the inside of which he found scratched the initials of Jack the Ripper's five victims, together the signature J. Maybrick, and the words 'I am Jack.' As with the diary, the watch has been subjected to scientific analysis and the scratches have been found to be compatible with the period 1888 to 1889, although these findings have been disputed. But the sudden appearance of the watch, so soon after the diary was made public aroused a great deal of suspicion.

Probably both fake tributes to the popularity of Ripperology.

PART 12

Conclusions

It would be unfair to judge the Victorians by our current standards. In particular none of the women in the cases reviewed should have been convicted by a fair-minded jury (Sgt Jones was able to challenge many jurors for partiality in the selection for Chesham) operating with an impartial judge (as we have seen one of the principal factors in miscarriages of justice), but they do range from probably guilty to undoubtedly innocent. So how do these cases rank in order of innocence? One must bear in mind that being guilty of something is not the same as judging the prisoner guilty of murder.

Elizabeth Pearson, probably guilty, but for the question marks noted in the discussion of the case, not beyond reasonable doubt.

Mary Ball, probably innocent of murder. Re-quoting the end of Muscutt: 'On what we know it was at worst a spur of the moment self poisoning which could have been prevented by Mary Ball, and at best a straightforward accident.

Priscilla Biggadike, probably innocent, Proctor being the guilty party.

Sarah Chesham, probably innocent.

Mary Lefley, looking at the unanswered questions, firmly innocent.

Sarah Barber, undoubtedly innocent of murder. Guilty, on her own confession, of conspiracy to pervert the course of justice by throwing away the bottle.

Anne Merritt, undoubtedly innocent. The woman is in abject poverty and fearful of the workhouse yet she is accused of poisoning her husband a few days before the two years are up which would have enabled her to claim £10 from the burial society.

Florence Maybrick, undoubtedly innocent.

What is clear is that in Victorian times, as now, a good experienced barrister, such as Sgt Jones in the first Chesham cases and Sir Charles Russell in the Maybrick case can, with all the handicaps they laboured under, destroy a malicious prosecution witness. Examples of such witnesses abound in our cases.

In the end they were all convicted under the system in practice as opposed to theory – the misogynistic bias of the legal process. The entire legal system during the Victorian period was male, middle-class (jurors had to be landowners to sit on juries in the early part of the period) and therefore had prejudices against the working class women who were usually sole defendants before the court at trial. Male lovers such as Proctor (Biggadike) and Ironmonger (Barber) were often sent for trial but usually dismissed or acquitted.

For the best illustration of a typical middle-class view of the lower classes see the Foreman expressing the entire jury's observations in the Happisburgh Affair (Chapter 6):

> It is lamentable to perceive in what a state of wilful wickedness and ignorance many of the lower order of society still remained. He said wilful for were some parish churches better attended, they would there learn their duty to both God and men, and then the jury and those present would be spared the witnessing of such horrible scenes as those which had brought them together on the present occasion.

The concept of fair trials for working class women accused of poisoning was meaningless since the classic trilogy for charge and conviction, proof of means, motive and opportunity, was virtually presumed. Whilst perhaps the majority of working class homes purchased arsenic for ridding themselves of vermin, the middle classes involved in the legal system either employed professional rat catchers or left the problem to the servants. If a wife was accused of poisoning her husband it was assumed that any purchase of arsenic was for criminal purposes; any form of pecuniary gain or marital discord, however slight, was assumed as a motive and of course the opportunity was always there. It is amazing that from 1840 to 1880 any accused woman was ever acquitted. Over this period the defendants were not allowed to give evidence in their own defence. There was no appeal from the trial verdict until the Court of Appeal was established in the twentieth century. If the jury were misdirected or got it wrong that was it. The Home Office were never concerned with the merits of the case (that was for juries) and poisoners were almost always hanged.

In writing this book I was constantly reminded of the gap between the law as it stood and its performance in practice. Most of the current international safeguards for defendants were already enshrined in British law by the mid-Victorian period, from the presumption of innocence to an impartial tribunal. The major outstanding item was the haphazard function of the right to have a lawyer if you could not afford one and its creation of a knock-on effect to the equal right to examine prosecution evidence and produce evidence on your behalf. This was a defect not cured until the provision of criminal legal aid in the immediate post-Second World War period.

In practice the operation of the justice system reminded me of the Greek justice system and the way it worked, particularly for foreigners, a couple of decades ago. For drug crimes no one was ever acquitted and in Greece the defendant was not allowed to give sworn evidence in court, on the theoretical grounds that this would give rise to perjury.

End Notes

In my first true crime book *In The Mind Of A Female Serial Killer* I noted 'I have compiled these notes with twin, sometimes conflicting objectives of ensuring that those interested can examine my sources, while avoiding prolixity and duplication. The basic sources of information for each of these women's stories and quotes from them will therefore be placed at the head of their section.' The one general source, where useful, is again Ancestry.com the genealogical search engine. Local papers are sourced in the text.

Prologue
1. R.J. Muscutt, *The Life, Trial and Hanging of Mary Ball*, Broadland Books (2011)

Introduction
1. P. Wilson, *Murderess*, Michael Joseph London (1971)
2. D. Bentley, *English Criminal Justice in the Nineteenth Century*, The Hambledon Press, London (1998)
3. P. Wilson For general treatment of this issue

Chapter 1
1. J.C. Whorton, *The Arsenic Century*, Oxford University Press (2010) The 'go to' source book for an overview of much of the primary material in this chapter. In particular the opening *Times* letter and other articles from contemporary press and magazines.
2. *Passim.*
3. See H. Barrell, *Fatal Evidence*, Pen & Sword (2017) for a biography.
4. A. Meharg, 'Science in culture', *Nature* (June2003)

Chapter 2
1. D. Bentley, *English Criminal Justice in the Nineteenth Century*, The Hambledon Press, London (1998)

Chapter 3
1. M. Scollan, *Sworn to Serve: Police in Essex*, Phillimore & Co Ltd (1993)
2. C. Watson, *Death's Gatekeepers: The Victorian Coroner's Officer* (2016)

Chapter 4
1. See https://en.wikipedia.org/wiki/Angel_Makers_of_Nagyrev for general treatment.
2. B. Bodó, *Tiszazug: A Social History of a Murder Epidemic*, Columbia University Press East European Monographs (2003)
3. G. Gullickson *Unruly Women of Paris: Images of the Commune*, Cornell University Press, (1996)

Chapter 6
1. A. Nevins, 'American Journalism and Its Historical Treatment', *Journalism Quarterly* (1959)
2. HO 45/1386

Chapter 9
1. J. L. Ainsley, *The Ordeal of Sarah Chesham*, University of Victoria (1997)

Chapter 10
1. J. Astley *Nuneaton Diaries 1810–1849* serialised in the *Nuneaton Observer* from manuscript held at Nuneaton library.

Chapter 13
1. K. Clarke, *Bad Companions*, The History Press (2013)

Chapter 24
1. The whole story of Lizzie Pearson is dealt with in *A Shadow of Doubt: The Story of Lizzie Pearson*, written by Mike Stowe of the Gainsford local history group.

Chapter27
1. Mary Lefley HO 144/136/A35525

Chapter28
1. A.W. MacDougall, *The Maybrick Case*, Andesite Press, originally published by Bailliere Tindall and Cox, London (1891)
2. V. Blake, *Crime Archive: Mrs Maybrick*, The National Archives (2006)

Chapter 29
1. Florence Maybrick HO144 /1638,1639,1640,1641 – 4 files!

Chapter 31
1. From http://www.jack-the-ripper.org/james-maybrick.htm

Index